T0328413

TAX, MEDICINES AND THE LAW

In 1783 a stamp duty was imposed on proprietary or 'quack' medicines. These often useless but sometimes dangerous remedies were immensely popular. The tax, which lasted till 1941, was imposed to raise revenue. It failed in its incidental regulatory purpose, had a negative effect in that the stamp was perceived as a guarantee of quality, and had a positive effect in encouraging disclosure of the formula. The book explains the considerable impact the tax had on chemists and druggists – how it led to an improvement in professional status, but undermined it by reinforcing their reputations as traders. The legislation imposing the tax was complex, ambiguous and never reformed. The tax authorities had to administer it, and executive practice came to dominate it. A minor, specialised, low-yield tax is shown to be of real significance in the pharmaceutical context, and of exceptional importance as a model revealing the wider impact of tax law and administration.

Chantal Stebbings is Professor of Law and Legal History at the University of Exeter. In the past she has served as Dean of the Faculty of Law at the University of Exeter, Visiting Professor at the University of Rennes, France, a Fellow of the Institute of Taxation and a General Commissioner of Income Tax. She has also held a British Academy Research Readership and a Leverhulme Major Research Fellowship. She was generously supported by the Wellcome Trust for this book, which is her fourth monograph for Cambridge University Press. She is the editor of the *Journal of Legal History* and the Chair of the Hamlyn Trust.

Tax, Medicines and the Law

FROM QUACKERY TO PHARMACY

CHANTAL STEBBINGS

CAMBRIDGE
UNIVERSITY PRESS

University Printing House, Cambridge CB2 8BS, United Kingdom

One Liberty Plaza, 20th Floor, New York, NY 10006, USA

477 Williamstown Road, Port Melbourne, VIC 3207, Australia

314-321, 3rd Floor, Plot 3, Splendor Forum, Jasola District Centre, New Delhi - 110025, India

79 Anson Road, #06-04/06, Singapore 079906

Cambridge University Press is part of the University of Cambridge.

It furthers the University's mission by disseminating knowledge in the pursuit of education, learning and research at the highest international levels of excellence.

www.cambridge.org
Information on this title: www.cambridge.org/9781108716994
DOI: 10.1017/9781139178990

© Chantal Stebbings 2018

First published 2018
First paperback edition 2018

A catalogue record for this publication is available from the British Library

Library of Congress Cataloging in Publication data
Names: Stebbings, Chantal, author.
Title: Tax, medicines and the law : from quackery to pharmacy / Chantal Stebbings.
Description: Cambridge; New York, NY: Cambridge University Press, 2018. | Includes bibliographical references and index.
Identifiers: LCCN 2017040365 | ISBN 9781107025455 (hbk)
Subjects: | MESH: Legislation, Drug – history | Taxes – history | Pharmacy – history | Fiscal Policy – history | History, 18th Century | History, 19th Century | United Kingdom
Classification: LCC RM41 | NLM QV 11 FA1 | DDC 615.109–dc23
LC record available at https://lccn.loc.gov/2017040365

ISBN 978-1-107-02545-5 Hardback
ISBN 978-1-108-71699-4 Paperback

For my husband,
Howard

Contents

Figures

Acknowledgements

This project was funded by two awards from the Wellcome Trust [WT089621AIA; WT095723MA]. I most gratefully acknowledge this generous support, without which the sustained period of research and writing would not have been possible. I would like to thank Kim Hughes of Cambridge University Press for her encouragement and patience; John Betts, Curator of the Royal Pharmaceutical Society Museum for facilitating this research so helpfully; to Chris Torrero of LGC Ltd and P.W. Hammond for their expert assistance with regard to the history of the Government Laboratory; to Richard Thomas for all his literary allusions; and to all friends and colleagues in legal history and tax law, whose comments, insightful questions and willingness to listen have informed this work. All errors remain, of course, my own. Finally, my very special thanks to my family – to Howard, to Jennie and Paul, Alex and Mark, whose enthusiasm, encouragement, understanding and wise counsel I have valued immensely.

In memory of my great-grandfather, Alfred Reilly (1869–1942), Chemist and Druggist, Nice, France.

Table of Statutes

Table of Cases

1

Proprietary Medicines and the Fiscal State

"Tax quackery with all my heart: It is but right that they who place greater confidence in the unknown hodge-podge of a stone mason or a gingerbread-baker, than in the skill of an honest and able regular practitioner, should pay a tax ad valorem, over and above the price of the stuff, for their folly and credulity."[1]

INTRODUCTION

The taxation of medicines within the British fiscal and legal systems began in 1783, the result of a confluence of various distinct and powerful forces. Socially, the country saw an unprecedented rise in the production and consumption of so-called 'quack' medicines sold for the purposes of self-medication. These were remedies promoted by a wide range of generally unqualified entrepreneurs who invented and sold them to the general public, with secret compositions and exaggerated claims for their efficacy in curing, preventing or relieving illness. These remedies were unproven, sometimes of little or no use, often dangerous, and they were consumed in prodigious quantities by a credulous public desperate for relief at a time when medical science was rudimentary. The trade had reached an unprecedented height in the later years of the eighteenth century.

The first formal legislative response to the phenomenon of proprietary medicines was to tax them. The state immediately took a keen fiscal interest in this exceptionally robust and thriving trade in medicines as a commodity and its potential financial yield. Economically, Britain in the late eighteenth

---

[1] William Chamberlaine, *History of the Proceedings of the Committee appointed by the General Meeting of Apothecaries, Chemists, and Druggists, in London, for the Purpose of obtaining Relief from the Hardships imposed on the Dealers in Medicine, by certain Clauses and Provisions contained in the new Medicine Act, passed June 3, 1802 etc,* (London: Highley, 1804), p. 20.

century faced an urgent need for increased public revenue and chose to meet
this need, in part at least, through the instrument of taxation. Together these
forces resulted in the forging of a fiscal relationship between medicines and
the state, because it is in this context that a tax – the medicine stamp duty –
was imposed on quack medicines, a description which, when cast in legislative language, extended to all proprietary and recommended medicines. The
tax was a minor one in fiscal terms, being highly specialised, raising relatively
little revenue, largely unremarked by the general public and familiar to only
a small proportion of revenue staff, who tended to leave it to its own devices.
This tax, which endured throughout the nineteenth century and was, still in
its original form, abolished in 1941, constituted the principal tax on medicines
in Britain.

The medicine stamp duty operated throughout a period of unprecedented
social, legal and economic dynamism.[2] Specifically, it spanned the epoch in
which the practice, profession and science of pharmacy developed. It saw the
construction of the legal foundations of a sophisticated tax system fit for a new
industrial age, and it experienced the enormous growth in the bureaucratic
authority of the state. To assume that taxation does no more than raise revenue
for the purposes of government underrates the power of tax. That a synergy
exists between tax and wider social, fiscal and legal movements was made
explicit in 1918 when Joseph Schumpeter observed that tax law is the prism
through which the social, political and economic values of any society are
distinguished, and that it shapes human behaviour and activity.[3] His premise
was that taxes created their own social and economic momentum, an idea
that has been adopted by the emerging discipline of fiscal sociology.[4] To fully
understand any social phenomenon, the role of tax cannot be ignored.

What lies at the heart of an appreciation of the broader effects of the medicine stamp duty in its wider legal context and in its specific field of operation,
namely pharmacy, is an understanding of the tax itself and that is a matter of

[2]   For the politics of nineteenth-century taxation, see the seminal work by Professor
      Daunton: Martin Daunton, *Trusting Leviathan* (Cambridge: Cambridge University Press,
      2001).
[3]   Joseph Schumpeter, 'The Crisis of the Tax State' (1918), in R. Swedberg (ed.), *The Economics
      and Sociology of Capitalism* (Princeton: Princeton University Press, 1991), pp. 99–140; John
      Tiley, *Revenue Law*, 6th edn (Oxford: Hart Publishing, 2008); Rebecca Boden, 'Taxation
      Research as Social Policy Research', in M. Lamb, A. Lymer, J. Freedman, S. James (eds.),
      Taxation: An Interdisciplinary Approach to Research (Oxford: Oxford University Press, 2005),
      pp. 105–21.
[4]   Isaac William Martin, Ajay K. Mehrotra, Monica Prasad (eds.), *The New Fiscal Sociology,
      Taxation in Comparative and Historical Perspective* (Cambridge: Cambridge University
      Press, 2009).

law. Constitutionally, taxes must be expressed in law. The imperatives that drive the legislators who draft and introduce the tax and the legal constraints under which they operate govern its shape. The legal form that a tax takes, the way it is formulated, the structures that are set up to administer it and the nature of provisions for its enforcement and collection together constitute its essential nature and the basis of its very existence.

This foundation makes any tax part of a legalistic discourse, which by its nature is highly technical. And although this character of a tax can seem arcane, being accessible and of interest only to doctrinal lawyers, and to tax lawyers at that, it is the legal factors shaping the tax that are responsible for the effects it can have. This fact makes the legal study of tax relevant beyond the narrow field of doctrinal law and its practitioners. Scholars pursuing other discourses in history, social policy, politics and government, seeking a full explanation of the dynamics of their field, could find their subject informed by its relationship with tax. What might appear unpromising issues of dubious relevance, namely questions of legislative drafting, statutory interpretation, bureaucratic administration and the practicalities of the implementation of tax, can illuminate the routine, the extraordinary and the intractable. A close doctrinal study of the law and practice of a tax, therefore, not only promotes the more profound understanding of the forces working towards the introduction of a specific tax and identifies the reasons for the nature of its substance and supporting machinery, but can also explain its potency outside the fiscal sphere. It can also reveal the reasons why certain taxes have difficulty in adapting to changing conditions and values.

This, then, is the story of a tax. The overall objective of this study is to explore the dynamics of the medicine stamp duty, to see the nature and extent of its contribution to the shaping of its operational context in law and in the practice of pharmacy. It explores the origins, nature and consequences of this fiscal relationship between medicines and the state as expressed in the medicine stamp duty. Its specific aims are twofold.

The first is to demonstrate that this apparently minor tax in the fiscal portfolio was far from insignificant, and through its history revealed broad themes of profound importance to the development of tax law and the wider legal order. An enduring tax on a specific commodity is rare in the history of taxation, especially one that remained essentially unreformed for the whole of its long life. The subject matter of taxes throughout fiscal history addressed social, political and economic imperatives and reflected the values of the age. Imposts on hats, gloves, carriages, servants, windows, hair powder and armorial bearings embodied a policy of taxation that had yet to reach the degree of sophistication that was to emerge in the later nineteenth century. But it is these very qualities of fiscal unimportance and restricted specialist operation which resulted in the tax's retention of its original form and its longevity and which together make the medicine stamp duty unique in its power to reveal much wider themes in the legal history of tax. These concern the fundamentals of taxation: the purposes and role of tax in society, the orthodox ideals of good taxation, the power of fiscal imperatives, the reality of the authority of law in the field of tax and the limits of bureaucratic power, how fairness was achieved in tax and the isolation of tax law within the English legal system. And these are themes that, in their detail, character and substance, reflect contemporary values and concerns. They transcend chronological differences and are of enduring relevance. Any historical understanding of these recurring questions in tax leads to a greater appreciation of the dynamics of these themes today.

The second aim of this study is to demonstrate that despite its relative financial insignificance, the medicine stamp duty and the way it was administered historically had a profound and unforeseen effect on the structures and practice of professional pharmacy, far beyond its original fiscal intent, namely the proprietary medicines it was first planned to address. It was the law of tax that determined the nature, processes and structure of an impost and, in turn, had an impact on the field of activity in which the tax operated. This study examines the effectiveness of the legal regime of the medicine stamp duty as a taxing and regulating instrument, the degree of its influence in the development of the pharmacy profession and its impact on the quality of medicines and the control of therapeutic medicines. The legalistic discourse is adopted and valued as shedding new light and revealing a novel perspective on the history of pharmacy. This study argues that tax is a potent force in the development of the practice of pharmacy, that it has a place within the social, political and economic forces that have been identified as shaping it in the nineteenth and twentieth centuries. Tax is the focus of this study, but it does not, of course, argue that the law of tax is the only, or even a major, factor in determining the historical course of pharmaceutical development. It acknowledges that tax is just one factor among many formative influences in this complex branch of medical history,[5] but maintains that it is one that can be addressed with value among the others identified by scholars in the medical humanities. Although tax and its legal doctrine constitute one dimension of the study of history, it is one that is frequently ignored, dismissed or regarded as merely incidental.[6]

[5] See generally Glenn Sonnedecker (ed.), *Kremers and Urdang's History of Pharmacy*, 4th edn (Philadelphia: J. B. Lippincott Company, 1976), pp. 99–121.
[6] Jan M. Novotny, 'Stamp Duties', (1955) 15 *Journal of Economic History* 288.

It has been neglected because it is, at best, perceived as technical and intractable, at worst because it is regarded as irrelevant, but always because of the dominance of other perspectives. This study seeks to redress the balance, to reveal a neglected force in a major aspect of nineteenth-century social development and to ensure tax takes its place in the intellectual infrastructure of pharmaceutical history, to provide new insights and fresh perspectives and to permit new connections to be made. It further seeks to address the remoteness of tax law to provide an accessible resource for scholars pursuing alternative discourses in the field of pharmaceutical history.

FINANCIAL IMPERATIVES IN EIGHTEENTH-CENTURY ENGLAND

At the time that the British government took the decision to tax medicines in the last quarter of the eighteenth century, it was in urgent need of increased public revenue. Politically the country was in turmoil and rife with faction.[7] Reeling from the loss of America in 1776, Lord North resigned in 1782, having served for more than a decade as Prime Minister and Chancellor of the Exchequer; the Marquess of Rockingham had died after just three months at the head of his administration; and the Earl of Shelburne's ministry of just eight months was defeated by a cynical alliance between Charles James Fox and Lord North. That ministry, headed by the Duke of Portland and only reluctantly accepted by George III, came into power on 2 April 1783. Financially, the country was in desperate straits. For much of the century it had been at war with France, Spain and, latterly, America, and the challenge facing successive administrations was that of raising sufficient public revenue to meet the escalating costs of these hostilities. The series of long and expensive wars had resulted in an enormous national debt, which reached £234 million in the wake of the American war. The annual tax revenues amounted to some £13 million, and of that more than half serviced the national debt. This financial crisis was of such magnitude that it could not be swiftly resolved. Indeed, when Sir Robert Peel became prime minister more than fifty years later, in 1841, he found a Treasury still empty from the financial aftermath of the wars of the previous century. The debt then claimed more than half of the total gross expenditure of the central government. Furthermore, the tax revenue had fallen as a result of the remission of some duties to promote the Whig principles of free trade, and the population struggled in the face of a series

---

[7] David Wilkinson, *The Duke of Portland, Politics and Party in the Age of George III* (Basingstoke: Palgrave Macmillan, 2003), pp. 48–52. See also John Cannon, *The Fox-North Coalition* (Cambridge: Cambridge University Press, 1969), pp. 82–8.

of bad harvests and depressed wages to pay the established taxes on everyday items of life. The financial trials seemed no less severe in the 1840s than they had been in the 1780s.

This challenging economic situation was exacerbated by an added call on the public revenue which was emerging in the early years of the new Victorian age. The economy of late-eighteenth-century Britain was characterised by the domination of agriculture, the modest scale and local nature of domestic commerce and industry,[8] the small and largely sessile population and the prime importance of land as the basis of political power. Only foreign commerce was important in scale and in its use of capital. The nascent industrialisation of the latter part of the eighteenth century grew and intensified apace, and by 1837 Britain was already in the process of transformation from an agricultural to an industrial economy. Technological advances had revealed the possibility of escape from the constraints of natural power, and from this stemmed the development, at an astonishing speed, of new heavy and manufacturing industry and a revolution in communications. Stimulating and sustaining these developments were the evolution of new markets, both domestic and foreign, and the availability of plentiful labour resulting from the trebling of the population. Britain's economy continued to grow throughout the nineteenth century, rising to such a degree of prosperity that by the last quarter of the century it could indeed claim to be the world's leading industrial nation.

Such rapid economic growth brought with it social problems greater than any the country had yet experienced. The new towns that developed rapidly in centres of industry, attracting workers from the countryside, soon became overcrowded and diseased, giving rise to severe problems of epidemic, criminality and vice.[9] Other problems of social welfare emerged from the appalling working conditions in mines and factories,[10] with the health, safety and education of children of particular concern. And underlying and intensifying these grave social concerns was the persistent question of poverty. The magnitude of these social welfare problems overwhelmed the essentially medieval legal and governmental infrastructure of early Victorian Britain.[11] To act on so many

[8]   See generally, M. J. Daunton, *Progress and Poverty* (Oxford: Oxford University Press, 1995).
[9]   Poor Law Commissioners, *Report on an Inquiry into the Sanitary Condition of the Labouring Population of Great Britain* (London: HMSO, 1842).
[10] First Report of the Central Board of Commissioners for inquiring into the Employment of Children in Factories, *House of Commons Parliamentary Papers* (1833) (450) xx 1 at p. 36.
[11] See generally S. G. and E. O. A. Checkland (eds.), *The Poor Law Report of 1834* (London: Pelican Books, 1974), Introduction; Derek Fraser, *The Evolution of the British Welfare State* (London: Macmillan, 1973); David Roberts, *Victorian Origins of the British Welfare State* (Hamden: Archon Books, 1969).

fronts, to gather the information necessary to initiate reform, to frame the legislation, set up commissions and the network of personnel in the field and to regulate and pay the officials concerned was costly. These were not one-off expenditures: what was required was a consistent flow of public revenue to meet what amounted to the increased expenditure of a new bureaucratic state.

The orthodox response to raising public revenue to meet such financial exigencies throughout the eighteenth century invariably included a combination of raising loans and levying taxes.[12] Accepting that the solution to the financial crisis lay in part at least with increased taxation, successive administrations sought to determine how far the existing imposts that formed part of the tax code could meet their pressing demands. In the late eighteenth century, direct taxation was inherently limited and constituted the exception rather than the rule. Such taxation was extraordinary, being limited to times of national emergency – generally war – and no sufficiently developed administrative machinery existed to extend its scope. The principal direct tax was the land tax, originally a tax on real and personal property and incomes but which by the end of the eighteenth century became a tax purely on land in the nature of a perpetual charge.[13] Although it was levied every year and constituted a real burden on landowners,[14] the tax reduced in importance and effectiveness, and in 1798 provision was made for its redemption.[15]

In the late eighteenth century, the fiscal system favoured indirect taxation and direct expenditure taxes, namely the taxation of a range of human events, transactions and commodities. There were various avenues in which public revenue could be raised in this way: taxes on a finished product, on the elements of its manufacture, on its sale, or on the seller, sometimes all at the same time, sometimes only one or more elements. The reason lay in dominant orthodox views as to the nature of desirable taxation, a fiscal ideology that excluded direct taxation from realistic consideration as a routine means

[12] See John Brewer, *The Sinews of Power* (London: Unwin Hyman, 1989), pp. 88–134.
[13] See generally B. E. V. Sabine, *A Short History of Taxation* (London: Butterworths, 1980), pp. 103–7; Thirteenth Report of the Commissioners of Inland Revenue, *House of Commons Parliamentary Papers* (1870) (C. 82) xx 193 at pp. 314–22; W. R. Ward, *The English Land Tax in the Eighteenth Century* (London: Oxford University Press, 1953); Paul Langford, *Public Life and the Propertied Englishman 1689–1798* (Oxford: Clarendon Press, 1991), pp. 339–66; J. V. Beckett, 'Land Tax or Excise: The Levying of Taxation in Seventeenth- and Eighteenth-Century England' (1985) 100 *English Historical Review* 285; William Phillips, 'No Flowers, By Request' (1963) *British Tax Review* 285.
[14] See R. A. C. Parker, 'Direct Taxation on the Coke Estates in the Eighteenth Century' (1956) 71 *English Historical Review* 247.
[15] Land Tax Perpetuation Act 1798 (38 Geo. III c. 60); Anon., *Considerations on the Act for the Redemption of the Land Tax* (London: J. Payne, 1798).

of raising public revenue. These were expressed in a number of canons, all stemming from the fundamental constitutional principle of consent to taxation, each of which inevitably led to a preference for indirect and expenditure taxation. These canons were set down by Adam Smith in his *Wealth of Nations* in 1776[16] to the effect that taxes should be voluntary and non-inquisitorial, that any direct assessment should be necessary and that the role of central government in assessment and collection should be kept to a minimum. It was also widely accepted that the poor should be taxed sensitively or not at all. Indirect and expenditure taxation went a long way towards satisfying these principles. Arguably, being directed to meet the nation's needs, all taxation was necessary. It was voluntary because, being imposed on luxuries rather than necessities, the individual had a choice whether to purchase the item and, accordingly, whether to bear the tax. By the same reasoning expenditure taxes were thought to constitute an accurate taxation of wealth and ensured that the poor were taxed as lightly as possible. Taxes on commodities were generally non-inquisitorial, that is, not requiring an intrusive inquiry into the personal financial affairs of individuals and so leaving any questions of means or income untouched by the officers of the executive. Furthermore, the costs of collecting indirect taxes were generally, although not invariably, lower than the costs of collecting direct taxes, requiring minimum effort by the executive who collected the tax from the merchant. This reflected a further immense advantage enjoyed by indirect taxes. As Adam Smith observed, taxes on commodities were 'not so much murmured against' because they were imposed in the first instance on the manufacturer or seller, who would increase the price of the commodity accordingly to pass the burden of the tax to the purchaser. The tax was thereby 'insensibly paid by the people'.[17] Thereafter, the duty could be increased, as small rises would barely be noticed. Such a low degree of public awareness promoted compliance.

Ideology and pragmatism, therefore, ensured that in the eighteenth century the public revenue was raised almost entirely through indirect and expenditure taxes.[18] These comprised the excise and the customs duties, a raft of assessed taxes and the stamp duties. Of these, the excise, introduced as part of the financial measures of the civil war in 1643, was the most productive. It applied

[16]   Adam Smith, *An Inquiry into the Nature and Causes of the Wealth of Nations* (R. H. Campbell, A. S. Skinner, W. B. Todd (eds.), 2 vols. (Oxford: Clarendon Press, 1976), vol. 2, pp. 825–8.

[17]   Adam Smith, *Lectures on Justice, Police, Revenue and Arms delivered in 1763* (Oxford: Clarendon Press, 1896), p. 243.

[18]   Patrick K. O'Brien, 'The Political Economy of British Taxation, 1660–1815' (1988) 41 *Economic History Review* 1.

to a wide range of domestically produced articles and raw materials intended for home consumption, and came to include beer, malt, spirits, soap, salt, candles, coal and paper, and was levied at the point of production or the point of sale. It also comprised various licences such as those to auctioneers, brewers, maltsters, tobacco dealers, vinegar makers and wine dealers. It raised the greatest proportion of revenue and its department was the largest by far of all the fiscal offices. Next in productivity came the ancient customs. They were imposed at the ports primarily on imported goods, notably spirits, beer, wine and tobacco, paid by the merchant and the cost passed on to the consumer.[19] They were set as a percentage on the value of the goods in the two Books of Rates, tables of duties agreed by Parliament and signed by the Speaker. The first Book of Rates was compiled during the speakership of Sir Harbottle Grimstone in 1660,[20] and it was supplemented in the time of Sir Spencer Compton to include in a second book goods not specified in the original.[21] Assessed taxes, which were strictly direct taxes, had the most various objects of charge in the seventeenth century, including burials, bachelors, glass, stone and earthenware bottles, windows and hearths, and throughout the eighteenth century taxes were imposed on armorial bearings, dogs, servants, silver and many other items.[22] The last in the portfolio of indirect taxes of the British fiscal system was the stamp duty. As with many of Britain's financial instruments, it had first been adopted from Holland and introduced into Britain in 1694 to help finance the war against France.[23] The duty was originally imposed on the vellum, parchment and paper on which legal transactions, agreements and proceedings were written.[24] As such it applied to documents such as insurance policies, documents in court proceedings, grants of honour, probate and

---

[19] For a history of the customs duties see First Report, Commissioners of Customs, *House of Commons Parliamentary Papers* (1857) (2186) iii 301 at pp. 358–76. See generally Edward Carson, 'The Development of Taxation up to the 18th Century' (1984) *British Tax Review* 237; John Craig, *A History of Red Tape* (London: Macdonald & Evans Ltd, 1955), pp. 91–6; William Phillips, 'Anything to Declare' (1965) *British Tax Review* 226.

[20] Referred to in the Act of Tonnage and Poundage 1660 (12 Car. II c. 4) s. 6.

[21] Act Amending the Act of Tonnage and Poundage 1724 (11 Geo I c. 7) s. 2. See Stephen Dowell, *A History of Taxation and Taxes in England*, 4 vols. (London: Longmans, Green and Co., 1884), vol. 2, pp. 17–20, 95–6.

[22] Report and Minutes of Evidence from the Select Committee on Inland Revenue and Customs Establishments, *House of Commons Parliamentary Papers* (1862) (370) xii 131 at q. 32.

[23] Stamp Act 1694 (5 & 6 Will. & M. c. 21). For the early history of the stamp duties, see Edward Hughes, 'The English Stamp Duties, 1664–1764' (1941) 56 *English Historical Review* 234; H. Dagnall, *Creating a Good Impression* (London: HMSO, 1994), pp. 3–14; See generally R. S. Nock, '1694 And All That' (1994) *British Tax Review* 432; Dowell, *History of Taxation*, vol. 3, pp. 321–46.

[24] 5 & 6 Will. & M. c. 21 s. 3.

letters of administration. The stamp duty was either a fixed amount depending on the nature of the item in question, or an ad valorem duty depending on the value involved, and ranged from one penny to forty shillings. It was immediately successful as a tax.

Not all the indirect taxes enjoyed an unrestricted potential for expansion. Customs duties had to be carefully managed due to their unique possible impact in the wider sphere of foreign trade and politics. Indeed, when Sir Robert Peel reintroduced the income tax in 1842, he did so to 'unlock the Free Trade cupboard.'[25] The excise was of equal, albeit domestic, sensitivity. Being imposed primarily on commodities perceived as necessities rather than luxuries as orthodox understanding of fairness demanded, and obtrusively administered by officers of central government, it had been immensely unpopular in the years after its introduction.[26] '[I]ts very name,' observed Blackstone, 'has been odious to the people of England'.[27] Although this resentment of the excise was diminishing by the close of the eighteenth century, and excise riots were rare,[28] governments were wary of straining this fragile popular acceptance too far. When Lord John Cavendish, Chancellor of the Exchequer in the Fox-North coalition, was searching for new sources of revenue in 1783, he said that the bad weather and poor harvests of recent years prevented him from raising the customs and excise duties, for the burden would ultimately fall on corn and that would cause national distress.[29] So while both customs and excise were increased during the eighteenth century, reaching their peak in the early nineteenth century before beginning their decline in the face of the movement for free trade,[30] it was done with caution. As to the assessed taxes, the danger in extending these lay in popular resentment of direct taxation and a perception that the British were overtaxed.

---

[25] G. M. Trevelyan, *British History in the Nineteenth Century and After* (1782–1919), 2nd edn (London: Longmans, Green & Co., 1937), p. 267. See generally J. H. Clapham, *An Economic History of Modern Britain: Free Trade and Steel 1850–1886* (Cambridge University Press, 1932), pp. 398–9; Brewer, *Sinews of Power*, p. 100.

[26] Edward Raymond Turner, 'Early Opinion about English Excise' (1916) 21 *American Historical Review* 314.

[27] Blackstone, *Commentaries on the Laws of England*, E. Christian (ed), 15th edn (London: T. Cadell and W. Davies, 1809), vol. 1, p. 319

[28] Michael J. Braddick, 'Popular Politics and Public Policy: The Excise Riot at Smithfield in February 1647 and its Aftermath' (1991) 34 *Historical Journal* 597; Stephen Matthews, 'A Tax Riot in Tewkesbury in 1805' (2002) *British Tax Review* 437.

[29] And, implicitly, any potential popular unrest: *Parliamentary Register 1780–1796*, vol. 10, 26 May 1783, p. 67 *per* Lord John Cavendish.

[30] See generally Graham Smith, *Something to Declare, 1000 years of Customs and Excise* (London: Harrap, 1980).

It was the stamp duty whose fiscal and political potential to produce more revenue was immediately understood and exploited in the latter part of the eighteenth century. Although it was by far the least productive of the four imposts,[31] it was held in especial favour. This was because it did not suffer from the drawbacks of the other taxes, and enjoyed practical advantages even beyond those normally associated with indirect taxes. There were two principal reasons why governments liked the stamp duty.

The first was that it enjoyed the invaluable advantage of easy and cheap management, and the reduction to a minimum of the expense of tax collection was the aspiration of any government and was firmly accepted as a desirable feature of any tax. Although the stamp duties were administered and controlled entirely by central government,[32] their implementation did not demand the extensive and expensive staff required by the customs and excise. Although the excise was the most productive tax, a large staff of salaried officers was necessary to undertake the constant visits to traders and manufacturers all over the country to inspect, check and assess the wide range of articles subject to the excise, and to undertake the considerable amount of paperwork to which such surveys gave rise.[33] In contrast to this, the administration of stamp duty was of refreshing simplicity.[34] The duties were collected as stamps sold. For most of the stamp duties, taxpayers would initiate the process by attending their local Stamp Office to purchase the stamp they required, or to have a chargeable document impressed with a stamp. Because they were required merely to provide the stamps requested, and not to give advice on the nature or value of the stamp an individual might need, the distributors did not need to be trained to the same degree as other revenue officials. By the end of the eighteenth century the machinery of stamp duty administration was well established. It could not rival the efficiency of the excise department, and serious deficiencies were identified in 1826, but thereafter it was regarded as generally robust, at least in London.

Second, stamp duties enjoyed minimal visibility and that brought with it popular toleration from their inception.[35] This acceptance continued into the

---

[31] See generally John Jeffrey-Cook, 'William Pitt and his Taxes' (2010) *British Tax Review* 376, 384.

[32] Control lay with the Board of Stamps, then the Board of Stamps and Taxes, and then from 1849, the Board of Inland Revenue.

[33] Report and Minutes of Evidence from the Select Committee on Inland Revenue and Customs Establishments, *House of Commons Parliamentary Papers* (1862) (370) xii 131 at qq. 1564–1616. See too John Pink, *The Excise Officers and their Duties in an English Market Town* (Surbiton: JRP, 1995).

[34] See Chapter 2.

[35] See generally, Charles Adams, *For Good and Evil, The Impact of Taxes on the Course of Civilisation*, 2nd edn (Lanham, Md: Madison Books, 2001).

late eighteenth century despite the opposition to the stamp duty in America still being fresh in the public mind,[36] and the stamp duty conforming to only one of the classic canons of taxation, namely that it was voluntary in that it was largely imposed on luxuries that individuals did not have to buy if they did not wish to. It was regarded as 'a painless process of extraction of the revenue'.[37] Reasonable increases could be introduced without undermining compliance, with taxpayers barely aware of the tax or its increase. It was, in Pitt's words, 'safely and expeditiously collected at a small expense',[38] 'easily raised, widely diffused, ... pressed little upon any particular class, especially the lower orders of society'.[39] Indeed, when Lord John Cavendish increased and extended the stamp duties in 1783 he remarked that he did so 'without materially affecting the poor' and minimising the risk of national unrest.[40] Furthermore, the simplicity of administration that made it so popular with the taxing authorities found equal popularity with the taxpaying public. Although it was administered by officers of central government – a feature that had made the excise the subject of popular loathing – the administration of the stamp duty in its interface with the public was unobtrusive, non-inquisitorial, simple, accessible and efficient. Whatever the problems experienced at the central office in London, the local offices that constituted the only contact the public had with stamp duty administration worked to its satisfaction. The items that had to bear a stamp were laid down in the charging statute, and the manufacturer or vendor simply had to purchase the stamps of the required value from the Stamp Office. Stamp offices were situated in the major towns all over the country and although it has been seen that the stamp distributors were not required to give the public advice, in practice they often did.

Examination of the fiscal policies of successive administrations in the late eighteenth century confirms that the stamp duty was valued as a stable, safe, convenient, albeit relatively small, source of revenue. As such, it was steadily

---

[36] The extension of the stamp duty to America was intensely opposed in that country, and although it was repealed, it formed a potent factor in the events leading to the Declaration of Independence: Dagnall, *Creating a Good Impression*, pp. 47–9. See too Lynne Oats and Pauline Sadler, 'Accounting for the Stamp Act Crisis', (2008) 35 *Accounting Historians Journal* 101.

[37] Report and Minutes of Evidence from the Select Committee on Medicine Stamp Duties, *House of Commons Parliamentary Papers* (1937) (Cmd. 54) viii 129 at q. 364 *per* Sir John Haslam, member of the committee.

[38] William Pitt, *The Speeches of William Pitt*, 4 vols. (London: Longman, Hurst Rees and Orme, 1806), vol. 3, pp. 122–5.

[39] *Ibid.* For Pitt's taxation policy see generally John Ehrman, *The Younger Pitt: the Years of Acclaim*, (London: Constable, 1969), pp. 248–58; Richard Cooper, 'William Pitt, Taxation, and the Needs of War' (1982) 22 *The Journal of British Studies* 94.

[40] *Parliamentary Register 1780–1796*, vol. 10, 26 May 1783, pp. 67, 70.

increased in scope. By the time the medicine stamp duty was introduced in 1783, the stamp duty applied to a large range of documents, including conveyances, licences, postage stamps, grants of probate, bonds, legal proceedings, legacies, newspapers, pamphlets, marine and fire insurances, bills of exchange, the admission to certain bodies such as the Inns of Court, promissory notes, receipts, contracts and inventories and the registration of births, marriages and deaths. Although the main category of stamp duties was always that on legal instruments, the tax had also been extended from the original range of legal documents to commodities in everyday use. Playing cards and dice, gold and silver plate, saddles, carriages, stage coaches, racehorses, hats, gloves, cosmetics, horses, pawnbrokers and publicans were all subjected to the tax. Not only was the scope of the stamp duties extended in this way, but the rates were regularly and comprehensively increased. When Lord John Cavendish did so in 1783, he admitted that it was unpleasant for any Chancellor of the Exchequer to increase taxes, but that he would endeavour to ensure the least inconvenience to the public. He calculated that his proposals would raise £560,000, '[t]he exact sum necessary to pay the interest on the loan of £12 million'.[41]

Facing a largely unabated financial challenge when, amid political disarray, he succeeded Lord John Cavendish as chancellor in December 1783, William Pitt's financial policy was equally dominated by the urgent need for fresh sources of public revenue and ensuring that established ones were made as productive as possible. His principal financial objective was to create a surplus so that he could reduce the country's enormous national debt, and he looked in part to taxation to achieve it.[42] Despite his introduction of conceptually innovative taxation in the form of the triple assessment of 1798[43] and the first general charge on income of 1799,[44] both unprecedented in that they breached the orthodox canon of voluntariness, William Pitt's taxation policy was firmly seated in eighteenth-century fiscal orthodoxy. He aimed to raise public revenue as efficiently and cheaply as possible, and to do so with the lightest impact on the people in general, and ensuring as far as possible that the tax burden was fairly shared according to ability to pay. To avoid taxing the

[41] *Ibid.*, p. 73.
[42] Michael Duffy, *The Younger Pitt*, (Harlow: Longman, 2000), pp. 81, 85–6.
[43] Based on multiples of a taxpayer's assessed tax charge of the previous year: Taxation Act 1798 (38 Geo. III c. 16).
[44] Duties on Income Act 1799 (39 Geo. III c. 13). For the history of income tax, see B. E. V. Sabine, *A History of Income Tax* (London: George Allen & Unwin Ltd, 1966); Peter Harris, *Income Tax in Common Law Jurisdictions* (Cambridge: Cambridge University Press, 2006); B. E. V. Sabine, 'Great Budgets: Pitt's Budget of 1799', (1970) *British Tax Review* 201; Thirteenth Report of the Commissioners of Inland Revenue, *House of Commons Parliamentary Papers* (1870) (C. 82) xx 193 at pp. 326–34.

poor as far as he could, he targeted luxuries rather than necessities, a policy enabled by the notable growth in consumerism in the eighteenth century.

Famously taxing 'as fast and as far as public opinion would allow',[45] acutely and pragmatically Pitt looked to indirect taxation.[46] In addition to increasing a raft of assessed taxes imposed on luxury goods, including the famous window and inhabited house taxes, and extending them to servants, carriages, coaches and carts, he introduced new taxes including those on bricks and tiles, horses of various kinds, game licences, non-working dogs, clocks and watches, armorial bearings, hats, packets of hair powder, perfumes and cosmetics and a new stamp duty on lawyers' certificates of qualification. He explored every item as a possible object of charge: corks, hops, guns, pins, fans, printed music, visiting cards, clocks, racecourses, ropes and so on.[47] As part of his policy to tax the business community properly, he introduced the highly unpopular shop tax and favoured extending the practice of imposing annual licences on shopkeepers and traders. Hawkers, hackney coachmen, publicans, dealers in gold and silver plate and sellers of tea, coffee and chocolate all had to purchase licences and this edict was extended to pawnbrokers, coachmakers, glove sellers and attorneys. Perfumers epitomised Pitt's fiscal policy. They were first taxed in 1786, having to purchase a licence and to pay stamp duty on all perfumes, pomatum, hair powder, cosmetics and other toilet articles they sold, articles that were indubitably luxuries. The longevity of Pitt's taxes was notable. Of his stamp duties, that on hats lasted for twenty-seven years, gloves for nine years and hair powder and perfumes each lasted for fourteen years; the game licences duty lasted 223 years.[48]

It was clear, therefore, that eighteenth-century governments in search of a commodity on which to impose the stamp duty looked to any widely used and clearly identifiable article that could bear a levy. As Lord John Cavendish observed in 1783, he chose as his objects of new taxation those he felt 'could well bear taxation, and be truly productive'.[49] It was in this search for a commercial activity that could be taxed for profit that the government's eye first fell in 1783 on the thriving, lucrative and rapidly growing trade in quack medicines.

[45] Jeffrey-Cook, 'William Pitt and his Taxes', 390.
[46] For a history of Pitt's taxes see Stephen Dowell, *A History of Taxation and Taxes*, 4 vols. (London: Longmans, Green and Co., 1884), vol. 2, pp. 182–200; Jeffrey-Cook, 'William Pitt and his Taxes', 376.
[47] Dowell, *History of Taxation* vol. 2, p. 186.
[48] The longest-lived stamp duty was that on playing cards, introduced in 1711 and abolished in 1960.
[49] *Parliamentary Register 1780–1796*, vol. 10, 26 May 1783, p. 67.

THE PHENOMENON OF QUACKERY

Quack medicines were ubiquitous in eighteenth-century England. Illness was rife in society at all levels and within a rudimentary practice of health care, the use of therapeutic medicines constituted an established element of medical treatment. The regular medical profession, underpinned by requirements of education, ethics and, in theory at least, monopoly, consisted of physicians, apothecaries and surgeons. The wealthy generally consulted a qualified physician, the elite of medical practitioners, whereas those of limited means would turn to an apothecary. After a one-to-one consultation, a physician would prescribe a medicine for the patient's particular condition, and that medicine would be made up on the physician's instructions by an apothecary. But when patients' resources did not permit recourse to orthodox medical practice, they turned to the ever-increasing number of unqualified individuals operating outside the regular medical professions and specialising in the invention, manufacture and sale of medicines. These individuals were popularly known as quacks,[50] and their medicines, defined in the public mind primarily according to the nature of the people who sold them, as quack medicines.

The term 'quack' was well known but fundamentally uncertain. There was no agreement or uniformity in its significance or use. What was a quack or quack medicine to one person might not be so regarded by another. It was a subjective term, generally used as a term of abuse, and was loosely used to describe an unorthodox medical practitioner, with connotations of amateurism and false premises.[51] In his *Dictionary* of 1755, Samuel Johnson defined a quack as '[a] boastful pretender to arts which he does not understand', '[a] vain boastful pretender to physick; one who proclaims his own medical abilities in publick places' and '[a]n artful tricking practitioner in physick'.[52] Writing some thirty years later, James Makittrick Adair, a regular physician based in

---

[50] There are differing views as to the genesis of the term 'quack'. One view is that it comes from the noise of ducks in the farmyard, others from the old Dutch word *quacksalver*: 'one who quacks (boasts) about the virtue of his salves' Quack also meant shouting.

[51] Roy Porter, *Quacks* (Stroud: Tempus Publishing Ltd, 2000), pp. 15–20. This book is the illustrated version of Professor Porter's major work on quackery: Roy Porter, *Health for Sale, Quackery in England 1650–1850* (Manchester: Manchester University Press, 1989); Irvine Loudon, 'The Vile Race of Quacks with which this Country is Infested', in W. F. Bynum and Roy Porter (eds.), *Medical Fringe & Medical Orthodoxy 1750–1850* (London: Croom Helm, 1987), p. 106.

[52] Samuel Johnson, A *Dictionary of the English Language*, reprint of the edition first published London: Kapton, 1755, (New York: AMS Press, 1967). The definition endured: see 'Pharmacopulus', 'On the Concealment of Discoveries in Medicines', (1831) 16 *The Lancet* 444; T. W. Eden, 'An Address on Ancient and Modern Quackery', (1899) 154 *The Lancet* 1350.

Bath and a celebrated critic of quacks, added 'a vender of nostrums, the powers of which he does not understand – in short, a swindler and a knave' in the
definition.[53] Whether they were perceived as quacks depended on the nature
of the products or services they provided for money, and the way they did
so. The term quack applied to a diverse range of practitioners and appeared
in varying degrees according to the individual concerned. It encompassed
the traditional mountebanks, charlatans, individual medicine vendors and
entrepreneurs who at best were astute businessmen, at worst simply crooks.[54]
However, the term also included members of the regular profession who
engaged in commercial activity. This, and the fact that quack remedies were
often concocted from ingredients and formulae used by the regular medical
profession in preparing the medicines they prescribed, served to make the
dividing line between quacks and regular practitioners, and between quack
medicines and orthodox medicines, extremely difficult to draw. The assumption that quack medicines were medicines sold by quacks was far too easy and
simplistic. So although the term quack was a familiar term that most people
believed they understood instantly and precisely, it was one that was particularly challenging to define.

Quack medicines, however, shared characteristics other than the nature
of their vendors. When these medicines were looked at as a genre of remedy, certain characteristics were understood to attach to them. Their first, and
pre-eminent, feature was their highly pronounced commercial nature. It was
made explicit in the fact and content of their advertisement. Quack medicines
were invariably aggressively promoted to the public, as they would only sur-
vive in a highly competitive marketplace and earn their proprietors a return
if they were robustly publicised. Indeed, the 'noisy' advertisement or 'puffing' of their products was also a central characteristic of the quack, and possibly gave rise to the name itself.[55] Publicity and advertising were acceptable
in the eighteenth century, a period when display was culturally important to
the whole of society, including the medical professions.[56] With the particular
agenda of the quacks, to attract, persuade and cajole an impersonal audience

53 James Makittrick Adair, 'Essay on Empiricism, or Quackery', *Medical Cautions for the
    Consideration of Invalids* (Bath: R. Cruttwell, 1786), at p. 138.
54 Itinerant vendors were less common in Britain than in the rest of Europe. Many quacks set-
    tled in towns and villages, and a large number were based in London: Leslie G. Matthews,
    'Licensed Mountebanks in Britain', (1964) 19 *Journal of the History of Medicine* 30, 43–4; C.
    J. S. Thompson, *The Quacks of Old London* (London: Brentano's Ltd, 1928), pp. 73–85. But
    see Porter, *Quacks*, pp. 63–5.
55 Eric J. Trimmer, 'Medical Folklore and Quackery' (1965) 76 *Folklore* 161, 162.
56 For example, apothecaries, chemists and druggists displayed colourful filled carboys in their
    shop windows to affirm the nature of their business and attract custom.

with authority and confidence, quacks used various techniques.[57] Initially, this was commonly done through stage shows, using such entertainments as tricks, spectacles, animals, comedy and dancing, often supported by distributing handbills to the watching crowds, providing entertainment and an atmosphere conducive to purchasing the quacks' wares. By the eighteenth century, the preferred method of publicising such medicines was through advertisements in the ever-increasing number of national and provincial newspapers.[58] Indeed, it was the central importance of advertising to the trade in medicines that forged the link with booksellers, newspaper proprietors and printers, who became some of their most active and important vendors.[59] Circulating libraries, perfumers and grocers also sold medicines.

A pamphlet published circa 1790, titled *An Account of Several Valuable and Excellent Genuine Patent and Public Medicines* sold by Mr W. Bacon in London to advertise his stock, describes twenty-four medicines in detail, lists a further eighty-eight, and refers to 'all other efficacious lozenges, corn salves and medicines'. The scope, efficacy, dosage and cost of the selected twenty-four are discussed in some detail, embellished by reported histories of the cured or relieved.[60] Large sums were expended by owners in advertising their medicines. For example, it is believed that the quack Samuel Solomon paid £5,000 a year to advertise his nostrum, the *Balm of Gilead*, all over the country.[61] Newspaper advertising increased throughout the nineteenth century, as did publicity in magazines, circulars and pamphlets, and was joined by advertising on huge hoardings, often near the principal railway lines, and posters on all forms of public transport.[62] Advertising remained the principal expense in connection with the trade; the London Chamber of Commerce estimated in 1914 that some £2 million was spent annually on it.[63]

[57] See Figure 1. For the promotional techniques adopted by quacks up to the eighteenth century, see Porter, *Quacks*, pp. 53–6, 87–114. See too Leslie G. Matthews, *History of Pharmacy in Britain* (Edinburgh: E. & S. Livingstone, 1962), pp. 290–4; Juanita Burnby, 'Pharmaceutical Advertisement in the 17th and 18th Centuries' (1988) 22 *European Journal of Marketing* 24.

[58] See for example, P.S. Brown, 'The Venders of Medicines Advertised in Eighteenth-Century Bath Newspapers' (1975 19 *Medical History* 352; Porter, *Quacks*, pp. 109–14.

[59] One advertisement for *Spilsbury's Drops* said that 'they may be supplied by their newsmen': *Felix Farley's Bristol Journal*, 6 December 1788. See too Tanya Schmoller, *The Life and Hard Times of a Sheffield Bookseller, Printer, Stationer and Supplier of Patent Medicines in the Mid-Eighteenth Century* (Newcastle upon Tyne: Tanya Schmoller, 1999).

[60] W. Bacon, *An Account of Several Valuable and Excellent Genuine Patent and Public Medicines* (London: *ca.* 1790).

[61] Porter, *Quacks*, p. 159.

[62] For the advertising of quack medicines in the mid-nineteenth century, see 'The Mode of Puffing Quack Medicines', (1849) 9 *Pharmaceutical Journal* (series 1) 163.

[63] Report and Minutes of Evidence from the Select Committee on Patent Medicines, *House of Commons Parliamentary Papers* (1914) (Cd. 414) ix 1 at qq. 6334, 6358.

The advertisements invariably made exaggerated and miraculous claims for the medicines' powers in curing, preventing or relieving every illness from the common cold to cancers and tuberculosis. Each medicine would list the names of the diseases it would relieve or cure, often an astonishing number of unrelated ailments. These claims were generally supported by fulsome testimonials from respectable middle-class individuals or, even better, the nobility or royalty.[64] Some medicines, particularly earlier in the eighteenth century, were panaceas, a single remedy claiming to cure all known human ailments. *Daffy's Elixir*, for example, a celebrated product, claimed to treat gout, kidney stones, shortness of breath, coughs, stomach cramps, scurvy, dropsy and rickets. Most, however, were specifics, addressing a particular ailment or group of ailments. In the eighteenth century most were directed to non-fatal diseases that were serious and debilitating or to minor complaints that were inconvenient or unpleasant such as digestive ailments and diseases of the eyes and skin. Susceptibility to the claims of the advertisements contributed to the continued popularity of such medicines. In Charles Dickens' *Our Mutual Friend*, published in 1864, Mr Twemlow feels unwell 'in consequence of having taken two advertised pills at about mid-day, on the faith of the printed representation accompanying the box (price one and a penny halfpenny, government stamp included), that the same "will be found highly salutary as a precautionary measure in connection with the pleasures of the table"'.[65]

The second characteristic of quack medicines was that of proprietorship, incorporating notions of exclusivity and secrecy, and this was revealed in the advertisements themselves. The product was named, and although this sometimes included aspirational terms such as 'Royal' or 'Imperial' or the name of a famous regular physician,[66] it usually reflected that of the inventor or proprietor. *Spilsbury's Antiscorbutic Drops* and *Dr James's Fever Powder* were celebrated examples.[67] The proprietor thus claimed the formula as his own and, accordingly, kept the composition secret, and so it was not disclosed in either advertisements or on the packaging of the medicine. Secrecy was a central characteristic of these medicines, adding to their mystique and reflecting the cultural values of the eighteenth century.

Some inventors went further to ensure ownership and secrecy. They formally obtained permission through the grant of letters patent from the Crown

[64] See the testimonials for *Spilsbury's Antiscorbutic Drops* in *Bath Chronicle*, 23 September 1784.
[65] Charles Dickens, *Our Mutual Friend*, Stephen Gill (ed.), (Harmondsworth: Penguin Books, 1971) p. 684. My thanks to Mr Richard Thomas for this reference.
[66] Porter, *Quacks*, pp. 104–5; Adair, 'Essay', p. 132.
[67] See Peter G. Homan, Briony Hudson, Raymond C. Rowe, *Popular Medicines*, (London: Pharmaceutical Press, 2008), p. 85.

'for the exclusive privilege to dose the public in his particular manner'[68] under the Statute of Monopolies 1623. Any person who had invented a medicine could obtain a monopoly for its manufacture and distribution for a period of fourteen years, as long as the medicine was new and that the person disclosed its composition to the Patent Office and paid the required fee.[69] There was in theory no secrecy in these patent medicines, as indeed the name implies, for the applicant had to give a specification or description of the invention, open to public scrutiny, so as to enable the public to have use of the invention at the end of the fourteen-year period.[70]

In practice, however, the disclosure was minimal and for all practical purposes the secrecy of the formula was maintained. Patents granted for medicines in the latter part of the eighteenth century reveal that the ingredients and method of manufacture were described (in some detail) in the specifications, some in general terms, some including precise amounts and concentrations. In some, however, only the ingredients were stated and not the amounts, proportions or concentrations, and sometimes the method of manufacture was omitted entirely. Because applicants were able to obtain a patent without full disclosure of the medicine's composition, a successful application for letters patent had significant benefits for a manufacturer. It preserved the essential secrecy of the composition; it still gave the owner legal protection against others who attempted to take advantage of the formula; it provided a significant cachet because the prestige of royal endorsement, albeit a purchased one, could be fulsomely and prominently exploited in advertising; and although the patent process included no element of quality control, of testing for efficacy or analysis for harmful ingredients, the formal nature of the grant of letters patent implied a degree of official approval of the medicine in question. The sale of patents for medicines thrived during the eighteenth century, and some 100 medical patents were taken out. Two examples of successful patentees, who were regular practitioners, were Dr Nehemiah Grew, who patented *Epsom Salts*, and Dr Thomas Henry, who patented antacids and medicines for nervous diseases.[71] Francis Spilsbury obtained a patent for his *Antiscorbutic Drops* in 1792.

Because the process for obtaining a patent was extremely costly with cumbersome procedures involving a number of useless yet expensive steps and corrupt officials requiring bribes to bend the rules, the great majority of medicines

[68] Dowell, *History of Taxation*, vol. 4, p. 366.
[69] Statute of Monopolies 1623 (21 Jac. I c. 3), s. 6.
[70] Sir William Blackstone, *Commentaries on the Laws of England*, 12th edn, 4 vols. (London: A. Strahan and W. Woodfall, for T. Cadell, 1794) vol. 2, p. 407 n. 7.
[71] Porter, *Quacks*, p. 21.

sold were not formally patented.[72] The inventors had never applied for one, had applied and been unsuccessful, or had successfully applied for one and it had expired. One of the most famous quack medicines, *Daffy's Elixir* was, for example, never patented. But to give their medicines an aura of official approbation, many medicine vendors falsely claimed a patent, most consumers being entirely unaware whether a particular medicine was formally patented.[73] The success of the trade supported this. Some individual quacks scraped a living through itinerant shows or small-scale local distribution of medicines, but many made their fortune in the eighteenth century. James Graham has been described as a 'superquack',[74] whereas Isaac Swainson made a fortune from his *Velnos' Vegetable Syrup*, said to treat venereal diseases, consumption, leprosy, cancer, tuberculosis, scurvy, smallpox and a range of other diseases, as did Nathaniel Godbold with his *Vegetable Balsam* for treating venereal disease and Joshua Ward and his *Pill and Drop*.

The collective name for such medicines varied. The word 'medicine' meant any remedy administered by a physician,[75] and so when qualified by the prefix 'patent' or 'proprietary,' it tended to signify a medicine supplied by an individual often outside the profession of regular medicine claiming ownership of the formula. By the eighteenth century the terms quack, proprietary, secret, patent, nostrum and empiric were used interchangeably. If drawn at all, any distinction tended to be one of scale. A nostrum suggested a poorer quack marketing his or her own concoction on a small scale, and a proprietary medicine being a named medicine manufactured and sold either by its inventor or by individuals who had purchased the formula and become the proprietors of the medicine in question, and marketed on a wider scale. By the nineteenth century many individual chemists prepared their own medicines which carried their name, and were marketed regionally, while the large manufacturing chemists of the late nineteenth century sold their 'branded' medicines nationally and dominated the field of self-medication. By the early twentieth century many of these latter concerns were operating on a considerable scale, representing huge financial investments and a significant workforce. Many

---

[72]	See the process described in William Holdsworth, A *History of English Law*, 16 vols., A. L. Goodhart and H. G. Hanbury (eds.), (London: Methuen & Co. Ltd; Sweet and Maxwell, 1965), vol. xv, pp. 35–7; *ibid.*, vol. xi, pp. 424–32. See too E. Wyndham Hulme, 'On the Consideration of the Patent Grant, Past and Present' (1897) 13 *Law Quarterly Review* 313; E. Wyndham Hulme 'On the History of Patent Law in the Seventeenth and Eighteenth Centuries', (1902) 18 *Law Quarterly Review* 280.

[73]	See *Gazeteer and New Daily Advertiser*, 31 January 1784.

[74]	Porter, *Quacks*, p. 13.

[75]	Johnson, *Dictionary* (1755).

had their own scientific laboratories and were actively engaged in ground-breaking research. The term 'patent medicine' strictly meant a medicine that had received a royal patent, but as a result of the practice of falsely claiming a royal patent, increasingly the term was used to refer to any medicine in the nature of a named, branded, proprietary remedy. As such, the term also took on the characteristics of these quack medicines, above all the secrecy of their ingredients and the extravagant advertising of their benefits.[76] As a result, the term 'patent medicines' came to be widely used, albeit entirely incorrectly, to describe all medicines of this kind. The use of the term would endure into modern popular usage[77] because it continued to evoke an impression of respectability, and although the fact that there was no statutory or legal authority for calling quack medicines 'patent' medicines was shown by the judgment in *Pharmaceutical Society* v. *Piper*,[78] the term was still seen in official reports right up to the abolition of the medicine stamp duty.[79] Because the expression was both inaccurate and misleading,[80] the term that is used henceforth in this study is 'proprietary medicines'.

The trade in proprietary medicines was at its height in the eighteenth century.[81] The demand for them seemed insatiable, and the public relied on them to an ever-growing degree. Quackery, observed James Makittrick Adair, 'has arrived to a truly alarming height'.[82] The prices charged show that proprietary medicines were directed primarily at the middle classes, but all sectors of society used them and they were part of the plurality of medical services available to and sought by the sick in eighteenth-century England. Certainly many celebrated individuals were known to use such remedies. Queen Anne, who was severely shortsighted, swore by the remedies of her oculist William Read, a tailor by trade[83]; George II employed Joshua Ward, who had once

---

[76] See for example Lee J. Vance 'Evolution of Patent Medicine' (1891) 39 *Popular Science Monthly* 76.

[77] Dowell, *History of Taxation*, vol. 2, p. 179.

[78] *Pharmaceutical Society* v. *Piper & Co.* [1893] QB 686.

[79] Thirty-sixth Report of the Commissioners of Customs and Excise, *House of Commons Parliamentary Papers* (1945–46) (Cmd. 6703) xi at p. 19. Note too that the medicines that came within the scope of the medicine stamp duty were still being called 'quack medicines' as late as 1909: *Parliamentary Debates* [hereafter *Parl. Deb.*] vol. 10, ser. 5, col. 1467, 9 September 1909 (HC).

[80] Dowell, *History of Taxation*, vol. 4, p. 365. See for example the marginal note to the introduction of the 1785 Act in *Journals of the House of Commons*, vol. 40, 4 July 1785, p. 1124.

[81] See generally Porter, *Quacks*; Thompson, *Quacks of Old London*. For the trade in eighteenth-century Ireland see James Kelly, 'Health for Sale: Mountebanks, Doctors, Printers and the Supply of Medication in Eighteenth-Century Ireland', (2008) 108C *Proceedings of the Royal Irish Academy. Section C: Archaeology, Celtic Studies, History, Linguistics, Literature* 75.

[82] Adair, 'Essay', p. 126.

[83] Matthews, 'Licensed Mountebanks', 43.

worked in the salt trade, to attend to his dislocated thumb;[84] Henry Fielding, Horace Walpole, Fanny Burney and Byron were all believers in various proprietary medicines.[85] The public's appetite for proprietary medicines was fed by a growing culture of consumerism, improved communications and increasingly sophisticated marketing. In 1748 the *Gentleman's Magazine* named more than 200 proprietary medicines and admitted the list was not complete.[86] Many were household names. *Dr Johnson's Yellow Ointment, Daffy's Elixir, Friar's Balsam* and *Velnos' Vegetable Syrup* were just a few, and *Dr James's Fever Powder* was astonishingly popular. Many would in due course make their owners extremely wealthy, a prime example being Thomas Holloway who, in the next century, made a great fortune from his *Holloway's Ointment*.[87]

Various powerful economic and social factors combined to create and sustain this intense demand for proprietary medicines from people of all classes, from the educated and wealthy to the poor and ignorant. First, in the eighteenth century, acute and chronic illnesses were widespread, death rates high and the age of mortality low. Insanitary conditions of life and poor nutrition rendered few people able to withstand the onslaught of such fatal diseases as smallpox, typhus and tuberculosis and of such debilitating conditions as gout, dropsy, skin and eye diseases and deafness.[88] In such an environment where to be ill and in pain was the norm, individuals naturally sought whatever relief they could obtain from whatever source, and were prepared to try almost anything. The state of medical science in the Western world was as yet undeveloped because the causes of disease were not understood. The remedies available to, and dispensed by, regular practitioners, were too few and too rarely effective in curing or relieving illness for regular medical practitioners to enjoy the exclusive confidence of the general public. Furthermore, the claims for the medicines chimed with popular medical knowledge.[89] The sick, the ignorant, the gullible and the desperate were the stock-in-trade of the proprietary medicines vendor.

Second, proprietary medicines were undoubtedly to some degree effective. The quacks argued that their remedies were beneficial, innovative and

[84] Porter, *Quacks*, p. 68; Thompson, *Quacks of Old London*, pp. 276–89.
[85] Porter, *Quacks*, p. 61.
[86] 'Pharmacopoeia Empirica' (1748) 18 *Gentleman's Magazine* 346.
[87] In 1879 he founded Holloway College for the Higher Education of Women in Egham in Surrey, which, as Royal Holloway College, became part of the University of London.
[88] Porter, *Quacks*, pp. 32–3.
[89] See J. Worth Estes, 'The Pharmacology of Nineteenth-Century Patent Medicines' (1988) 30 *Pharmacy in History* 3.

based on experience rather than theory.[90] Indeed, some remedies were no more harmful, or less effective, than the medicines prescribed by the regular physicians and prepared by the apothecaries. Some proprietary remedies, such as *Dr James's Fever Powder* and the quinine preparation *Jesuit's Bark* were accepted by regular practitioners as having some effectiveness.[91]

Third, although proprietary medicines were not particularly cheap – newspaper advertisements of the late eighteenth century show the prices commonly of between two shillings and sixpence, and five shillings – they did have the advantage of convenience. They were ready-made remedies, with no need for any formal consultation beforehand. They could be purchased anonymously from numerous fixed retail outlets, usually booksellers and publishers,[92] but also apothecaries, and chemists and druggists, and even by post, and could be bought in sufficient quantity for future use.

Finally, numerous other minor factors have been identified as contributing to the flourishing of the trade in proprietary medicines in England.[93] These included ineffective professional bodies, an economic theory that opposed regulation, patients with commercial power exercising real choice from the wide range of health-care options available in the eighteenth century and taking active responsibility for their own treatments, an undeveloped ethical context, the growing importance of good health in the face of increased secularisation, the influence of newspaper advertising in informing potential consumers as to the nature, cost and availability of medicines, an overarching increase in consumerism generally and the growth in the national market for manufactured goods. A weak and profiteering Crown bore some responsibility too, through its earlier practice of granting patents to newly invented medicines. The Crown was driven by financial motives, but because its actions gave such remedies credibility, it materially encouraged the trade.

---

[90] Empiricism, meaning the application of observation, experiment and practical experience rather than theory in determining the cause and treatment of illness, was claimed by many quacks as the basis of their treatments. The term empirics was applied both to the quacks themselves and to the medicines they sold.

[91] Adair, 'Essay', p. 134.

[92] For example, Charles Elliot, an Edinburgh bookseller and publisher, was a customer of, and agent for, the London chemist, Francis Spilsbury: Peter Isaac, 'Charles Elliot and Spilsbury's Antiscorbutic Drops', (1997) 27 *Pharmaceutical Historian* 46; Schmoller, *Sheffield Bookseller*.

[93] Porter, *Quacks*, pp. 31–52 and the authorities there cited.

THE TAXATION OF PROPRIETARY MEDICINES

In this dynamic setting of a prosperous and flourishing trade in proprietary medicines, a volatile political climate, severe financial exigencies in government and an established policy of raising money in times of crisis through the taxation of commodities, the Chancellor of the Exchequer in the new coalition ministry, the 'ineffective'[94] Whig Lord John Cavendish, introduced the medicine stamp duty in 1783. He did so in his first budget only days after the ministry was formed. It was not strictly a war budget, as the preliminaries of peace with France and Spain had been signed five months earlier, and the Treaty of Versailles between the three parties would be signed the following September, but it addressed the parlous financial state of the country resulting from those hostilities. The medicine stamp duty was undoubtedly a minor feature of Lord John Cavendish's budget, but nevertheless part of a comprehensive increase in the scope of stamp duty taxation.

The Medicine Stamp Duty Act 1783, the third of three stamp duty Acts passed in that year, taxed proprietary medicines for the first time.[95] There were two aspects to the tax. First, all persons who sold medicines in Great Britain[96] had to purchase an annual licence.[97] The licence cost twenty shillings in London and five shillings elsewhere,[98] although it was simplified in 1864 and 1875, when a uniform rate of five shillings per annum was introduced to apply to the whole country.[99] Second, any medicine they sold had to pay stamp duty on the enclosure, namely the container. So the stamp, which was a strip of paper, had to be fixed to the bottle, packet, phial or box to show that the duty had been paid before sale, and in such a way that the medicine could not

---

94 David Wilkinson, *The Duke of Portland, Politics and Party in the Age of George III* (Basingstoke: Palgrave Macmillan, 2003), p. 52.

95 23 Geo. III c. 62 (1783). The first two Acts were the 23 Geo III c. 49 (imposing new stamp duties on bills of exchange, promissory notes and receipts) and the 23 Geo. III c.58 (imposing new and additional duties on stamped velum, parchment and paper and repealing some exemptions from the duty).

96 The duty did not extend to Ireland. Stamp duties applied to Scotland only after 1808, but the consumption of proprietary medicines in that country was always considerably less than in England.

97 23 Geo III c. 62, ss. 1, 5.

98 *Ibid.*, s. 1. The medicine licence was relatively cheap compared with the £15 licence to act as a pawnbroker or the £10 licence required to run a coach: Fourteenth Report of the Commissioners of Inquiry into the Collection and Management of the Revenue arising in Ireland, Scotland; etc. Board of Stamps, *House of Commons Parliamentary Papers* (1826) (436) x 69 at p. 443.

99 Customs and Inland Revenue Act 1875 (38 & 39 Vict c. 23), s. 8. The rate remained the same until the abolition of the duty.

be consumed by the purchaser without damaging the stamp. The notion of stamping the wrapper of an article subject to duty was not new. In the case of the 1711 tax on playing cards, the pack of cards would be enclosed in a wrapper that had already been sent to the Stamp Office to be stamped. The duty was on a graduated scale charged according to the amount for which the medicine was sold, and duty added on. Cavendish put on as high a duty as the trade could bear, namely 8 per cent.

The tax was not a stamp duty in the traditional sense. Adam Smith said that the stamp duties on cards and dice, which were similar in nature to the future medicine stamp duty, were 'properly taxes upon consumption'[100] with the burden falling on the consumer. It was certainly true that there existed an official perspective that the stamp duty was unsuitable as a tax on articles such as medicines, gloves or perfumery because the purpose of the stamp duty was to give law proceedings and other documents an authority in law. As Mr Sheridan observed in 1786,

> [t]he system of extending taxation by stamps, to such articles as the principle of a stamp duty would not apply to, was absurd in the extreme: stamping law proceedings and other documents was a good idea; then the stamp gave a weight, a sanction, and authority, where so applied; but could that be said of gloves, or of all the trumpery of a perfumer's shop to which they were now about to extend stamp duties; would a stamp legalize pomatum, or give valid- ity to lavender water?[101]

For Stephen Dowell too, it was an essential requirement of real stamp duties to be charged on deeds or other written instruments.[102] Dowell was assistant solicitor to the Board of Inland Revenue for more than thirty years in the second half of the nineteenth century, when the medicine stamp duty was at its most pervasive and dynamic.[103] His writings on the history of all the taxes is of real significance regarding the nature and practice of taxation in the late nineteenth century. His contemporary, knowledgeable and practical experi- ence reflected in his writing is invaluable. In his *History and Explanation of*

[100] Smith, *Wealth of Nations*, p. 863.
[101] *Parliamentary Register* 1780–1796, vol. 20, 4 May 1786, p. 157.
[102] Stephen Dowell, *A History and Explanation of the Stamp Duties* (London: Longmans, Green and Co., 1873), pp. 6–7. Those stamp duties where no stamp was involved, as in the case of the duties on advertisements, stage coaches, horses and hackney carriages, were known internally as 'unstamped duties' of stamps: *ibid.*, pp. 8–9; Dowell, *History of Taxation*, vol. 2, p. 188; *ibid.*, vol. 3, p. 322.
[103] See A. F. Pollard, 'Dowell, Stephen (1833–1898)', rev. Patrick Polden, *Oxford Dictionary of National Biography*, eds. H.C.G.Matthew and Brian Harrison, vol. 16 (Oxford: Oxford University Press, 2004), pp. 778–9.

the Stamp Duties, published in 1873, he called the medicine stamp duty a 'statutory stamp duty' and not a stamp duty 'properly so termed'.[104] It had, he said, 'no real claim to the appellation of stamp duties', having been placed under the care of the Stamp Commissioners entirely for the purposes of administration and collection.[105] It was, in fact, neither a true stamp duty nor a true excise. For this reason he excluded the medicine stamp duty from that volume of 1873, a work of more than 300 pages. In his *History of Taxation and Taxes* in 1884 he included the tax on proprietary medicines not under the head of stamp duties but under the head of taxes on articles of consumption, specifically as 'manufactures'.[106]

The Act of 1783 did not attempt to define the medicines brought into charge, doubtless because it was clear that there were considerable difficulties in doing so sufficiently robustly for legislative taxing purposes. The constitutional principle of consent to taxation demanded that a tax be imposed only in express and clear words. There was clear tension between this requirement and the term 'quack medicine' even though it was undoubtedly familiar to the public and was used consistently in official government correspondence, in newspaper reports and contemporary pamphlets.[107] It was also freely used in all pre-legislation discussion, and when he introduced the tax, Lord John Cavendish expressly called it a tax on quack medicines, knowing it would be well understood by his audience in the House. The object of charge – quack medicines – was thus clear to the public. Indeed, in a wedding announcement of 1785 the groom was described as a 'Collector of the Quack Medicine Duty'.[108] Nevertheless, however great its 'Notoriety and Designation',[109] the term 'quack medicine' was virtually impossible to define. It was a slang expression, with no clear meaning, and as such was certainly far too loose to be used in an instrument as formal as a taxing statute. The Stamp Office itself acknowledged that it was 'unfit to be introduced into an Act of the Legislature'.[110]

The difficulty inherent in the definition of key terms was to shape the entire history of the medicine stamp duty. Unable to use the popular terms of 'quack'

[104] Dowell, *Stamp Duties*, p. 7.
[105] *Ibid.*, p. 6.
[106] Dowell, *History of Taxation*, vol. 2, pp. 396–8.
[107] *Stamp Office: Observations upon the present Medicine Act and Proposals for an Improvement of that Duty*, 21 May 1785: The National Archives (TNA): T1/624/514. The term is used, for example, in the *Public Advertiser*, 12 July 1783; *Morning Herald and Daily Advertiser*, 11 July 1783, reporting the passing of the Act in those terms.
[108] 'Marriage', *Morning Post and Daily Advertiser*, 8 September 1785.
[109] *Stamp Office: Observations upon the present Medicine Act and Proposals for an Improvement of that Duty*, 21 May 1785: TNA: T1/624/514.
[110] *Ibid.*

and 'quack medicines', the legislature had to develop some objective test. The one chosen for the Act of 1783 was the status of the vendor: medicines sold by medically unqualified persons were chargeable, whereas those sold by medically qualified persons were exempt. The Act was thus directed to the sellers, and not to the medicines they sold. Unqualified persons wishing to sell any medicines had to be licensed, and all licensed persons had to pay tax on all the medicines they sold. This was made clear in the public notice issued by the Stamp Commissioners themselves in September 1784.[111] Only the character of the seller was of legislative import, and the key factor was the presence or absence of medical qualification.

The exemptions to the Act reflected the essence of the new tax. Those 'regularly bred to the [medical] profession',[112] namely those who had served an apprenticeship to a surgeon, apothecary, chemist and druggist, or who had served as a navy or army surgeon were exempt from the requirement to purchase a licence, and therefore from the stamp duty itself.[113] There existed a second exemption, which was not related to medical qualification. It applied to individuals who had kept a shop 'for the vending of drugs and medicines only, not being drugs or medicines sold by virtue of His Majesty's Letters Patent' and had done so for three years before the passing of the Act.[114]

The Act failed entirely in its aim to raise revenue by taxing all medicines, proprietary, formally patented and regular, if sold by an unqualified person, and to protect the regular medical profession.[115] It failed because the scope of the charge was too limited and the exemptions, in playing to vested interests, were too wide. The handful of patent medicines properly so called was arguably taxable whoever sold them. Medically qualified practitioners, such as surgeons and apothecaries, sold proprietary medicines as much as unqualified vendors did and yet were exempt. Beyond the medically qualified and established shopkeepers there existed only unqualified medicine vendors who had recently begun trading, so the reach of the tax was severely circumscribed. The effect was that the only proprietary medicines that were subject to the tax were the very few patent medicines strictly so called, and all medicines sold by unqualified individuals who had not kept a shop for more than three years. Consequently, proprietary medicines in general escaped the charge and this,

[111] *St. James's Chronicle* or *British Evening Post*, 11 September 1784.
[112] *Parliamentary Register 1780–1796*, vol. 10, 26 May 1783, p. 71, *per* Lord John Cavendish.
[113] 23 Geo III c. 62 ss. 1, 2. Physicians were not included in this exemption because they were not permitted to dispense medicines.
[114] *Ibid.*, s. 1.
[115] *Stamp Office: Report of Several Defects in the present law affecting duties*, 15 February 1785: TNA: T1/624/504.

along with widespread evasion, resulted in the complete fiscal failure of the 1783 Act. It was also realised that exempting established shopkeepers of three years' standing was not only far too great a concession to vested interests but would result in even this reduced yield being unsustainable. It would decline year after year as more shopkeepers came within the exemption. This was not a case of a new tax experiencing early problems of administration. The Act was untenable. To prove effective, the legislation urgently needed far greater thought and a radical recasting. Reform was imperative.

Only two years later, in the surge of fiscal activity that characterised his ministries, William Pitt introduced a new Act.[116] Regarded as an astute and highly able chancellor, Pitt was certainly a prodigious and effective tax legislator and reformer, introducing seventeen new taxes during his ministries, reforming existing ones and thoroughly overhauling the structures for the administration of the taxes.[117] Many tax reforms of the eighteenth century resulted from suggestions from the revenue authorities themselves, and the medicine stamp duty was no exception.[118] A mere four months after the 1783 Act came into force, the Stamp Commissioners put proposals for a new statutory regime to the Treasury, based on common sense and their experience of the first disastrous Act.[119] The objective was to extend the duty 'both to Persons and Things not within the description of the present law, tho' certainly meant by the Legislature',[120] to bring in a significant revenue. Pitt agreed with their view that although the duty was 'in some respects incomplete', it 'merits attention, as an object of revenue that may admit of much extension and improvement'.[121] Recasting the Act 'for the sake of convenience and the public service',[122] the Medicine Stamp Duty Act 1785[123] framed the duty in the form it was fundamentally to retain until its abolition some 160 years later.

---

[116] In July 1785 the first Medicine Stamp Duty Act was addressed by the House and a revised Act considered: *Journals of the House of Commons*, vol. 40, 15 July 1785, p. 1144.

[117] See Jeffrey-Cook, 'William Pitt and his Taxes', 376.

[118] Note that throughout this book the terms 'revenue authorities', 'board' and 'commissioners' are used, largely interchangeably, to describe the organs of the executive responsible for the administration of taxes.

[119] *Stamp Office: Report of Several Defects in the present law affecting duties*, 15 February 1785: TNA: T1/624/504; *Stamp Office: Observations upon the present Medicine Act and Proposals for an Improvement of that Duty*, 21 May 1785: TNA: T1/624/514.

[120] *Stamp Office: Report of Several Defects in the present law affecting duties*, 15 February 1785: TNA: T1/624/504.

[121] First Report from the Committee Appointed to Enquire into the Illicit Practices Used in Defrauding the Revenue, 38 *House of Commons Sessional Papers of the Eighteenth Century* 23 (24 December 1783).

[122] Quoted in Dowell, *History of Taxation*, vol. 4, p. 367.

[123] 25 Geo. III c. 79 (1785).

The inevitable difficulties inherent in the definition of key terms and sub-jective popular perceptions remained, making it challenging to lay down in statutory language the target of the tax and thereby causing enormous problems for the legislators. It was a difficulty Cavendish had sidestepped by charging the sellers rather than the medicines and using an absence of formal medical qualification as the determinant. Pitt, however, addressed the prob-lem directly. He adopted a different and more realistic approach, acknowledg-ing that for any chance of success it was necessary clearly to set out the object of charge – the medicine – and to attach the duty to it irrespective of whether it was sold by qualified or unqualified persons.[124] In terms of nomenclature, the term 'patent medicine' was carefully avoided in the legislation, although in the House of Commons' *Journals*, the proposed Act was consistently called the Patent Medicine Licences Bill.[125] The words 'nostrum' and 'proprietary medicine' were used 'as generally denominative of the proper Objects of this Tax'.[126] Clearly these were thought synonymous with the popular sense of 'patent medicines' and the understood meaning of 'quack medicines'. In the newspapers it was called the Medicine Duty Bill.[127]

The Act, as the Stamp Commissioners had recommended,[128] charged every container of medicine sold in Great Britain, namely

> every packet, box, bottle, phial, or other inclosure, containing any drugs, oils, waters, essences, tinctures, powders, or other preparation or composition whatsoever, used or applied, or to be used or applied, externally or internally, as medicines or medicaments for the prevention, cure, or relief of any disor-der or complaint incident to, or in anywise affecting, the human body, which shall be uttered or vended in Great Britain.[129]

The Act proceeded to refine this general and comprehensive charge, explain-ing it more precisely in an official description of the remedies that were to be taxed.[130] It imposed the charge on the container of medicine if the maker or seller made or sold it under letters patent, or claimed a secret art, or an

---

[124] The revenue authorities' practice in implementing the *known, admitted and approved* remedy exemption after 1903 was ultimately recognised as undermining this principle: see Chapter 2.

[125] *Journals of the House of Commons*, vol. 40, July 1785, pp. 1124, 1141, 1144.

[126] *Stamp Office: Observations upon the present Medicine Act and Proposals for an Improvement of that Duty*, 21 May 1785: TNA: T1/624/514.

[127] See, for example, *The Times*, 20 July 1785.

[128] *Stamp Office: Observations upon the present Medicine Act and Proposals for an Improvement of that Duty*, 21 May 1785: TNA: T1/624/514.

[129] 25 Geo. III c. 79 s. 2 (1785). The tax did not, and never would, apply to veterinary medicines, even though there was a great deal of quackery in that trade.

[130] *Ibid.*, s. 16.

exclusive right in doing so, or recommended it to the public as an effective remedy, or if it was expressly named in a supplementing schedule, which contained more than eighty named preparations, including famous ones such as *Bateman's Drops, Daffy's Elixir* and *Turlington's Balsam.*

Although not an elegant taxing code, it accepted the insuperable difficulties of definition and instead embodied a pragmatic and realistic approach. Carefully and accurately it identified the universally recognised characteristics of the medicines it was desired to tax, namely secrecy, ignorance, deception, publicity and proprietary claims. In including secrecy as a central characteristic of dutiable medicines, Pitt showed an understanding of these powerful social and cultural beliefs and astutely tapped into a traditional popular distrust of secrecy (as opposed to privacy)[131] and thereby actively promoted compliance with the tax and diffused popular opposition to it. Because the threefold test of liability of medicines, namely secrecy, proprietary claim and recommendation, was disjunctive, the possession of any one sufficing to bring a preparation into charge, the scope of the charge was very wide, indeed comprehensive. It covered all patented, secret, proprietary, advertised and scheduled medicines. This test proved to be as useful as any that could be conceived over the next 150 years.[132]

As under the 1783 Act, the rate was determined by the value of the medicine and reflected the prevailing pricing policy. Medicines up to the value of 1 shilling paid 1½ d duty, the only change to the rates of 1783; up to a value of 2s.6d the duty was 3d; up to 5 shillings the duty stood at 6d; and over 5 shillings the duty was 1 shilling.[133] This amounted to some 8 per cent of the value of the medicine.[134] The requirement for any vendor selling dutiable medicine to obtain an annual licence remained,[135] although the fees were amended slightly to bring the cost of a licence in Edinburgh in line with that in London at £1, and it remained at 5 shillings in the provinces.[136]

Because the duty was grounded in the nature of the taxed medicine, it followed that no exemptions could properly be given. Indeed, the Stamp Office had stressed that once the objects of the duty were clearly identified, it was essential that no vendors be exempt from paying it. There was, they said, to be no 'Privilege of Person', but everyone who sold a chargeable medicine,

---

[131] Porter, *Quacks*, p. 44.

[132] *Parl. Deb.*, vol. 205, ser. 5, col. 752, 26 April 1927, *per* Ronald Mcneill, financial secretary to the Treasury.

[133] 25 Geo. III c. 79 s. 2 (1785).

[134] *Parliamentary Register 1780–1796*, vol. 10, 26 May 1783, p. 71, *per* Lord John Cavendish.

[135] 25 Geo. III c. 79 ss. 5, 7 (1785).

[136] *Ibid.*, s. 5.

whether medically qualified or not, would have to obtain a licence and stamp the product.[137] Nevertheless, Pitt wished to ensure that legitimate medical and pharmaceutical practice was not undermined. The 1785 Act therefore distinguished between legitimate and proprietary medicines, protecting the former and taxing the latter. He did so by including three exemptions, which reflected the different approach of his legislation in that they related to medicines sold by their ordinary or scientific names, with no element of quackery in the sense of secrecy, exclusivity or advertising.

The first exemption, which was intended primarily to protect foreign trade, applied to imported medicines that were already subject to customs duties, mainly natural drugs such as roots and barks, and certain chemicals such as alum.[138] These drugs were essentially the raw materials for the manufacture of medicines, and they were specified in the two Books of Rates of 1660 and 1714.[139] The first Book of Rates named some 200 drugs, and the second named 86.[140] Even though the Books of Rates became obsolete in the late eighteenth century, and the specific exemption was largely subsumed by the second exemption for pure drugs vended entire and was condemned in 1912 as 'absolutely useless',[141] the exemption was repeated in the subsequent medicine stamp Acts.

The second exemption was for medicines that were 'entire' and were sold by a medically qualified or licensed person.[142] These were pure and crude drugs used to make medicines. Aspirin, balsam, aloes, camphor, cloves, menthol, nutmeg, rhubarb, senna and turmeric, for example, came within this exemption. Any element of admixture would negate the exemption.[143] So a single drug dissolved in alcohol to make a tincture was chargeable, as was a single drug that was mixed with colouring or perfume, or indeed any medicinally

---

[137] *Stamp Office: Observations upon the present Medicine Act and Proposals for an Improvement of that Duty*, 21 May 1785: TNA: T1/624/514.

[138] 25 Geo. III c. 79 s. 3 (1785).

[139] The two Books of Rates could be found in the Statutes at Large, appended to the Act of Tonnage and Poundage 1660 (12 Car. II c. 4) and the Act Amending the Act of Tonnage and Poundage 1724 (11 Geo. I c. 7).

[140] For full list see *Board of Customs and Excise and Predecessor: Private Office Papers, The Medicine Stamp Duties 1783–1936*, TNA CUST 118/366 at pp. 157–60.

[141] Report and Minutes of Evidence from the Select Committee on Patent Medicines, *House of Commons Parliamentary Papers* (1914) (Cd. 414) ix 1 at q. 193, *per* Sir Nathaniel Highmore, solicitor to the Customs and Excise.

[142] 25 Geo. III c. 79 s. 3 (1785).

[143] *Smith v. Mason & Co.* [1894] 2 QB 363, 371. It was held in *Knoll v. Renshaw* [1916] 1 KB 700 that if a drug was mixed with medically inert materials it was no longer a drug vended entire and the vendors were not entitled to the benefit of the exemption. See 'Legal Hints for Pharmacists, Medicine Stamp Duty', (1898) 60 *Pharmaceutical Journal* (series 3) 192.

inert substances. The category of qualified persons was taken from the 1783 Act, signifying surgeons, apothecaries, chemists and druggists who had served regular apprenticeships, and surgeons serving in the navy or army. Primarily it ensured that the single drugs that doctors and chemists needed to make up their prescriptions could be obtained by them free of duty from qualified or licensed individuals. However, because doctors and chemists obtained such drugs under their scientific names and not as secret, proprietary, patent or recommended medicines, this exemption was little more than a declaration of the law. This exemption for pure drugs was also, however, introduced in the interests of the poor. It had been suggested by the Stamp Commissioners on the basis that pure drugs were sold by many shopkeepers and medicine vendors 'to the great Convenience and Advantage of the lower Orders of the People in distant and bye parts of the Kingdom', and that it would be 'highly unreasonable and impolitic' to impose the duty on such medicines.[144]

The third exemption relieved composite medicines that were *known, admitted and approved* remedies for illnesses where they were sold by a quali-fied person.[145] It could not be claimed if the medicine was secret, propri-etary, patent or recommended as an effective remedy. This exemption was probably introduced to make it quite clear that ordinary medicines were no longer chargeable, and would become immensely important to the modern pharmacist.[146]

The exemptions relating to imported medicines and to medicines sold entire by qualified practitioners were not problematic because they would generally not fall within the description of chargeable medicines. Neither class of medicine would normally be secret, patent, exclusive or recom-mended and so would not be liable to duty anyway. They were expressly exempted so as to confirm that the trade in imported drugs would not be harmed by the duty, and that the drugs that medical practitioners used in preparing their prescriptions could be obtained duty-free from qualified or licensed individuals.[147] The third exemption for *known, admitted and approved* remedies was problematic, because it was not an exemption in the proper sense of the term. A preparation that was not secret, proprietary, patent or recommended would not have been subject to duty anyway, so the exemption was legally otiose.

---

[144] *Stamp Office: Observations upon the present Medicine Act and Proposals for an Improvement of that Duty*, 21 May 1785: TNA: T1/624/514.

[145] 25 Geo. III c. 79 s. 4 (1785).

[146] See Chapter 2.

[147] *Board of Customs and Excise and Predecessor: Private Office Papers, Medicine Stamp Duty 1783–1936*: TNA: CUST 118/366 at p. 9.

THE FINANCIAL RATIONALE FOR THE TAX

The evidence strongly suggests that the introduction of the medicine stamp duty in the late eighteenth century was financially motivated, and that it was maintained throughout the nineteenth century and nearly half of the twentieth, above all to generate public revenue. First, and most obviously, this was affirmed by its fiscal context. It was one of a number of stamp duties imposed on a diverse range of commodities, most of which could have no underlying social policy ambitions, and which were accordingly unambiguously introduced to meet urgent national financial exigencies. Lord John Cavendish anticipated an annual yield of £15,000 from the medicine stamp duty,[148] a return equally sought by Pitt, which, although small in the context of the overall public revenue,[149] would have constituted a welcome, worthwhile and secure contribution in the context of the parlous state of Britain's finances. Everything Cavendish said in his budget confirmed a financial motivation for the tax, and indeed payment of the interest on the newly floated loan of £12 million was the only express justification that he gave for imposing any of his new taxes in 1783.[150] His observation that quack medicines were 'very proper objects of taxation'[151] arguably referred to the extensive nature of the trade and the grasping of a market opportunity. Indeed, contemporary commentators saw the tax as motivated solely by financial necessity. Francis Spilsbury, medicine vendor and vociferous critic of the tax, said Lord John Cavendish was 'biassed with the pleasing prospect of gold pouring into the Treasury'.[152] And when William Pitt recast the tax, he did so by adopting in their entirety the reforming measures the Stamp Commissioners proposed to make the law workable 'as an object of revenue', that is, to make it profitable[153] and 'productive'.[154] In 1802 Henry Addington, then Chancellor of the

---

[148] *Parliamentary Register 1780–1796*, vol. 10, 26 May 1783, p. 71.

[149] It was less than 1 per cent of the entire stamp duty yield, which itself was the smallest producer of the four main taxes of customs, excises, taxes and stamps.

[150] Only in relation to the taxation of the registration of births, marriages and deaths did he mention that it was a matter of policy and not merely finance: *Parliamentary Register 1780–1796*, vol. 10, 26 May 1783, p. 72.

[151] *Ibid.*, p. 71.

[152] Francis Spilsbury, *Discursory Thoughts Disputing the Construction of His Majesty's Hon. Commissioners and Crown Lawyers, relative to the Medicine and Horse Acts … with Remarks on the Late Trials Concerning the Medicine Act*, 2nd edn, (London; Dispensary, Soho Square, 1785), p. 40.

[153] *Stamp Office: Observations upon the present Medicine Act and Proposals for an Improvement of that Duty*, 21 May 1785: TNA: T1/624/514.

[154] *Stamp Office: Report of Several Defects in the present law affecting duties*, 15 February 1785: TNA: T1/624/504.

Exchequer, called for an increase in the duty expressly to help meet an urgent need for increased revenue.[155] Nineteenth-century commentators were in no doubt that the medicine stamp duty had been introduced to augment the national revenue.[156]

Second, at the time the medicine stamp duty was introduced, the orthodox understanding of the nature of taxation was as an instrument of government whose sole purpose was to raise money to meet government expenditure. This was confirmed when the Stamp Office adopted the conventional determinant of the success of a tax, and declared that with an annual yield of just a quarter of the anticipated return, the 1783 medicine stamp duty was a failure.[157] Indeed, the yield of the first medicine stamp duty at the end of its first year of operation was so low that it was immediately recognised as a complete failure rather than simply a new tax experiencing early problems of administration. The tax's success – or lack of it – was consistently measured entirely in terms of its monetary yield.

Third, there was every indication at its inception that the tax would be a financial success. It was undoubtedly viable in principle and the potential yield was realistic. The tax base was clear: the trade in proprietary medicines was extensive and was so evidently a species of commercial enterprise that it was naturally an object of taxation. Indeed, from that perspective, proprietary medicines were almost predisposed to be taxed. The nature of the tax was such that, according to prevailing theories of fair taxation, it was likely to ensure compliance: an indirect, non-inquisitorial assessment through an increased cost of the commodity paid by the public almost unknowingly, despite the fact that the bottle, packet or box of medicines bore a physical stamp reminding the purchasers that they were paying the duty. The fact that the tax was likely to be socially acceptable to the public would help ensure compliance, and therefore yield. Although proprietary medicines were very popular, and indeed widely regarded as a necessity rather than a luxury, the perception of the quack vendors as ignorant, cheating and often foreign itinerant rogues, preying on the misfortunes of others, persisted. When the tax was introduced,

•

---

[155] A new Act, 42 Geo. III c.56 (1802), was passed within three weeks of the introduction of the bill: *Board of Customs and Excise and Predecessor: Private Office Papers, The Medicine Stamp Duties 1783–1936*: TNA CUST 118/366 at pp. 12, 17. There was virtually no reported debate, with the discussion addressing mainly the limitation of informations, an issue not included in the final Act. The Act passed on its third reading with no reported discussion.

[156] E. N. Alpe, *Handy Book of Medicine Stamp Duty* (London: Offices of 'The Chemist and Druggist', ca. 1888), p. 7.

[157] *Board of Customs and Excise and predecessor: Private Office Papers, Medicine Stamp Duty 1783–1936*: TNA CUST 118/366 at p. 6.

one newspaper observed that even if the quacks evaded the tax by reducing the price of medicines to 6d per box or phial, they would still make a profit of some 600 per cent or 800 per cent, as well as 'the certainty of a greater sale'.[158] In an age that valued reason and public order, this perception was reinforced by the element of secrecy in the sale of medicines, particularly when allied to extravagant advertising and uncertain results. To keep the ingredients of medicines secret could only be to prevent others manufacturing them and thereby diminishing the profits of the inventor. This was 'naked self-serving, sanctimoniously masquerading under the cloak of humanity',[159] and created widespread and intense grievance. This made the quack a legitimate target for taxation, and ensured that the taxation of proprietary remedies was not universally unpopular.

In every way, therefore, the medicine stamp duty conformed to the orthodox paradigm of eighteenth-century taxation as a revenue-raising instrument of government. Furthermore, a strong case can be made for a financial rationale to the retention of the medicine stamp duty until the middle of the twentieth century, although the basis was more pragmatic than ideological. Other than the acute need for increased public revenue in the middle years of the nineteenth century, there were three principal factors responsible for its retention, all of which were yield-related.

The first lay, paradoxically, in a changed fiscal landscape. Throughout the nineteenth century, indirect taxes lost a great deal of their financial importance when the policy of the eighteenth century to raise public revenue primarily through indirect taxation was seen to have failed. The revenue had increased, but not enough to meet the pressing financial needs of the government. As early as 1799 William Pitt realised that the indirect taxes could never raise enough to remain the principal pillar of British tax revenue. He saw that the future lay in direct taxation, and in that year he was forced to introduce a general charge on all leading branches of income, namely the new income tax.[160] While that tax too failed in that it did not achieve the intended yield, it constituted a momentous step in fiscal history in that it unambiguously breached the principle of voluntaryism. Henry Addington's remodelling of the income tax in 1803 was such that he has been described as the true author of the modern income tax.[161] It was his introduction of the schedular system and deduction of tax at source that made the income tax viable. When Sir Robert

---

[158] *London Packet or New Lloyd's Evening Post*, 22–24 October 1783.
[159] Porter, *Quacks*, p. 44.
[160] Duties on Income Act 1799 (39 Geo. III c. 13).
[161] A. Farnsworth, *Addington: the Author of the Modern Income Tax*, (London: Stevens and Sons, 1951).

Peel reintroduced income tax in 1842 after a suspension of some twenty-five years, he began the formative period of modern British taxation. Although the yield of the income tax was small in comparison with the other taxes in the nineteenth-century fiscal portfolio, it was widely understood that permanent direct taxation embodied the financial future and it began a clear shift in the ideology of taxation.[162] It was a perception that proved accurate. Direct taxation became increasingly effective, and by 1860 it was understood to constitute the fiscal future for a modern state. The customs and excise continued to yield significant sums for the Treasury, and against a backdrop of considerable national prosperity, there would seem little reason for the retention of those minor taxes on commodities such as the medicine stamp duty, which were suited to the fiscal policies and social habits of the previous century.

It was, however, a matter of considerable political and fiscal difficulty to ensure that the income tax achieved its full potential. To augment the public revenue and address the financial demands of the country, it would have to reach the new fund of commercial wealth. The task of making the income tax work effectively, bringing new forms of property such as joint stock company shares and debentures into charge, with outdated administrative machinery and problems of popular resentment and non-compliance, and to do so in a context of unprecedented commercial, financial and social dynamism, fully occupied the Treasury and the revenue boards throughout the century. With the energies of the revenue boards directed to the development of the income tax and the death duties, there was a tendency to leave the established indirect taxes of customs, excise and stamps, and the assessed taxes, to function as they always had. This inertia with regard to the indirect taxes served to leave the medicine stamp duty, despite its flaws, well alone.

The second factor in the retention of the medicine stamp duty lay in the resilience to changing fiscal fashion of the advantages of the stamp duty in particular and the indirect taxes in general. The characteristics which had made them attractive to eighteenth-century governments lost none of their appeal. Although indirect taxes came to represent a much smaller fraction of the public revenue, they were maintained throughout the nineteenth and twentieth centuries, and continue to the present day. The momentum of the nineteenth-century tax reforms left the medicine stamp duty untouched. It yielded a small and safe amount and was administered cheaply and without apparent difficulty. Indeed, in 1927 the cost of collection was stated to be

[162] First Report of the Commissioners of Inland Revenue, *House of Commons Parliamentary Papers* (1857) (2199 sess. 1) iv 65 at p. 94.

'absolutely negligible'.[163] It could be increased with relative ease, a point that was illustrated by a doubling of the rates in 1915 with no justification other than to contribute to the financial demands arising from the first world war.[164] This was a temporary increase, but was renewed annually to 1927, at which time the increased rates were made permanent. After a decade of the higher rates with no decrease in consumption, it was clear that the trade could bear the tax comfortably[165] and the outcome was taken as proof that the tax was 'a legitimate source of revenue'.[166]

Third, no government would disregard any useful and convenient fiscal instrument. The orthodox measure of the success of a tax, namely its monetary yield, was undiminished in the nineteenth century, and as a result there was an engrained institutional reluctance to abolish a tax that worked. Any yield, however small, was valued as a contribution to government finances and was not lightly to be relinquished. Even where a tax was unpopular, or even dangerous in its effects, if the yield outstripped the expense of administering it, it was to be retained. A striking example was the window tax in the early Victorian period.[167] The reluctance of the revenue boards to abolish even the smallest tax was increased by their understanding that the public perception of taxation throughout the nineteenth century was that it was too heavy[168] and that the introduction of any new tax would inevitably be unpopular, raising real concerns as to compliance. This preference for the status quo is a feature of the executive attitude to taxation that remains at the present day. Furthermore, because the medicine stamp duty, along with the other indirect taxes that proliferated in the eighteenth century, was used to pay the interest on long-term loans, it was firmly entrenched and more difficult to repeal.[169]

There was every indication that the yield would be maintained. The public appetite for self-medication remained undiminished,[170] and the trade in

---

[163] *Parl. Deb.*, vol. 205, ser. 5, col. 753, 26 April 1927, *per* Ronald Mcneill, financial secretary to the Treasury.

[164] Finance (No. 2) Act 1915 (5 & 6 Geo. V c. 89). For the administrative problems caused by the increase, see F. H. Rawlings, 'Letters: Medicine Stamps', (1986) 16 *Pharmaceutical Historian* 8.

[165] *Parl. Deb.*, vol. 205, ser. 5, col. 750, 26 April 1927, *per* Ronald Mcneill, financial secretary to the Treasury.

[166] *Ibid.*, col. 751.

[167] Chantal Stebbings, 'Public Health Imperatives and Taxation Policy: the Window Tax as an Early Paradigm in English Law', in J Tiley (ed), *Studies in the History of Tax Law*, vol. 5, (Oxford: Hart Publishing, 2011), p. 43.

[168] See the famous description of taxation in Britain by Sydney Smith, 'Article III, Statistical Analysis of the United States of America', (1820) *The Edinburgh Review* 77–8.

[169] Brewer, *Sinews of Power*, p. 119.

[170] See *Parl. Deb.*, vol. 269, ser. 3, cols. 596–7, 12 May 1882 (HC); 'Pharmaceutical Quackery', (1846) 6 *Pharmaceutical Journal* (series 1) 51.

proprietary medicines went from strength to strength in the nineteenth century, growing fivefold between 1850 and 1900, with new preparations coming on to the market almost daily. In 1846 a catalogue of patent medicines sold by 'the leading establishment or emporium of quackery in the kingdom' from premises in Oxford Street in London listed more than 700 medicines, many of which promised cures for the widest range of often acute diseases.[171] The character of proprietary medicines changed as the century progressed. Individual enterprising vendors became less prominent, large manufacturing chemists began to produce medicines of high quality, based on rigorous scientific research, and the sale of branded medicines was found in the chemists and druggists and other retailers.[172] This demand for prepacked branded medicines was further stimulated by growth in the urban population and their incomes, severe public health problems, improvements in communications and advertising and the development of foreign markets.[173] Indeed, in terms of the history of English pharmaceuticals, the nineteenth century is characterised by widespread and unregulated retailing of medicines.[174] It was well known that the 'unquenchable medicinal thirst'[175] of the British endured, to the extent that as late as 1936 the minister of health could say that 'we are rapidly becoming a nation of confirmed medicine drinkers'.[176] The growth in the number of licences issued for the sale of dutiable medicines reflects the increase in the trade.[177] The reduction in the licence fee in 1875 to a uniform five shillings[178] encouraged large numbers of unqualified vendors to enter the trade in proprietary medicines to a point 'almost incredible'.[179]

As a result of the continued growth in the trade in proprietary medicines, the yield of the medicine stamp duty increased steadily if not spectacularly.

[171] 'On the Injury Inflicted on the Public by the Legalized Sale of Quack Medicines', (1848) 51 *The Lancet*, 699, 700.
[172] Louise Hill Curth, 'Introduction: Perspectives on the Evolution of the Retailing of Pharmaceuticals', in Louise Hill Curth (ed.), *From Physick to Pharmacology, Five Hundred Years of British Drug Retailing* (Aldershot: Ashgate, 2006), pp. 7–8. Hilary Marland, 'The 'Doctor's Shop': The Rise of the Chemist and Druggist in Nineteenth-Century Manufacturing Districts' in Louise Hill Curth (ed), *From Physick to Pharmacology*, 79.
[173] See generally George B. Griffenhagen and James Harvey Young, *Old English Patent Medicines in America*, (Washington DC: Smithsonian Institution, 1959).
[174] Hill Curth, 'Introduction', in *From Physick to Pharmacology*, p. 3.
[175] *Board of Customs and Excise and Predecessor: Private Office Papers, The Medicine Stamp Duties 1783–1936*: TNA CUST 118/366 at p. 124.
[176] *Ibid.*, p. 124.
[177] Dowell states that 12,339 licences were issued in Great Britain in 1870; 15,022 in 1876; 18,754 in 1881 and 19,404 in 1883: Dowell, *History of Taxation*, vol. 4, p. 372.
[178] Customs and Inland Revenue Act 1875 (38 & 39 Vict. c. 23) s. 8.
[179] 'Medicine Stamp Duty', (1893) 23 *Pharmaceutical Journal* (series 3) 597; 'The Medicine Stamp Act', (1894) 24 *Pharmaceutical Journal* (series 3) 327.

After its 'reconstruction'[180] by Pitt in 1785 it was described as 'amazingly productive',[181] yielding more than £12,000 at the end of its first year, and that
remained more or less constant until 1800, when it rose to more than £14,000.
Although not a high yield, it was approaching its original promised yield of
£15,000 by 1801.[182] In 1807, out of a stamp yield of more than £4 million on
some 25 different articles it raised £33,522.[183] This was just 1% of the total stamp
duty yield, but was by no means the smallest producer. Until 1855 the amount
raised by the tax remained constant at between £30,000 and £40,000[184] with
the vendors' licences raising just less than £5000 a year.[185] The annual receipt
remained constant throughout the 1850s, yielding an average gross annual
amount of slightly more than £40,000. This was admitted to be a 'trifling'
sum.[186] The 1860s saw a steady increase with a net receipt close to £70,000 pa
by the end of the decade due to the buoyant economy.[187] Substantial increases
continued throughout the 1870s as the appetite for proprietary medicines
increased apace, and by 1875 it had exceeded £100,000.[188] By 1890 it was yielding more than £200,000 per year[189] and in 1902 it tipped over the £300,000

---

[180] This was the term used by the modern revenue boards: *Board of Customs and Excise and
Predecessor: Private Office Papers, Medicine Stamp Duty 1783–1936*: TNA CUST 118/366
at p. 6.

[181] 'Editorial', *Morning Chronicle and London Advertiser*, 26 September 1785. Pitt's fiscal policies
were remarkably successful. In a decade, he increased the public revenue by some £6 million,
of which £1 million came from his new taxes: see Duffy, *The Younger Pitt*, p. 82.

[182] *Board of Customs and Excise and Predecessor: Private Office Papers, Medicine Stamp Duty
1783–1936*: TNA CUST 118/366 at p.11. For the sums raised under the two Acts in the eighteenth century, see *Journals of the House of Commons*, vol. 41, 21 March 1786, pp. 393, 407. For
the sums raised from 1800 to 1855 see First Report of the Commissioners of Inland Revenue,
House of Commons Parliamentary Papers (1857) (2199 sess. 1) iv 65 at p. 213.

[183] An Account of the net Produce of the Duties of Stamps Paid into the Exchequer in the Years
ended 5 April 1807, 1808 and 1809, *House of Commons Parliamentary Papers* (1810) (270) xiii
135. For the sums raised by individual articles subject to the duty, see Hughes, 'English Stamp
Duties', 264.

[184] Return of the Annual Amount received in the last Ten Years for stamps issued for Patent
Medicines, *House of Commons Parliamentary Papers* (1844) (307) xxxii 439; Fourteenth Report
of the Commissioners of Inquiry into the Collection and Management of the Revenue arising
in Ireland, Scotland; etc. Board of Stamps, *House of Commons Parliamentary Papers* (1826)
(436) x 69 at p. 302.

[185] See First Report of the Commissioners of Inland Revenue, *House of Commons Parliamentary
Papers* (1857) (2199 sess. 1) iv 65 at p. 224.

[186] *Ibid.*, p. 87.

[187] Fourteenth Report of the Commissioners of Inland Revenue, *House of Commons Parliamentary
Papers* (1871) (C. 370) xvii 647 at p. 672.

[188] Eighteenth Report of the Commissioners of Inland Revenue, *House of Commons Parliamentary
Papers* (1875) (C. 1329) xx 513 at p. 533.

[189] Thirty-third Report of the Commissioners of Inland Revenue, *House of Commons Parliamentary
Papers* (1890) (C. 6187) xxvi 397 at p. 415.

mark.[190] The steady increase continued throughout the first decade of the twentieth century, particularly over the years of the first world war due to the doubling of the rates in 1915,[191] raising more than £1 million by 1919.[192] The receipts of the tax reached their peak in the 1920s, at £1,333,512 in 1928–9, but then began to plateau and to diminish during the 1930s. In 1931–2 it fell to less than £1 million for the first time in more than a decade.[193] By 1935–6 it had declined to £747,930[194] and by the end of the 1930s it was yielding in the region of £725,000.[195]

CONCLUSION

Throughout its long life the medicine stamp duty retained as its legal basis the fundamental framework and principles laid down by William Pitt in 1785 and remained unchanged in its essentials. Indeed there were virtually no changes in its substance until its abolition in 1941.[196] An Act of 1802 extended the schedule of dutiable medicines, to considerable professional objection, addressed specific evasions, ensured the charge reached all the medicines Parliament intended while retaining the three exemptions under the 1785 Act, made penalties more stringent, introduced a revised scale of rates that was to endure for the whole of the nineteenth century and made the collection of the tax more secure.[197] Although the schedule of dutiable medicines was revised the following year, administrative reforms formed the core of that Act in 1803.[198] The wide general definition of dutiable medicines and the statutory exemptions remained untouched, and the revised schedule of the 1803 Act was repeated

---

[190] Forty-fifth Report of the Commissioners of Inland Revenue, *House of Commons Parliamentary Papers* (1902) (Cd. 1216) xxii 365 at p. 479. For tabulated figures for 1891–92 to 1901–02 see *ibid.*, p. 485.

[191] Finance (No 2) Act 1915, (5 & 6 Geo. V c.89) s. 11. The duty was raised from 1½d upwards to 3d upwards. This was continued annually by express provision in each Finance Act, until the Finance Act 1927 (17 & 18 Geo. V c. 10) s. 2 made the new higher rates permanent.

[192] Tenth Report of the Commissioners of Customs and Excise, *House of Commons Parliamentary Papers* (1919) (Cmd. 503) xiii 597 at p. 610.

[193] Twenty-third Report of the Commissioners of Customs and Excise, *House of Commons Parliamentary Papers* (1931–32) (Cmd. 4195) vii 583 at p. 593.

[194] Report and Minutes of Evidence from the Select Committee on Medicine Stamp Duties, *House of Commons Parliamentary Papers* (1937) (Cmd. 54) viii 129, Memorandum of C. J. Flynn of the Board of Customs and Excise, p.165.

[195] Thirtieth Report of the Commissioners of Customs and Excise, *House of Commons Parliamentary Papers* 1938–39 (Cmd. 6098) x 415 at p. 517.

[196] See generally Leslie G. Matthews, 'The Medicine Stamp Acts of Great Britain' (1986) 16 *Pharmaceutical Historian* 2.

[197] 42 Geo. III c. 56 (1802).

[198] 43 Geo. III c. 73 (1803).

in the Medicine Stamp Duty Act 1804.[199] It named some 550 medicines and now included all foreign medicines except drugs. The medicines included in these schedules were regarded as 'authentic lists of the most popular shop medicines in use at the time', being medicines taken without prior expert medical advice.[200] Simple drugs, such as senna and rhubarb, and confectionary were exempted.

After a period of eight years with no legislation concerning the medicine stamp duty, a new Stamp Act was passed in 1812.[201] This Act was regarded as the principal Act relating to the medicine stamp duty until its repeal in 1941. It reiterated the usual administrative provisions, retained the three exemptions, rectified a minor error made eight years earlier in the 1804 Act to confirm that residents of Edinburgh who sold dutiable medicines had to purchase a licence,[202] but its most important substantive provision was to bring artificial waters into charge. The schedules of 1803 and 1804 had imposed the charge on 'Waters, Artificial Mineral' but as it had not been clear whether soda water came within this charge, the 1812 Act expanded the provision in the schedule to make its scope explicit. However, the Act exempted from the requirement for a medicine vendor's licence all shopkeepers, in practice confectioners and victuallers, who sold no dutiable medicines other than artificial waters to be drunk on their premises. The labels or covers of the bottles, however, had to be duly stamped.[203] An Act of 1815, which was a general measure relating to duties on deeds, law proceedings and written and printed instruments, amended the law relating to the articles of confectionary that had been made liable to the medicine stamp duty under earlier legislation.[204] The Act provided that ginger and peppermint lozenges and other confectionary were exempt from the duty as long as they were not sold as medicines by being recommended as beneficial for a human ailment, and confirmed that no medicine licence was required for selling the exempt lozenges.[205] Whether this amendment was due to professional pressure or the king's well-known partiality for ginger and peppermint lozenges is unclear. The final change to the substantive law occurred in 1833 when artificial mineral waters were entirely exempted from the charge.[206]

---

[199] 44 Geo. III c. 98 (1804).
[200] *Board of Customs and Excise and Predecessor: Private Office Papers, The Medicine Stamp Duties 1783–1936:* TNA CUST 118/366 at p. 19.
[201] 52 Geo. III c. 150 (1812).
[202] *Ibid.*, s. 3.
[203] *Ibid.*, s. 4.
[204] Stamp Act 1815, (55 Geo. III c. 184).
[205] *Ibid.*, s. 54.
[206] Stamps, etc., Act 1833 (3 & 4 Will. IV c. 97) s. 20.

There was some serious discussion as to its reform in the 1830s, when Henry Goulburn, the Chancellor of the Exchequer, proposed retaining the exemption for pure drugs but abolishing the exemptions for drugs named in the Books of Rates and for *known, admitted and approved* remedies[207] on the basis that neither 'had any real value in practice',[208] a considerably enlarged schedule, and the extension of the duty to Ireland. More radical proposals were made six years later by Mr Spring Rice, to the effect that the schedule of dutiable medicines should be abolished altogether and reliance placed entirely on a general charge on secret, proprietary, patent and recommended medicines, retaining just one exemption for pure drugs vended entire.[209] Neither Goulburn's nor Spring Rice's proposals became law, primarily because they formed just a small part of a wider, and impracticable, scheme for the consolidation of all the stamp duties.

The eighteenth-century medicine stamp duty was a new impost on a thriving commercial activity. The charge was as clear as the subject matter allowed; despite some complexity within the exemptions they were regarded as protecting the regular medical profession. The tax was as well administered as any of the taxes, depending as it did on the established processes of the Stamp Office; it was generally accepted by the public, and, after 1785, it consistently raised its predicted yield. Indeed as a tax, within its own modest confines, the medicine stamp duty was a success. Its yield was safe if not spectacular, not only exceeding the cost of its administration but also consistent. Evasion and avoidance were minimal, primarily, although not solely, because the rates were, in the long term, low. This sufficed to secure its place within the British fiscal establishment for some 160 years. Its final form, however, in all its essentials, was settled in 1785 and remained unchanged until its abolition in 1941. The inertia in the substantive reform of the law undermined these achievements of the tax, and had the most profound consequences on the tax and on those subject to it. Not only did it have far-reaching effects on the administration of the tax and the practice of pharmacy in the nineteenth and twentieth centuries, it also led inexorably and inevitably to the development of the law almost entirely through bureaucratic action. And this, it will be seen, ultimately led to its fiscal failure and subsequent abolition.[210]

---

[207] *Board of Customs and Excise and Predecessor: Private Office Papers, The Medicine Stamp Duties 1783–1936:* TNA CUST 118/366 at pp. 26–8.

[208] *Ibid.,* p. 26.

[209] For the medicine stamp duty sections of the Stamp (Consolidation) Bill 1836, as amended in Committee, see *Board of Customs and Excise and Predecessor: Private Office Papers, The Medicine Stamp Duties 1783–1936:* TNA CUST 118/366 at Appendix III.

[210] See Chapter 5.

FIGURE 1 Isaac Swainson promoting his Velnos' Vegetable Syrup, 1789, Wellcome Library, London.

FIGURE 2 Medicine duty stamp, temp. George III.

2

The Medicine Stamp Duty and the Authority of Law

"Attempts have been made over a period of years, with a certain amount of success, to apply the law equitably and to secure by administrative action some relation between the spirit of the Statutes and the conduct of modern business."[1]

INTRODUCTION

The administration of a tax is arguably as important as its substance, if not more so. The reason is that taxpayer compliance is of essential importance in the success of any tax, and the degree of compliance has been demonstrated to be intimately connected to the manner of a tax's administration. It is administration that is the public face of tax law. As a result, the most robustly drafted tax can fail for want of sensitive administration, and the most flawed legislation can be made to work through administrative practice. The role of administration in tax is a matter that has exercised bureaucrats, legislators, lawyers and the taxpaying public throughout its history.

As with all British taxes, implementation of the medicine stamp duty was ordained entirely by statute. It was dictated in theory because it was a fundamental constitutional principle, established from the earliest days of Magna Carta and affirmed in the Bill of Rights 1689, that the consent of the taxpayer was a prerequisite to lawful taxation. This consent was parliamentary consent, and from it stemmed the requirement that a tax be expressed in an Act of Parliament. A tax could be imposed only with such statutory authority and never by implication. It followed from this that the charge to tax had to be laid down expressly, clearly and unambiguously in the Act for the charge to be lawfully imposed. The implementation of the medicine stamp duty was

---

[1] *Parliamentary Debates* [hereafter *Parl. Deb.*], vol. 373, ser 5, col. 64, 8 July 1941 (HC), *per* Ernest Brown, Minister of Health.

dictated by statute in practice, because the extent and nature of its practical implementation was determined by the quality, comprehensiveness, accuracy, clarity and precision of the legislation. Legislative provision in relation to implementation had two facets: the first was the statutory framework for the tax's administration. The second, and the perspective that was ultimately the most problematic and addressed the major theme of the authority of law within the fiscal system, was the statutory expression of the charge to tax itself.

THE ADMINISTRATIVE MACHINERY

Detailed statutory provisions were laid down for the implementation of every type of tax and the stamp duty was no exception. Sometimes the purely administrative provisions formed part of the parent Act imposing the charge, and sometimes they were included in a separate management Act. The former was the model originally adopted for the stamp duty, the latter for the assessed taxes and the income tax. The medicine stamp duty was very much a stamp duty like any other. The rates of the duty, the cost of the licences and the provisions for its administration and enforcement were all standard form and shared by other stamp duties on a wide variety of documents and commodities.[2] For example, the medicine stamp duty of 1783 was very similar in structure and provision to the advertisement duty, and the taxes on hair powder and perfumes followed exactly the same form as that on medicines. Furthermore, standard-form regulations of all former stamp Acts were expressly provided to apply, including the 'usual indulgences of the Stamp Revenue', namely discounts for prompt payment and allowances for damaged stamps.[3] The approach of all the revenue departments in the eighteenth and nineteenth centuries, not least the Stamp Office, was highly pragmatic. Methods and procedures that had been tested and found to work in practice and were likely to ensure compliance were adopted wherever possible. Such benefits of experience, however, were often outweighed by the difficulty in amending the law in particular instances when they formed part of a standardised and widely used structure. Problems resulting from specific provisions were inevitably found in the full range of taxes using the standard form.

The tax's nature as a stamp duty – albeit not one of the traditional kind – placed the medicine tax within the portfolio of the Stamp Commissioners,

---

[2] The provisions as to informers were standard form and well known: James Ridgway, *Ridgeway's Abstract of the Budget for 1785*, 2nd edn, (London: James Ridgway, 1785), p. 47.

[3] *Stamp Office: Observations upon the present Medicine Act and Proposals for an Improvement of that Duty*, 21 May 1785: The National Archives (TNA): T1/624/514; 25 Geo. III c. 79, ss. 14, 18 (1785).

a board of between five and seven central government officials charged with the 'government, care, and management' of all the stamp duties.[4] They were well remunerated, being paid a salary of £1000 pa, with the chairman receiving a further £500 pa to preside over the board of Commissioners and attend on the Lords of the Treasury.[5] They were originally located in Lincoln's Inn, which was convenient for the lawyers who were the principal payers of the first stamp duties on legal documents, and in 1787 they moved to the newly built Somerset House.[6] They remained there through their various mergers and reorganisations culminating in the creation in 1849 of the Board of Inland Revenue, which administered the medicine stamp duty. The duties on licences for the sale of medicines were transferred to the Board of Excise in 1864, but from 1908 the medicine stamp duty was to be 'deemed' an excise duty for all purposes and was transferred to the care and management of the new combined Board of Customs and Excise.[7] This administrative rearrangement reflected the true nature of the medicine stamp duty as a tax on a commodity, but it did not bring with it the degree of regulation of the trade that the orthodox excise duties did.[8]

The original medicine stamp duty legislation instructed the Board of Stamps to do all 'things necessary to be done for putting this Act in execution'.[9] Within the Stamp Office there originally existed a medicine duty office consisting of a salaried registrar and distributor of medicine licences and labels whose task was to collect the duty through the sale of licences and stamped labels.[10] The purchase of a licence to sell dutiable medicines marked the start of the direct and formal interaction between the medicine vendor and the tax authorities, and any person who applied for a licence had to give his or her name, address and place of business. Licences were originally obtainable

---

[4] 25 Geo. III c. 79 s. 6 (1785).
[5] For the patent appointing the Stamp Commissioners, see Thirteenth Report of the Commissioners of Inquiry into the Collection and Management of the Revenue arising in Ireland, Scotland; etc., *House of Commons Parliamentary Papers* (1826) (435) x 1 at pp. 17–19.
[6] In the mid-nineteenth century it moved to the New Wing of Somerset House, and in 1935 to Bush House: H. Dagnall, *Creating a Good Impression* (London: HMSO, 1994) pp. 68–75.
[7] Revenue (No. 2) Act 1864 (27 & 28 Vict. c. 56) s. 6; Excise Transfer Order 1909 made under the authority of the Finance Act 1908 (8 Edw VII c. 16) s. 4. The Stamp Office continued to print the labels until 1933, when the Stationary Office took over the task.
[8] C. Stebbings, 'Traders, the Excise and the Law: Tensions and Conflicts in Early Nineteenth Century England', in John Tiley (ed.), *Studies in the History of Tax Law*, vol. 4. (Oxford: Hart Publishing, 2010) p. 139 at pp. 141–48.
[9] Medicine Stamp Duty Act 1785 (25 Geo. III c. 79) s. 6.
[10] Sixth Report from the Select Committee on Finance: the Stamp Office, *House of Commons Parliamentary Papers, Sessional Papers of the Eighteenth Century* (1797), vol 108 at p. 34; *Minutes on Medicine, Card and Dice Duties, 1811–36*: TNA IR 83/203.

from the Stamp Office in Lincoln's Inn, which was open daily for the purpose, and thereafter from any distributor of stamps, collector of inland revenue or from Somerset House in London.[11] At first, adopting the original procedure of the early stamp duties, the makers or sellers of dutiable medicines were responsible for sending the labels of the medicines, bearing such information as the board directed, namely the maker or seller's name and the sale price of the article, to the board to have them stamped.[12] The labels were then stamped in the Stamp Office and returned to the seller, through local distributors when outside London, who then affixed them to the medicines. At that point the medicines could be offered for sale. An Act of 1802 made a useful administrative reform in permitting the makers of medicines to obtain stamps directly from the board instead of having to send their own labels to the office to be stamped.[13] That suggested that the trade had grown too much for the old system to cope with.[14] From the perspective of the medicine vendor, the administrative process was then straightforward.[15] It was a mechanical if detailed exercise, undertaken in London and in stamp offices all over the country, and the officials involved were not required to give any kind of legal advice as to the value of the stamp to be purchased in each case.[16] As an aid to effective administration, the makers and sellers of dutiable medicines had to inform the board of the places of manufacture or sale and lists of their medicines and their prices, and to keep this information up to date.[17]

The first medicine stamps under the eighteenth-century legislation were in the shape of a cross, and the duty was printed at the intersection of the four arms of the cross in a circle bearing a crown. In 1802 the old cruciform shape of stamp was replaced by a rectangular form. Like the earlier newspaper stamps, rather than being embossed, the medicine stamps were recess-printed on damp paper from line-engraved plates, in red or black on white paper, with a crown in the middle of the rectangle, enclosed by a circle on which the

---

[11] *Taxes, Precedent Book, 1892–1910*: TNA IR 83/61.

[12] 23 Geo. III c. 62 s. 6 (1783); 25 Geo. III c. 79 s. 9 (1785).

[13] 42 Geo. III c. 56 s. 10 (1802).

[14] Leslie G. Matthews, 'The Medicine Stamp Acts of Great Britain', (1986) 16 *Pharmaceutical Historian*, 2.

[15] For the mechanics of the stamping process in the mid-1820s, see Fourteenth Report of the Commissioners of Inquiry into the Collection and Management of the Revenue arising in Ireland, Scotland; etc. Board of Stamps, *House of Commons Parliamentary Papers* (1826) (436) x 69 at pp. 98–109, 130–1, 559–61.

[16] For the work of the distributors and registrar of the medicine stamp duty in the 1820s see *ibid.*, at pp. 157–71, 559–61.

[17] 25 Geo. III c. 79 s. 15 (1785). Alpe suggested that this regulation was 'probably never very strictly enforced': E. N. Alpe, *Handy Book of Medicine Stamp Duty* (London: Offices of 'The Chemist and Druggist', ca. 1888), p. 18.

amount of duty was stated in words. On either side of the circle were printed the details of the rate of duty. The stamp also bore the words 'Stamp Office' or, in the latter part of the nineteenth century, 'Inland Revenue'.[18] At the time of the 1802 Act, the Stamp Office allowed the manufacturers of medicines to print either the name of their product or their own name on the medicine stamp label itself.[19]

ENFORCEMENT

Stamp fraud was a real danger to the public revenue and had been common since the early eighteenth century.[20] It was a particular problem with all new taxes because, as Pitt observed in 1786, frauds and evasions were invariably introduced at the inception of any tax.[21] The glove tax of 1785, for example, was immediately 'generally evaded'.[22] Lord John Cavendish had anticipated difficulties in implementing his new medicine tax insofar as it applied to non-patented proprietary medicines in point of identification, but was confident that collection would become more efficient 'as experience would enable government to discover the means by which evasions should be practised'.[23] He was, perhaps, somewhat sanguine. Most evasions consisted simply of selling dutiable medicines without a valid licence, or selling dutiable medicines without a stamp, or both. Evasion was sometimes deliberate. Examples included pasting a label that resembled the medicine stamp over the cork of the bottle, so that at first glance it appeared to bear the duty and suggest to the purchaser that it was made by the vendor named on it,[24] or removing a stamp from a bottle of medicine after it had been sold and affixing it to another bottle of medicine[25] or exhibiting stamped boxes of medicines in the shop window as decoys, while others were kept unstamped inside, for sale.[26] More often than not, however, evasion was committed through ignorance or misunderstanding, the

---

[18] See Figure 2. For the technical aspects of printing the stamps and a discussion of their appearance, see Dagnall, *Creating a Good Impression*, pp. 32–3, 61–2, 86; George Griffenhagen, *Medicine Tax Stamps Worldwide* (Milwaukee, Wisc: American Topical Association, 1971), pp. 6–26; 'Medicine Licence and Stamps', (1904) 65 *Chemist and Druggist* 211.

[19] For a definitive philatelic history, see Michael J. A. Tanner, *Great Britain Medicine Stamp Duty, A Philatelic History* (The Revenue Society, 2013).

[20] For evasions by attorneys, see Hughes, 'English Stamp Duties, 1664–1764', 249–50.

[21] *Parliamentary Register 1780–1796*, vol. 20, 29 March 1786, p. 7.

[22] *Ibid.*, 4 May 1786, p. 157, *per* Mr Sheridan.

[23] *Ibid.*, vol. 10, 26 May 1783, p. 71, *per* Lord John Cavendish.

[24] 'Proceedings under the Medicine Stamp and Licence Acts', (1852) 12 *Pharmaceutical Journal* (series 1) 506.

[25] 'Fraudulent Use of a Patent Medicine Stamp', (1874) 5 *Pharmaceutical Journal* (series 3) 237.

[26] 'A Limited Company Fined', (1903) 70 *Pharmaceutical Journal* (series 4) 654.

latter being unsurprising, considering the opacity of the provisions of charge. The forging of stamps, however, was an evasion of an altogether more serious nature.

Acutely aware of taxpayers' sensitivities to perceived intrusions of the fiscal state into their private lives, the government drew short of establishing an inspectorate of medicines with power to visit all the warehouses and shops where dutiable medicines were made, stored or sold to ensure that they were properly wrapped in stamped labels.[27] Instead, a number of preventative measures of a mechanical nature were adopted. The simplest was to require that the stamp be fixed to the medicine container such that it could not be opened without tearing the stamp.[28] Again, any parcel sent to a retailer by public conveyance, or which was about to be exported, containing twelve or more medicines was required to bear the word 'medicines', with authority for a magistrate to open any unmarked parcel if there was material suspicion that it contained unstamped preparations.[29] A new provision of wider scope, notable stringency and particular importance in ensuring collection essentially introduced the concept of collection at the source. This feature would remain in force until the abolition of the tax in 1941, and would later prove to be of a significance quite unforeseen in 1802.[30] It meant that the duty had to be paid and the medicines stamped by the proprietor, compounder or first vendor before the preparation was sold or exposed for sale, either wholesale or retail, or delivered out of his or her possession for sale at home or abroad.[31] The stamps were generally affixed to the medicines by the manufacturers and sent out to retailers ready for sale.

It was, however, by making it fraught with financial risk that evasion was primarily addressed. Severe statutory penalties for non-compliance were imposed. A person selling dutiable medicines without a licence or without a stamp affixed would be fined £5 for every medicine so sold.[32] If a stamp was

[27] *Stamp Office: Observations upon the present Medicine Act and Proposals for an Improvement of that Duty*, 21 May 1785: TNA: T1/624/514.

[28] 52 Geo. III c. 150 s. 2 (1812). See Figures 3 and 4.

[29] 43 Geo. III c. 73 s. 3 (1803). The need for such authority was a concession resulting from the complaint of the association that the original powers of search in the bill were too wide and impractical: William Chamberlaine, *History of the Proceedings of the Committee appointed by the General Meeting of Apothecaries, Chemists, and Druggists, in London, for the Purpose of obtaining Relief form the Hardships imposed on the Dealers in Medicine, by certain Clauses and Provisions contained in the new Medicine Act, passed June 3, 1802 etc*, (London: Highley, 1804), pp. 18–19.

[30] See below, pp. 73–77.

[31] 42 Geo. III c. 56 s. 3 (1802).

[32] 23 Geo. III c. 62 ss. 4, 7 (1783); 25 Geo. III c. 79 ss. 8, 10 (1785).

used twice the penalty was £10 for each offence,[33] and if any vendor failed to keep the Stamp Commissioners informed of the place of manufacture and sale and to keep up-to-date lists of medicines for sale, he or she could be fined £10.[34] The penalty was to be levied on the offender's goods, but if it could not be paid the offender had to go to prison for three months or until the sum was made good.[35] These penalties were kept under review, and the Act of 1802 made them even more stringent, generally doubling them but quadrupling them in some instances to act as a deterrent to evasion, thereby to make the collection of the tax more secure.[36] It was not worth the risk. Penalties for forging a stamp were of an entirely different order because forgery constituted a felony punishable by death.[37] Indeed, the capital nature of the offence confirmed that forgery was a major concern from the earliest days of the stamp duty,[38] and the Stamp Office embraced technical innovations to address it.[39] Despite carrying the severest of penalties, forgery was practised,[40] and towards the end of the nineteenth century there was extensive forgery of British medicine stamps in France.[41] One of the earliest cases of counterfeiting was *R* v. *Collicott*.[42] Collicott, a wholesale vendor of proprietary medicines, was accused of selling *Dr Jebb's Pills* with forged stamped labels. The labels were printed with the words 'Stamp' and 'Office' at each end, as genuine stamps were, but in the circle, instead of the duty and the crown, it bore the words 'Jones, Bristol', cut out and the hole obscured by sealing wax. The effect was convincing. He was tried at the Old Bailey Sessions in 1812. Despite arguing that the stamp was so unlike a true medicine stamp that it could not be a forgery, and some technical shortcomings in the framing of the indictment, he was ultimately found guilty and sentenced to death. It is unknown whether the penalty was carried out or

---

[33] 23 Geo. III c. 62 ss. 8, 9 (1783); 25 Geo. III c. 79 ss. 11, 12 (1785).

[34] 25 Geo. III c 79 s. 15 (1785).

[35] *Ibid.*, s. 22.

[36] 42 Geo. III c. 56 ss. 9, 12, 13, 14 (1802). With regard to the administrative reforms of the 1802 Act generally, see Matthews, 'The Medicine Stamp Acts', 2.

[37] 23 Geo III c. 62 s. 11 (1783); 25 Geo. III c. 79 s. 17 (1785).

[38] See Dagnall, *Creating a Good Impression*, pp. 13, 20.

[39] See for example Sir William Congreve's short-lived Compound Plate Printing and the enduring perforated date-bearing stamp of Henry Bessemer: Dagnall, *Creating a Good Impression*, pp. 20–1, 50–4. The medicine label plates were valuable items and great care was taken as to their custody and security: *Board's Order Book, 1860–93*: TNA IR 83/21 at p. 125.

[40] For the counterfeiting of British medicine stamps in America and France in the nineteenth century, see Griffenhagen, *Medicine Tax Stamps Worldwide*, p. 12.

[41] *Parl. Deb.*, vol. 36, ser. 4, col. 908, 27 August 1895 (HC).

[42] *R.* v. *Collicott* (1812) 4 Taunt. 300; 2 Leach 1048.

reduced to transportation or penal servitude for life, but E. N. Alpe, writer on the medicine stamp duty, observed that 'probably this unfortunate man was hanged'.[43]

The detection and prosecution of breaches of the medicine stamp duty legislation was by means of the system of 'laying an information'. This method of enforcement was favoured in many areas of the legal system in the eighteenth and nineteenth centuries and was an integral element in criminal law in the absence of a sophisticated police force and, in the context of the medicine trade, no pharmaceutical inspectorate.[44] At first, the informer was either a member of the public or a revenue officer. Because medicines were generally sold by display in a shop window, it was easy to see whether they were stamped. The informer would thus pose as a customer and purchase a dutiable medicine. If it was sold without the necessary stamp, or if the vendor was found not to have a valid licence, the infringement would be reported to the revenue authorities and proceedings would be taken against the vendor. Informers were attracted by indemnity and the fact that the heavy penalties the legislation imposed would, if the prosecution were successful, be divided between the public revenue and the person who informed.[45] This provision was a 'Revenue safeguard',[46] and the usual division was that each would receive one half.

This system of lay informers was intensely unpopular, and was abolished in 1803.[47] Thereafter, and until the twentieth century, the only persons who could lawfully 'lay an information' were officers of the revenue authorities, who had no pecuniary interest whatever in the proceedings. They would periodically be sent by the board to make purchases at different shops to seek out articles unlawfully offered for sale without a stamp, usually targeting vendors suspected of evading the tax. They were carefully instructed in their duties. For example, they were told to ensure that they did not purchase those regular medicines properly dispensed and bearing a label, handwritten or printed, indicating the name or use of the medicine. This was a common practice, and was not the object of the tax. Only if such medicines were previously made up,

---

[43] Alpe, *Handy Book*, p. 140.
[44] See generally Leon Radzinowicz, *A History of English Criminal Law and its Administration from 1750*, 4 vols., (London: Stevens & Sons Ltd., 1956), vol. 2, pp. 138–55.
[45] 23 Geo. III c. 62 s. 12 (1783); 25 Geo. III c. 79 s. 19 (1785). However, if the penalty was prosecuted for after six months or more, the whole sum went to the revenue: 25 Geo. III c. 79 s. 21 (1785).
[46] *Board of Customs and Excise and Predecessor: Private Office Papers, Medicine Stamp Duty 1783–1936*: TNA CUST 118/366, p. 6.
[47] 43 Geo. III c. 73 s. 4 (1803).

kept ready for sale and sold with any kind of leaflet or instruction as to their beneficial effects for a human ailment were they liable to the tax.[48]

The revenue authorities had extremely broad powers of enforcement. When the officer of the board suspected a vendor of an offence, the latter would be called in for an explanation or, as the solicitor to the Stamp Department put it in 1826, would 'tease the parties with letters'.[49] An example from 1848 read: 'I give you this intimation in order to afford you an opportunity of offering any explanation or statement of extenuating circumstances, with a view to induce the Commissioners either to forgo the proceedings or to mitigate the penalty'.[50] It was entirely up to the revenue authorities if a prosecution was instituted or not. If they were convinced by the explanation, they could decide to drop the matter entirely. They also had the power to settle with the offender. So they could fine the vendor £10, and if the vendor agreed to pay it, then no proceedings would be instituted. If the vendor refused to settle, proceedings would be brought. The solicitor to the Stamp Department would issue an Exchequer writ against the vendor – hence the common expression that an individual had been 'exchequered'. The cases would be heard in the first instance by a local magistrate. Prosecutions were expensive if they were taken to their conclusion, and the whole sum would be met by the defendants if they were found guilty, since they were liable to pay the costs. The revenue authorities, however, had the power to vary the sentence of the court.[51]

From the inception of the tax, the revenue authorities did not hesitate to prosecute where they deemed it necessary. In September 1784 the Stamp Commissioners published a notice in the national press.[52] They said that they had received information to the effect that many vendors of medicines who were within the meaning of the Act had not renewed their licences and were selling their medicines without the necessary stamps, and reiterated that such persons would face immediate prosecution in the Court of Exchequer. It

---

[48] *Further Instructions to Surveyors of Taxes in making Detections against Persons Evading the Stamp Duties, Assessed Taxes and Income Tax Circulars, 1812–40,* 20 November 1837: TNA IR 78/1, p. 154.

[49] Fourteenth Report of the Commissioners of Inquiry into the Collection and Management of the Revenue arising in Ireland, Scotland; etc. Board of Stamps, *House of Commons Parliamentary Papers* (1826) (436) x 69 at p. 227, *per* Godfrey Sykes, solicitor to the Stamp Department.

[50] 'The Medicine Stamp Act – Fraud and Attempt at Extortion', (1848) 8 *Pharmaceutical Journal* (series 1) 409.

[51] Report and Minutes of Evidence from the Select Committee on Patent Medicines, *House of Commons Parliamentary Papers* (1914) (Cd. 414) ix 1 at q. 205, *per* Sir Nathaniel Highmore, solicitor to the Customs and Excise.

[52] See for example *St James's Chronicle* or *British Evening-Post,* 11–14 September 1784.

seems that most vendors had taken out licences when the tax was first introduced, but were failing to renew them as they became aware of the problems
and doubts associated with the administration of the duty.[53] The parliamentary returns of Exchequer informations reveal the profile of prosecutions for
breach of the medicine stamp duty legislation. Within a period of just eight
months in 1829–30 392 breaches were prosecuted. Prosecutions for selling
medicine without a licence were double those for selling without a stamp.
Of the total, 77% were compounded for an average of £3 each, 7% dropped
entirely, and the rest moved to penalty. None was further proceeded on in the
Court of Exchequer.[54] In 1856 the Inland Revenue instituted 130 prosecutions
for non-compliance with the legislation.[55]

Defences to criminal prosecutions for breach of the legislation were few.
An accused vendor would have to show he or she came within an exemption,
as for example the surgeon Jeremiah Taylor, who escaped prosecution when a
Stamp Officer was heard to say that he would not be pursued because, being a
surgeon, the medicine he sold did not come within the Medicine Stamp Act.[56]
Under the reformed duty of 1785, the accused would have to show either that
the medicine was not of the kind chargeable under the legislation, either by
its nature or because it came within one of the exemptions, but inadvertence
or ignorance of the law were never a defence, however unclear that law was.

LEGISLATIVE DRAFTING

A fundamental prerequisite to the implementation of the tax by the revenue
authorities was to identify those medicines that were, by law, subject to the
charge. The objects of charge were laid down in the statutes themselves, but
the statutory language had to be interpreted to ascertain its meaning and
establish whether any given medicine was or was not subject to the tax. Every
phrase in every provision of charge and exemption had to be interpreted, and
the effect of the interrelationship between them assessed in order to implement the tax. The ease and accuracy with which this could be achieved

---

[53] Francis Spilsbury, *Discursory Thoughts Disputing the Construction of His Majesty's Hon.
Commissioners and Crown Lawyers, relative to the Medicine and Horse Acts...with Remarks
on the Late Trials Concerning the Medicine Act*, 2nd edn, (London; Dispensary, Soho Square,
1785), p. 20.

[54] Return of Exchequer Informations from 1829–30, *House of Commons Parliamentary Papers*
(1830) (317) xxix 439.

[55] First Report of the Commissioners of Inland Revenue, *House of Commons Parliamentary
Papers* (1857) (2199 sess. 1) iv 65, 88.

[56] London Metropolitan Archives MJ/SP/1786/04/042 and 072.

depended entirely on the quality of the legislative drafting. It was this perspective of the statutory framework of the medicine stamp duty, and indeed of any tax, that was ultimately the most problematic.

The provisions of all the stamp Acts had to be interpreted. This was a difficult task, due to the ever-growing number of stamp Acts and the archaic and complex nature of the provisions within them. By the end of the eighteenth century alone there were more than 100 . Even the judges in the eighteenth century were divided as to the interpretation of certain provisions in the legislation. Pitt's Stamp Duty Consolidation Act 1804[57] remedied this to some extent by repealing all previous stamp duties and reintroducing them in a new, clear and consolidated statute. However, the law remained confused and complex. In 1826 an official inquiry observed that the number and breadth of the stamp duty Acts led to 'considerable confusion, and consequent difficulty in forming accurate conclusions, as to the real state of the law upon some branches of the Stamp Revenue'.[58] A decade later there had been little progress. In 1836 the 230 stamp Acts then in force were described as forming 'a complete farrago of legislation' containing 'such contradictory provisions that even the most subtle lawyers find themselves entangled in coming to decisions on them, and individuals become the victims subjected to penalties never intended to be inflicted on them'.[59] It was not until 1870 that effective consolidating and simplifying legislation was enacted, in the three Stamp Acts of that year.[60] The first set out what the duties were, the second repealed the existing legislation and the third addressed the management of the duties.

The medicine stamp duty legislation was no exception. Wide and loose drafting was its defining pattern from its first introduction, and caused enormous problems of interpretation and convenience, enforcement and compliance.[61] In respect of the quality of drafting the original Act of 1783 was a disaster. It has been seen that the term 'quack medicines', which the evidence confirms was the intended object of charge, could not be used in an Act of Parliament, and that accordingly the Act imposed the tax on all medicines

---

[57] 44 Geo. III c.98 (1804).

[58] Fourteenth Report of the Commissioners of Inquiry into the Collection and Management of the Revenue arising in Ireland, Scotland; etc. Board of Stamps, *House of Commons Parliamentary Papers* (1826) (436) x 69 at p. 198.

[59] *Parl. Deb.*, vol. 32, ser. 3, col. 336, 13 March 1836 (HC) *per* Thomas Spring Rice, Chancellor of the Exchequer.

[60] The three Stamp Acts of 1870 (33 & 34 Vict. cc. 97, 98, 99) and those of 1891 (54 & 55 Vict. cc. 38, 39) did not amend the substance of the medicine stamp duty.

[61] For the inconsistent and uncertain administration of the newspaper stamp duty, see Lynne Oats and Pauline Sadler, 'The Abolition of the Taxes on Knowledge', in John Tiley (ed.), *Studies in the History of Tax Law Volume 2* (Oxford: Hart Publishing, 2007), pp. 299–301.

sold by unqualified persons licensed under the Act or sold under letters patent.[62] Qualified individuals were to pay no duty on any medicines they sold other than patent medicines properly so called.[63] Whatever the merits of this approach, the wording of the Act, ambiguous as it was, did not warrant this interpretation. Having provided that medically qualified individuals and established shopkeepers were exempt from its provisions, there followed a proviso to the effect that 'they had dealt in drugs or medicines only, not being drugs or medicines sold by virtue of his Majesty's letters patent'.[64] This raised a number of problems. It was not clear whether the proviso related exclusively to the shopkeepers' exemption, or included the medically qualified; it was not clear whether the word 'only' meant that the vendor had to sell medicines and no other commodities to be exempt, or whether it referred to the subsequent provision about patent medicines – namely that the vendor would not be exempt if he or she sold medicines that included patent medicines. The question was an important one, because most of those who sold medicines sold other commodities as well, such as tobacco, tea, cosmetics and dyes. The most common sellers of medicines were booksellers, who obviously sold books as well as medicines.[65] Furthermore, it was arguable that the charge when it applied did not extend to all patent medicines popularly so called, but was limited to those patent medicines with patents that were still in force. Most proprietary medicines advertised in the newspapers as patent medicines did not possess a valid patent. Indeed, Francis Spilsbury identified only five, namely *Analeptic Pills*, *Ague Tincture*, *Spa Elixir*, *Samaritan Water* and *Fryar's Drops*, leaving some sixty others that had once had a patent, or that claimed a patent and which were popularly called patent medicines. These were, on a strict interpretation, outside the meaning of patent medicine in the Act.[66] Spilsbury's argument

[62] See Chapter 1.
[63] Anon, *A Concise Abstract of the Most Important Clauses in the following Interesting Acts of Parliament* (London: J. Walker, 1785), p. 89; Spilsbury, *Discursory Thoughts*, p. 5; *Board of Customs and Excise and Predecessor: Private Office Papers, Medicine Stamp Duty 1783–1936*: TNA CUST 118/366, p. 6.
[64] 23 Geo III c. 62 s. 1 (1783).
[65] See Francis Spilsbury's defence of the booksellers against the interpretation of the Stamp Commissioners: Francis Spilsbury, *The Power of Gold Displayed, in the Humane Proposal of the Right Hon. William Pitt, Chancellor of the Exchequer, to bring forward an Act to put his Majesty into the disagreeable situation of signing a decree, that no sick or lame person, or diseased cattle, in Great Britain, shall have a medicine of repute without paying tribute; which the writer contends, is not justifiable either by the law of God, or man, and is a disgraceful impost, as it places the life of a human being in competition with a three-penny or six-penny stamp*, 1st edn (London: Dispensary, Soho Square, 1785).
[66] Spilsbury, *Discursory Thoughts*, p. 4. In 1784, before he obtained a royal patent for his medicine, and being a chemist, he advertised it as being sold free of duty: *Bath Chronicle*, 23 September 1784.

that the Act applied only to patent medicines in the strict sense of the term could legitimately be sustained by the wording of the legislation, and indeed he stated that the solicitor to the Stamp Commissioners agreed with him.[67]

While it was undoubtedly the case that it was difficult to define proprietary medicines sufficiently precisely to tax them, that Lord John Cavendish had said he could not 'draw a line relative to medicines, so as not to hurt the medical regular practice'[68] and that only patent medicines could be distinguished and taxed with certainty because they were formally specified on record,[69] such a strict interpretation could not have reflected the intention of the legislature. With only five patent medicines properly so called in existence in 1783, this interpretation would have rendered the Act nugatory[70] and so doomed it to failure. The intention must have been to spread the tax net wider to have any realistic chance of raising the amount of revenue envisaged. Indeed, as Spilsbury observed, his interpretation would not find favour with the Stamp Commissioners, as it would have 'blighted their hopes of a golden harvest'.[71] When it was put to them by the owners of proprietary medicines, the response was, according to Spilsbury, '[i]f, gentlemen, you mean to make use of chicanery arguments, the act will not produce any sum of consequence. I shall leave the public to judge who has been the greatest adept in chicanery'.[72]

The reason for the complete financial failure of the first Medicine Stamp Act lay in its defective drafting, and this was made clear in a report from the Stamp Commissioners to the Treasury.[73] It failed 'for want of more precise and definite Terms with respect to the Articles intended to be Taxed'.[74] Instructed by the Treasury to conceive an effective way of bringing proprietary medicines into charge, the revenue board proposed a realistic and pragmatic approach that looked to the characteristics of the tax rather than the nature of the vendor and thereby extended the duty 'both to Persons and Things not within the description of the present law, tho' certainly meant by the Legislature'.[75]

[67] Spilsbury, *Discursory Thoughts*, p. 4.
[68] *Ibid.*
[69] *Ibid.*
[70] *Ibid.*, p. 22.
[71] *Ibid.*, p. 4.
[72] *Ibid.*
[73] *Stamp Office: Report of Several Defects in the present law affecting duties*, 15 February 1785: TNA: T1/624/504; *Stamp Office: Observations upon the present Medicine Act and Proposals for an Improvement of that Duty*, 21 May 1785: TNA: T1/624/514.
[74] *Stamp Office: Observations upon the present Medicine Act and Proposals for an Improvement of that Duty*, 21 May 1785: TNA: T1/624/514.
[75] *Stamp Office: Report of Several Defects in the present law affecting duties*, 15 February 1785: TNA: T1/624/504.

Because the reference to patent medicines had caused so much uncertainty and evasion it was replaced at the board's suggestion by a broader terminology of charge.[76] It has been seen that the general charging clause in 1785 essentially taxed every preparation used internally or externally as a medicine to prevent, cure or relieve any human ailment,[77] if it was patented, secret, proprietary or recommended to the public as an effective remedy or if it was expressly named in a supplementing schedule, which consisted of a long list of the principal named preparations.[78] The Act also allowed the three exemptions for some imported medicines already paying customs duties, for pure drugs sold by qualified chemists or licensed individuals and for mixed drugs that were *known, admitted and approved* remedies sold by medically qualified individuals.[79] This framework was deliberately conceived and adopted to 'obviate any doubts which may arise in the construction' of the measure.[80]

Although the recast Act of 1785 was a material improvement in terms of substance and, to some extent, clarity of language, significant uncertainty remained. Difficulties stemmed from the unavoidable challenges of definition, but also from the need to bring all proprietary medicines within the charge while ensuring that regular medicines and practitioners were not inadvertently caught. The legislation was consequently excessively complicated in its structure, with its list of expressly charged medicines in the schedule, a comprehensive general charge on all medicines, a refinement of the meaning of medicines in order to impose the general charge on proprietary medicines only and the three express exemptions to mitigate the impact of the tax in the interests of regular medicines even though the exemptions were implicit in the general charge. Furthermore, the express repetition of some clauses to emphasise the exclusion of some regular medicines added another element of impenetrability. This method of charge, called a 'duplicate method' by the revenue authorities, was continued throughout the subsequent medicine stamp duty legislation.[81] The interrelationship between the provisions was bound to cause problems of interpretation and construction. The impenetrability of the drafting was not helped

[76] *Stamp Office: Observations upon the present Medicine Act and Proposals for an Improvement of that Duty*, 21 May 1785: TNA: T1/624/514.

[77] Medicine Stamp Duty Act 1785 (25 Geo. III c. 79) s. 2.

[78] *Ibid.*, s. 16.

[79] *Ibid.*, ss. 3, 4.

[80] *Ibid.*, s. 16.

[81] *Board of Customs and Excise and Predecessor: Private Office Papers, The Medicine Stamp Duties 1783–1936*: TNA CUST 118/366 at p. 56.

by the practice inherent in all stamp Acts of using standard-form catch-all clauses and applying them to a range of different articles from newspapers to gloves to medicines.

Neither were the lessons of poor drafting swiftly learned. The Act of 1802 was rushed, being hastily drafted with insufficient thought and precision within a large clutch of bills at the end of a Parliament. And because it was drafted with little consultation with the chemists and druggists, the new schedule of dutiable medicines included some preparations that strictly were exempt according to the general provisions. Because the legislation was left virtually untouched for the entire duration of the tax – it will be recalled that the Act in force in 1941 was that of 1812, which itself was in its essentials identical to that of 1785 – the problems of drafting were left unaddressed. Complexity, uncertainty and ambiguity became more acute as the statutory regime became out of date and antiquated. Most of the medicines brought into charge in the early decades of the tax were those expressly named in the schedule. That list was for the most part clear and unambiguous, but as those medicines fell into disuse and new ones were introduced with no revision of the schedule, the general charging provision came into prominence. It was this clause, however, that was full of words and phrases that were vague and uncertain. Key terms such as 'medicine', 'enclosure', 'preparation', 'recommended' and 'ailment' were left undefined in the Act itself. Similarly the exemptions were unsatisfactory. Apart from the obsolescence of the exemption for imported medicines already paying customs duties and named in the Books of Rates, the exemption for pure drugs was very wide, and that for *known, admitted and approved* remedies was undefined. Almost from its inception, therefore, and increasingly so throughout its life, the legislation imposing and regulating the medicine stamp duty was chaotic, impossibly wide, repetitive, overlapping, vague, uncertain and persistently out of date. Although much of nineteenth-century tax law came within this description to some degree, the medicine stamp duty fell squarely within it and as such constituted the most extreme example of an unsound statutory framework in British tax.

This was immediately clear. Among the first prosecutions under the legislation were the actions taken in 1785 against Messrs Newbery, Dicey and Wray, who were all tried for selling medicines without a licence. It was said that the prosecutions were brought 'with a liberal spirit'[82] and with the

---

[82] Spilsbury, *Discursory Thoughts*, p. 48. Spilsbury said that the case was heard by Baron Skinner in Westminster Hall on 5 March 1785.

primary intention to determine the correct construction of the 1783 Act.[83] In relation to the first defendant, Mr Newbery, who had kept a shop for the sale of medicines for more than three years and so prima facie was exempt from the requirement to purchase a licence, it was argued on a strict interpretation that he fell outside the exemption because he had sold a patent medicine properly so called, namely *Dr James's Analeptic Pills*, and thereby breached the specific terms of the exception.[84] Condemning the ambiguity of the Act, from which it was difficult to ascertain 'any clear sense or meaning', counsel for the defence looked to its spirit rather than its letter.[85] Arguing the innocence of his client on either interpretation, he said that '[t]he intention of the legislature was to impose a duty upon patent medicines, and to restrain booksellers, perfumers, and other shopkeepers, from selling medicines without a licence and stamps; but that the general dealers in drugs or medicines should be exempted'.[86] Ultimately, so unclear was the meaning of the legislation in relation to the specific point as to the sale of patent medicines properly so called by an established shopkeeper and being a question of 'nice import',[87] that a special verdict was found so that the opinion of the court could be taken upon it, but the purposive interpretation of counsel for Newbery was welcomed as 'fair and reasonable'.[88] A similar case against Messrs Dicey & Co had the same outcome, but in the prosecution of Messrs Wray, regular wholesale and retail chemists and druggists, the decision was clearer. They were found guilty of selling medicines without a licence, on the basis that they also dealt in articles of perfumery as well as medicines.[89] They had sold toothbrushes along with their medicinal tooth powder and so were not vendors of medicines 'only' under the Act of 1783. This finding supported the interpretation of the Stamp Commissioners and disproved the view, maintained by Spilsbury and others, that the exemption was denied if the vendor sold patent medicines, not if the vendor sold other articles.[90]

[83] *The New Annual Register* (London: Thomas McLean, 1785), pp. 20–1.

[84] *Ibid.*, p. 20. See Newbery's newspaper advertisement where he states that he sells his non-patent medicines free of duty as he was a medicine vendor within the statutory exemption: *Morning Post and Daily Advertiser*, 4 September 1784.

[85] *New Annual Register*, p. 20.

[86] *Ibid.*, p. 21.

[87] *Ibid.*

[88] *Ibid.*

[89] *Ibid.*

[90] Spilsbury, *Discursory Thoughts*, pp. 49, 51.

REVENUE PRACTICE

Statutory Interpretation by the Board

In the first half of the nineteenth century administration of the medicine stamp duty legislation amounted primarily to the implementation of the schedule, because most dutiable medicines were chargeable under that part of the Act, and indeed the Registrar of Medicine Duty admitted in 1825 that he did not look beyond it.[91] Despite some problems of drafting in the schedule, it was by its very nature relatively straightforward and unambiguous. As the century progressed, however, the medicines listed in the schedule became out of date as they were discontinued or were no longer popular. By 1888 more than 200 preparations named in the schedule were still available, but in many cases under different names or with a different formula. By 1937 the list of medicines in the schedule had become largely obsolete. Of the very few still available when the tax was abolished in 1941 were *Daffy's Elixir* and *Hooper's Female Pills*. As the schedule became outdated, so the duty was increasingly imposed under the general charge. So loosely worded was the charge that the task of assigning a meaning to the statutory language and thereby deciding the scope of the charge, which fell in the first instance to the Stamp Commissioners, increased dramatically in difficulty. The Commissioners making up the board were expressly given all necessary powers to execute the taxing Acts.[92] If the language posed any problems it was for the Commissioners to resolve them in the first instance.

Where questions of law arose and there was any doubt as to the chargeability of a medicine, the Commissioners could seek the expert advice of the board's solicitor.[93] So if any legal question arose before them concerning the collection of the duties or the nature of the stamps, they would ask the solicitor to

---

[91] Fourteenth Report of the Commissioners of Inquiry into the Collection and Management of the Revenue arising in Ireland, Scotland; etc. Board of Stamps, *House of Commons Parliamentary Papers* (1826) (436) x 69 at p. 561, *per* Louis Legoux, Registrar and Distributor of Medicine Licences and Labels.

[92] See for example the Inland Revenue Board Act 1849 (12 & 13 Vict. c. 1) ss. 1, 3; Thirteenth Report of the Commissioners of Inquiry into the Collection and Management of the Revenue arising in Ireland, Scotland; etc., *House of Commons Parliamentary Papers* (1826) (435) x 1 at pp. 17–19.

[93] *Further Instructions to Surveyors of Taxes in making Detections against Persons Evading the Stamp Duties, Assessed Taxes and Income Tax Circulars*, 1812–40, 20 November 1837: TNA IR 78/1 at p. 154.

attend them and seek his advice.[94] When called for, which was frequently the case, his view was almost invariably adopted. His constant practice, and that of his staff, made him knowledgeable as to the detail of the legislation, 'for a man can never learn the Stamp Acts without he is daily engaged upon them'.[95] If on the other hand the members of the board felt they needed scientific assistance, to decide for example whether a drug was a pure drug for the purposes of the exemption, or a wine so medicated that it was a medicine rather than a wine,[96] they could call on the services of the Government Laboratory.[97] In some instances the revenue authorities could look to definitive judicial interpretation of provisions in the Act by analogy but this was rare. The meaning of the words 'expose to sale', for example, could with some degree of confidence be held to mean an exposure to the view of a purchaser, as had been held in relation to the same words in the Margarine Act 1887[98] and the Public Health Act 1875.[99]

With recourse to this expert legal and scientific advice, the members of the board assigned a meaning to vague and uncertain provisions, words and phrases. They did so with confidence on the basis that they had been closely involved in drafting the legislation and so understood precisely the intention underlying it and, therefore, what the 'correct' interpretation was.[100] They made rulings on a daily basis, to keep up with the thriving trade in proprietary medicines and the constant invention of new products. In so doing, the revenue authorities established a body of guidelines to which they adhered to and which resolved the inadequacies of the statutory language and enabled them to implement the law. This revenue practice addressed all the words and phrases that were unclear in the legislation, and, accordingly, the fundamental

---

[94] Fourteenth Report of the Commissioners of Inquiry into the Collection and Management of the Revenue arising in Ireland, Scotland; etc. Board of Stamps, *House of Commons Parliamentary Papers* (1826) (436) x 69 at p. 756, *per* Godfrey Sykes, solicitor to the Stamp Department.
[95] *Ibid.*, at p. 757.
[96] See for example *Board of Inland Revenue decisions on medicine stamp duty*, 1892: TNA DSIR 26/138.
[97] See Chapter 4.
[98] 50 & 51 Vict. c. 29 s. 6; *Crane v. Lawrence* (1890) 25 QBD 152.
[99] 38 & 39 Vict. c. 55, s. 116; *Ollett v. Jordan* [1918] 2 KB 41.
[100] See for example *Stamp Office: Observations upon the present Medicine Act and Proposals for an Improvement of that Duty*, 21 May 1785: TNA: T1/624/514. But see Thirteenth Report of the Commissioners of Inquiry into the Collection and Management of the Revenue arising in Ireland, Scotland; etc., *House of Commons Parliamentary Papers* (1826) (435) x 1 at p. 43, *per* James Sedgwick, chairman of the Stamp Commissioners, where he observed that in his recent experience legislation was a matter for the Treasury and the solicitor, and that the board was not involved.

concepts underlying the tax. So numerous were the doubts and difficulties in their drafting, that an extraordinary degree of bureaucratic involvement in the interpretation of the law was required.

The precise meaning of every word, every phrase and every combination of provisions had to be established. Under the Act of 1783, in which the status of the vendor was of the essence, the scope of the exemption for the medically qualified was key. The Stamp Commissioners interpreted the exemption for the medically qualified so as to permit them to sell proprietary medicines without a licence, but with the requirement that they pay the duty on any patent medicines they sold, even though the Act exempted them entirely, on the basis that it was the government's intention to tax all patent medicines, and yet protect regular medicines or drugs. Where chemists and druggists sold proprietary medicines and other items such as tobacco, they were held not to be liable to the duty on their medicines.

Under the Act of 1785, however, which established the nature of the modern tax, the difficulties of interpretation pervaded the entire tax. Five key terms and phrases had to be assigned a meaning. First, the charge attached to 'every packet, box, bottle, pot, phial, or other inclosure' containing the dutiable medicine. The board interpreted this to mean a container that was sealed in some way, with glue or string. Any container not so sealed, maintained the board, was not a container within the meaning of the Act and escaped the charge. Accordingly, when medicines were sold loose in a paper bag, or when customers brought their own bottles to be filled with a liquid mixture or where the vendor sold a single pill into the hand, they were not liable to duty. This was a generous interpretation by the board.[101]

Second, the charge was expressed to apply only to 'preparations'. This was taken to mean that some active processing had to have taken place. For this reason, simple unmedicated and unprepared herbs were held not to be within the charge.[102]

Third, the Act provided that a preparation was only chargeable if it was used as a medicine, but the term 'medicine' was not defined. It was clear that instruments and appliances such as ear trumpets and trusses were not within the

---

[101] Ultimately there was judicial authority for what constituted a package under section 6 of the Margarine Act 1887 (50 & 51 Vict. c. 29): *Toler* v. *Bischop* (1896) 65 LJMC 4.

[102] *Taxes Precedent Book 1892–1910*: TNA IR 83/61. If they were ground into a powder, they would be chargeable: Report and Minutes of Evidence from the Select Committee on Medicine Stamp Duties, *House of Commons Parliamentary Papers* (1937) (Cmd. 54) viii 129, Memorandum of C. J. Flynn of the Board of Customs and Excise, p. 162. Pure herbs could also come within the statutory exemption for single drugs. Medicated herbs were expressly included in the general charge.

charge, even if recommended as beneficial for human ailments, because they were not used as medicines. But the term raised particular problems where preparations were recommended for the relief of an ailment but were used as a food, confectionary or as a beverage. These cases were numerous, with sometimes very fine distinctions, and the board had to decide whether these articles were within the charge to medicine stamp duty or not. There were a number of borderline preparations, notably *Guinness*, *Bovril* and *Ovaltine*, all of which were advertised as beneficial to general health and as preventing colds and influenza. The board took the view that they were consumed and used as foods and beverages within the normal diet, and not as medicines, so they escaped the charge. An example of the difficulties in drawing the line was *Savory & Moore's Digestive Candy*. The revenue authorities thought it was not liable because it was not held out as a medicine nor recommended, and that an aid to digestion was not a use as a medicine.[103] When, however, a food was combined with a medicinal drug and recommended for the relief of a human ailment, it was liable. For example, the preparations *Maltine with Cod Liver Oil* and *Maltine with Cascara Sagrada* were both held liable to the duty by the board, even though *Maltine* with no additions was regarded as a food and not subject to duty.[104] Some such preparations came to be adjudicated upon by the regular courts. In *Harding* v. *Migge* in 1909 the court held that a 'brain and nerve food' sold in tablet form under the name of *Antineurasthin* to cure nervous diseases, headaches, neuralgic pains and other ailments was on the borderline between a food and a medicine, but it was sold as a medicine and so liable to the medicine stamp duty.[105] Although the product consisted mainly of egg whites, with a small percentage of mineral matter, the terms of the maker's published pamphlet and the dosage instructions on the box made it clear that it was held out as a medicine. It was to be consumed before or after a meal and so was extraordinary rather than ordinary in consumption. It was medicinal in nature and, as such, it was dutiable.

On similar reasoning toilet articles were prima facie not liable to the tax, but if they were sold as a medicine or recommended as preventing, curing or relieving an ailment then they came within the charge.[106] Toothpastes recommended for cleaning teeth or to be used as a mouthwash would not be chargeable, but would be chargeable if they were recommended for the prevention or cure for decay, toothache or gum disease. But when a hairdresser

[103] *Board of Inland Revenue decisions on medicine stamp duty*, 1892: TNA DSIR 26/138.
[104] *Ibid.*
[105] *Harding* v. *Migge* (1909) 73 JP 493.
[106] *Taxes, Precedent Book, 1892–1910*: TNA IR 83/61.

was prosecuted for selling *Rowland's Odonto* without a licence, and although he argued this was equivalent to a mere soap, the fact that the medicine stamp duty legislation expressly included tooth powders and similar products, he was accordingly convicted.[107] Again, such articles came to be adjudicated on in the courts. In *Fincher v. Duclercq* in 1896[108] Duclercq was prosecuted for selling *Ludovic's Pine Tar Soap* unstamped and without a licence, having recommended the soap as beneficial for the prevention and cure of a number of skin and lung conditions and other ailments. The informations were dismissed because no evidence was given before the justices as to the composition of the soap. Whether the soap constituted a medicine within the legislation was a question of fact for the justices to decide, and no evidence was put to them that it was, although such evidence could have been possible. *Lifebuoy Soap* escaped the charge, even though it was recommended as a safeguard against germs that might enter the human body and cause disease, because it was not recommended for any specific complaint or part of the body.[109]

Fourth, the general charge provided that for a preparation to be chargeable it had to be 'used or applied internally or externally'. In the context of preparations that were burned and the fumes inhaled to treat respiratory diseases, such as asthma cigarettes, the board adopted a liberal interpretation and decided that that requirement was not satisfied because it was not the preparations themselves that were 'used' but the product of their burning.[110] This view was based on the opinion of the board's solicitor and was followed from 1876. This was not extended to products such as smelling salts, which were themselves inhaled as such.[111]

Fifth, the preparation had to be intended for the relief of an 'ailment'. Again, in the absence of any guidance in the Act itself, there were challenging borderline cases. As a matter of practice the board decided that afflictions such as baldness, dandruff, sunburn, freckles or chapped lips were not 'medical' enough and so did not come within the charge. In the light of this hairdressers and perfumers were permitted to sell hair lotions and skin creams free of duty, even though they were recommended for the relief of such minor

[107] 'Is Rowland's Odonto a Patent Medicine?', (1873) 4 *Pharmaceutical Journal* (series 3) 435.
[108] *Fincher v. Duclercq* (1896) 60 JP 276.
[109] Report and Minutes of Evidence from the Select Committee on Medicine Stamp Duties, *House of Commons Parliamentary Papers* (1937) (Cmd. 54) viii 129 at qq. 28–34 *per* Sir Charles FitzRoy, solicitor to the Board of Customs and Excise.
[110] *Taxes, Precedent Book, 1892–1910:* TNA IR 83/61.
[111] *Board of Customs and Excise and Predecessor: Private Office Papers, The Medicine Stamp Duties 1783–1936:* TNA CUST 118/366 at p. 36.

conditions.[112] On the other hand, obesity was regarded as an ailment within the meaning of the Medicine Stamp Act.[113]

Once these five prerequisites to the charge had been clarified, that is that the article was a preparation sold in a sealed enclosure to be used internally or externally as a medicine to relieve an ailment, the provisions of the general charge, namely secrecy, ownership and recommendation, had to be interpreted to establish liability. To do so the board closely examined the words used not only on the medicine label itself, but on any writing related to it such as newspaper advertisements or price lists, or accompanied it in the form of an explanatory handbill or dosage instructions. Any expression suggesting that the medicine was secret, that the recipe belonged to a particular person or that it would relieve any ailment would render it liable.[114] This was confirmed in 1894 in the case of *Smith v. Mason & Co.*,[115] pursued by the revenue authorities because it 'involved a question of a considerable sum' to them.[116] The company carried on the business of chemist and druggist and distributed a free price list in which *Dr Gregory's Stomachic Powder* and *Tincture of Nux Vomica* were recommended as beneficial for certain ailments, a recommendation that was repeated in relation to the tincture in a handbill in which it was wrapped. When prosecuted for selling these unstamped, the court held that to incur liability to the medicine stamp duty, it was not necessary that the public notice or advertisement be affixed or delivered with the medicine.[117]

The question whether the use of the possessive case or the use of a name in parentheses amounted to a proprietary claim gave rise to considerable discussion. The board took the view that medicines bearing an individual's name, such as *Dr Gregory's Powder, Brown's Cough Mixture, Liver Pills, prepared only by Smith*[118] or *Dr Hunter's Liver Mixture*, followed by the name of the vendor, such as 'Wm. Jones, Chemist, London,' or *Rhubarb Pills (Smith), Rhubarb Pills (Smith's)*, generally implied a claim to some proprietary right and were, accordingly, liable.[119] The only exception was where

[112] *Ibid.*, p. 48.
[113] Report of the Government Chemist, *House of Commons Parliamentary Papers* (1912–13) (Cd. 6363) xxix 453 at p. 465.
[114] *Taxes, Precedent Book, 1892–1910*: TNA IR 83/61. See Figure 5.
[115] *Smith v. Mason & Co.* [1894] 2 QB 363.
[116] 'Proceedings under the Medicine Stamp Acts', (1894) 24 *Pharmaceutical Journal* (series 3) 1042.
[117] On an appeal from the magistrates' decision by way of case stated under the Summary Jurisdiction Act 1879 (42 & 43 Vict c.49) s. 33.
[118] *Board's Order Book 1860–93*: TNA IR 83/21.
[119] *Board of Customs and Excise and Predecessor: Private Office Papers, The Medicine Stamp Duties 1783–1936*: TNA CUST 118/366 at p. 167.

the ingredients were so well known to all chemists and druggists that the name in the possessive case amounted to nothing more than a description of the product. For example, the board acknowledged that the statement that *Dr Gregory's Powder* was 'successful' amounted to a recommendation, and that the use of a physician's name in this way amounted to an assertion of a proprietary right in the recipe, but that the presumption was rebutted by the fact that the ingredients of the medicine were well known to all chemists, so that the use of the name was merely descriptive.[120] It was very easy to breach the law unknowingly in this way. A London chemist, Bishop, in 1894 sold a preparation he called *Aromatic Iron and Quinine Tonic* and on its label it stated that it was prepared by 'S. Bishop, chemist'. Thus far the preparation would not have been liable to duty. However, the chemist had a small notice in his shop window that read 'Bishop's Iron and Quinine Tonic'. That sufficed to imply that the tonic – indeed all those tonics in the shop – was a proprietary medicine and was thus liable. He was fined five shillings, with costs.[121] Knowledge of the 'power of the apostrophe' gave rise to perceived opportunities for evasion. In 1895, a bottle exposed for sale unstamped bore the label *Windle's Solution of Cod-Liver Oil* and a statement that 'No preparations are genuine unless protected by this label, a counterfeit of which is a forgery'. When a revenue officer purchased it, the vendor took the bottle behind a screen and wrapped it, and when unwrapped it was seen that the *''s'* in *Windle's* had been removed. The vendor was fined £3 3s and costs.[122]

The statutory provision that gave rise to the most intense controversy and debate was that which charged medicines if they were recommended for the prevention, cure or relief of human ailments. The interpretation of the word 'recommended' by the board was of great importance, and indeed became the main test of liability, if only because most commercially sold medicines were chargeable within it.[123] The recommendation had to be printed or written, and could be direct or implied. An oral recommendation, such as the vendor commending the medicine to the purchaser at the time of sale, would not

---

[120] *Board's Order Book 1860–93*: TNA IR 83/21 at p. 163. See generally 'The Possessive Case', (1904) 65 *Chemist and Druggist* 650; Xrayser, 'The Reign of the Apostrophe' *ibid.*, 685.

[121] 'Proceedings under the Medicine Stamp Duty Acts', (1894) 25 *Pharmaceutical Journal* (series 3) 429.

[122] 'Sale of Proprietary Medicine Unstamped', (1895) 55 *Pharmaceutical Journal* (series 4) 171.

[123] Report and Minutes of Evidence from the Select Committee on Medicine Stamp Duties, *House of Commons Parliamentary Papers* (1937) (Cmd. 54) viii 129 at q. 111 *per* C. J. Flynn of the Board of Customs and Excise.

incur liability.[124] The recommendation could be on the label, on any associated printed matter, written on a notice in the shop window or on the shop window itself.[125] A recommendation was easily found. So, for example, even if a medicine were simply described as 'successful', then that was enough to be regarded as a recommendation and the medicine dutiable.[126] A statement on a label that a cough syrup was 'a safe and effectual remedy for children' amounted to a recommendation and made the preparation chargeable.[127] There were attempts to avoid the tax by ingenious wording of the labels to avoid a positive recommendation. For example, *Dr Collier's Orange Wine of Quinine* was recommended 'as being superior to bark, the properties of which are too well known to require comment'.[128]

Less evident was the effect of the long-established commercial practice to sell a medicine with a reference either to the ailment it purported to relieve or prevent, or to the organ of the body it maintained it would benefit. Cough mixtures, fever powders, eye lotions, antibilious pills, liver pills, corn paint and stomach tinctures were ubiquitous. In strict law they were all chargeable. A reference to the ailment was regarded as including an implied recommendation for medical treatment, and a reference to the organ of the body was understood to include the diseases that organ might be subject to. However, if such medicines were neither proprietary nor expressly recommended, which was in practice unusual, the revenue authorities tacitly agreed not to charge them on the basis that such names were mere descriptions of the medicines, not recommendations.[129] *Barratt & Co's Cough Killers* was held to be liable on the grounds of proprietary claim and express recommendation, not on the inclusion of the name of the ailment.[130] This leniency – adopted for the convenience of the public to enable them to select the medicine they needed for their particular condition – was embodied in the Board of Stamps and Taxes' instructions to its officers in 1848 and was confirmed in a circular of 1887.

In 1903, however, this sensible practice was brought to an abrupt end, and the board was forced to modify its view following a rare instance of judicial

---

[124] Unless, for example, publicised by a town crier: *Board of Customs and Excise and Predecessor: Private Office Papers, The Medicine Stamp Duties 1783–1936*: TNA CUST 118/366 at p. 39.

[125] See 'Legal Hints for Chemists, The Stamp Acts', (1897) 59 *Pharmaceutical Journal* (series 4) 469.

[126] *Board's Order Book, 1860–93*: TNA IR 83/21 at p.163.

[127] *Board's Decisions 1892*: TNA DSIR 26/138.

[128] 'Informations under the Medicine Stamp Act', (1848) 7 *Pharmaceutical Journal* (series 1) 361, 362.

[129] Alpe, *Handy Book*, p. 87.

[130] *Board of Inland Revenue decisions on medicine stamp duty*, 1892: TNA DSIR 26/138.

interpretation of the medicine stamp duty legislation. In the case of *Ransom v. Sanguinetti*[131] Mr Sanguinetti, a chemist, was prosecuted for selling a box of medicated lozenges unstamped. The label bore his name and address, the description 'Pure gum Pastilles', 'Influenza' and the phrase 'Delightfully Soothing to Singers and Public Speakers'. The board instituted a prosecution, but the justices, taking the view that the proceedings were 'frivolous', dismissed the case. They did so on the basis that the latter phrase was not clearly connected with the word 'influenza', and did not itself mention any ailment, just as the word 'influenza' alone did not constitute a recommendation that the lozenges were beneficial for that ailment. The chairman of the bench said he thought 'it might be a waste of money and time' to state a case, but the revenue authorities pressed for it and said it was 'a matter of great importance'.[132] On appeal the High Court disagreed with the finding of the magistrates and held that the inclusion of the word 'influenza' could have no meaning other than to state that these lozenges were good for influenza, and that amounted to a clear recommendation that they were beneficial for the relief of a human ailment, and so within the charge.

The effect of the decision was to make any medicine sold under a description that referred to the ailment liable to the duty.[133] 'Cough mixture', 'corn paint' or 'headache powders', for example, would now be liable in practice as well as in theory.[134] During the proceedings the revenue authorities' practice was criticised and the Solicitor General made it clear that that their interpretation of a descriptive title of a medicine would no longer be sanctioned. As a result, the board announced that their lenient practice would end.[135] If the ailment was mentioned, that was a recommendation, and liability would ensue.[136] Furthermore, although the board said that because the recommendation had to be for the relief of a human ailment, the mere mention of an organ of the body would not of itself render the medicine liable.[137] The board would not, therefore, regard as chargeable medicines such as 'liver pills,' or 'chest mixture' or 'throat pastilles,' even with reference to their general action, such as 'a good, general tonic,' 'beneficial for improving the health generally,'

---

[131] *Ransom v. Sanguinetti* (1903) 67 JP 219.
[132] 'Alleged Recommendation on Label', (1902) 68 *Pharmaceutical Journal* (series 4) 306.
[133] *Parl. Deb.*, vol. 125, ser. 4, col. 9, 8 July 1903 (HC).
[134] *Taxes, Precedent Book, 1892–1910*: TNA IR 83/61; *Instructions*: TNA IR 78/289.
[135] *Board of Customs and Excise and Predecessor: Private Office Papers, The Medicine Stamp Duties 1783–1936*: TNA CUST 118/366 at p. 75.
[136] 'Liability to Medicine Stamp Duty', (1903) 70 *Pharmaceutical Journal* (series 4) 828; 'Liability to Medicine Stamp Duty', (1903) 71 *Pharmaceutical Journal* (series 4) 868.
[137] *Instructions*: TNA IR 78/289.

'astringent mixture' or 'aperient pills'.[138] If, however, there was a word to suggest the manner in which the medicine would act on the organ itself, it was
liable. Preparations such as 'blood purifier' or 'liver invigorator' would be taxable. The board drew short of saying that remedies named solely after the
organ were not within the charge, stating instead that 'duty will not be pressed
for', a phrase suggesting that on a narrow reading of both the statute and the
judgment of the court, liability would arise, but that the board chose not to
adopt such an interpretation.[139]

Although the post-1903 practice was developed as a compromise, to allow a
description of the article to aid the consumer, but not one that suggested that
it was to be used for a particular complaint, the decision in *Sanguinetti* and
the board's consequent change in practice alarmed the trade considerably.
There was a fear that there could be a return to the old practice in which some
chemists and druggists, when first understanding that the chief basis of liability was based on recommendation on the label, refrained from labelling their
medicines at all, and so gave the customer no written instruction as to use or
dosage. Customers had to rely on remembering the chemist's verbal directions. The dangers of this were plain to see.[140] Not only was there widespread
concern about the danger to the public health of having to label medicines
with no indication of their purpose,[141] but there was concern as to the effect of
the decision on the 'Penny Trade'. The effect of the ruling was to make liable
to duty even the smallest amounts of pills, powders and medicines described
by reference to the ailment, and this would severely affect such sales by the
pennyworth, which were so important in poorer districts. The prices would
rise, and the vendors considerably inconvenienced by having to reprint and
affix labels.

Although it was almost invariably the terms in the general charge that caused
the most severe problems of interpretation, there was one article expressly
named in the schedule that challenged board and taxpayer alike. That was
the provision relating to artificial mineral waters. The schedules of the 1803
and 1804 legislation had imposed the charge on 'Waters, Artificial Mineral',[142]
but the 1812 Act was more explicit, bringing into charge 'Waters, videlicet – All

[138] *Ibid.; Taxes, Precedent Book, 1892–1910:* TNA IR 83/61; *Board of Customs and Excise and Predecessor: Private Office Papers, The Medicine Stamp Duties 1783–1936:* TNA CUST 118/366 at p. 76.

[139] *Taxes, Precedent Book, 1892–1910:* TNA IR 83/61.

[140] (1857) 17 *Pharmaceutical Journal* (series 1) 201. See too 'Letter to the Editor', (1870) 11 *Pharmaceutical Journal* (series 2) 575.

[141] 'The Stamp Acts and Domestic Remedies', (1903) 71 *Pharmaceutical Journal* (series 4) 18.

[142] 43 Geo. III c. 73 (1803); 44 Geo. III c. 98, schedule B (1804).

artificial Mineral Waters, and all Waters impregnated with Soda or Mineral alkali, or with Carbonic Acid Gas, and all Compositions in a liquid or solid State, to be used for the Purpose of compounding or making any of the said Waters'.[143] This had the effect of charging all artificial mineral waters, whether or not they were medicinal, and accordingly soda water and other waters sold as beverages became liable. In 1833 this provision was repealed, with the intention of exempting soda water, a very popular beverage, from the charge.[144] From then on it was assumed that any medicinal waters or compounds for making them that were recommended for human ailments would be dutiable under the general charging clause, which included the words 'and also all other medicines, waters, chemical and officinal preparations whatsoever to be used for the relief of any disorder ....' This, the board firmly believed, had been the intention of the legislators.[145]

The interrelationship between the repealed schedular charge and the extant general charge following this repeal caused real problems of statutory interpretation. The question was whether all artificial mineral waters, medicinal or not, were now exempt, or whether medicinal ones were subject to the tax under the general charge, and non-medicinal (such as soda water) were exempted from the original charge by the 1833 Act. In an attempt to resolve this question, the board sought the opinion of counsel in 1834. William Henry Maule of the Temple took the view that artificial mineral waters were not liable under the general charge, even if they had been recommended for the relief of a human ailment, because they had been liable under the schedule, and that specific charge had been repealed.[146] The response of the revenue authorities to this opinion was revealing. Because counsel's opinion differed from their own view, which they confidently believed was the view of the government, they sought the opinion of the Law Officers of the Crown. They argued that the 1833 Act did not repeal the duty on all artificial mineral waters. On the true construction of the Act, the repeal of the clause in the 1812 schedule left the general charge unaffected, and the question to be resolved was whether artificial mineral waters that were proprietary or recommended for the relief of a human ailment were liable under the general charge. The Attorney General and Solicitor General, however, agreed with learned counsel. They were of the opinion that 'whatever the secret intention of the framers might be', the effect of the 1833 Act was to exempt artificial

---

[143] 52 Geo. III c. 150, schedule (1812).
[144] Stamps, etc., Act 1833 (3&4 Will. IV c. 97) s. 20.
[145] *Stamp Duty, Law Officers' Opinions*, vol. 1, 1828–1908: TNA IR 98/11 at S. 62.
[146] *Ibid.*

mineral waters entirely from the stamp duty, the words in the general charge not being applicable to them.[147]

The matter was only definitively resolved by a court of law as late as 1878 in the case of *Attorney General v. Lamplough*.[148] The litigation concerned the liability to the tax of *Lamplough's Pyretic Saline*, a water composed of tartaric acid, bicarbonate of soda and chlorate of potash, the last ingredient being a medicine. It was advertised as a cure for a number of ailments, and was sold without any stamp duty being paid. It undoubtedly would come within the words of the general charge, and the Crown argued that the effect of the repeal by the 1833 Act of the express charge in the schedule on all artificial mineral waters was as though no such clause had ever been included, leaving the general charging clause unaffected and the *Pyretic Saline* liable under it. The defendant contended that because this would mean that the repeal of the express charge was a nullity, the correct view was that when the schedular charge was repealed, the water was no longer chargeable to tax at all. The High Court accepted the Crown's argument and held that the water was liable under the general charge. Kelly CB, however, dissented, taking the defendant's view that the *Pyretic Saline*, being a water impregnated with carbonic acid gas, was taxable under the words in the 1812 schedule but that it ceased to be liable when those words were repealed in 1833. The schedule and the general charge were mutually exclusive. On appeal, the judgment of the High Court was reversed, and the dissenting opinion of Kelly CB formed the basis of the Court of Appeal's decision that the *Pyretic Saline* was not liable to the tax: the water came within the schedular charge even if it did not satisfy the requirements of the general charge. It followed that it was not chargeable under the general charge, and because the schedular charge had been repealed, the water was not liable to the tax.

The effect of the decision was that effervescent waters similar in composition to *Lamplough's Pyretic Saline* – in other words, all unmedicated artificial mineral waters and soda waters – were exempt from duty despite being recommended for human ailments. The revenue board had been unable legally to assert its own view of the legislation, which it was convinced was correct and reflected the intention of Parliament, although it had tried to do so for nearly half a century. As a result, the number of artificial mineral waters sold with fulsome recommendations for their medical benefits increased enormously. These were intended as medicines and not mere beverages, but

[147] *Ibid.*
[148] *Attorney General v. Lamplough* (1878) LR 3 Ex D 214.

escaped the charge. Famous examples were *Eno's Fruit Salts*, *Epsom Salts* and *Andrew's Liver Salts*. None was subject to the duty.

Extra-Statutory Concessions

Although a considerable proportion of revenue practice consisted of assigning a meaning to uncertain key terms in the legislation, a significant proportion consisted of operational methods developed by the revenue authorities to make the law workable in the changing context of pharmaceutical and commercial usage. Inadequate drafting left gaps in the legislation that made implementation impossible. In an attempt to create a workable tax code applicable to proprietary medicines, the revenue authorities acted on their own initiative and made decisions entirely outside the statutory provisions to the effect that in certain specific instances the charge to tax should attach or not.

In many instances such decisions were specific and relatively narrow in their effect. For example, the legislation expressly provided that if at any point since a medicine's invention a proprietary right had been claimed in it – perhaps by selling it with a proprietary name – thereby rendering it liable to the tax, then that liability endured even after the medicine had become common property and its formula widely known and open to anyone to manufacture. In other words, once taxed, forever taxed. The practice of the board, however, was to ignore this requirement and regard such medicines, even though named, as non-dutiable. By 1936 some twenty-one medicines of this kind existed, including *Gregory's Powders* and *Hamilton's Pills*.[149] A further example of a specific concession was the board's treatment of lozenges before their exclusion from the tax in 1815.[150] These were essentially confectionary in nature, but because they were expressly included in the schedule, strictly they were liable to duty, whether sold as medicines or not. The practice, however, was to tax named lozenges, such as the famous *Ching's Worm Lozenges*, as proprietary medicines, but to allow unnamed ones, such as simple peppermint lozenges, to escape the charge. The only condition the board added was that such lozenges should be sold in small amounts with no printed recommendation.[151] In other instances, however, the practice of the board was of much wider scope and significance, often with only the most tenuous connection with the statutory

---

[149] *Board of Customs and Excise and Predecessor: Private Office Papers, The Medicine Stamp Duties 1783–1936*: TNA CUST 118/366 at p. 41.
[150] Stamp Act 1815 (55 Geo. III c. 184) s. 54.
[151] Chamberlaine, *History of the Proceedings*, pp. 31–2.

provision or even none at all. These came to be known as extra-statutory concessions, and four were of particular importance.

Known, Admitted and Approved *Remedies*

The first example of a board practice that transcended the words of the statute was one of particular significance: it began as an instance of the board disregarding a statutory provision and became one of ignoring a judicial decision. The practice in question was the board's approach to the statutory exemption for *known, admitted and approved* remedies sold by a qualified surgeon, apothecary, chemist or druggist. Throughout the nineteenth century the board, and indeed the chemists and druggists, discounted this exemption, understanding that because it was implicit in the charging provision, it was merely declaratory in nature and had no separate substantive effect so as to take out of the charge a medicine that would otherwise be within it.[152] The exemption had been included simply to make it absolutely clear that established remedies that formed the stock of qualified practitioners were not within the very wide general charge to the tax, as long as they were not secret, patent, proprietary or recommended to the public.[153] Even though a barrister, George Price, engaged by the Association of Chemists and Druggists, had drawn attention to the exemption in 1830,[154] the understanding of the statutory exemption as a dead letter of no practical importance continued throughout the nineteenth century and arguably reflected a complete disregard of an express statutory provision.[155] Had the consolidation of the stamp duties proposed in the 1830s taken place, it would have been repealed, and the board's instructions to officers of 1848 and 1897 simply ignored it.

Despite this long-established and widely accepted practice, in 1903 the pharmaceutical profession challenged its validity through a deliberate test case, reported as *Farmer v. Glyn-Jones*.[156] William Glyn-Jones, the secretary of the Chemists' Defence Association and himself a qualified chemist and

---

[152] Report and Minutes of Evidence from the Select Committee on Patent Medicines, *House of Commons Parliamentary Papers* (1914) (Cd. 414) ix 1 at q. 19, *per* Sir Nathaniel Highmore, solicitor to the Customs and Excise.

[153] *Board of Customs and Excise and Predecessor: Private Office Papers, The Medicine Stamp Duties 1783–1936*: TNA CUST 118/366 at p. 56; Stephen Dowell, *A History of Taxation and Taxes*, 4 vols. (London: Longmans, Green and Co., 1884), vol. 4, p. 367.

[154] *Board of Customs and Excise and Predecessor: Private Office Papers, The Medicine Stamp Duties 1783–1936*: TNA CUST 118/366 at p. 31 and see Appendix IV.

[155] *Ibid.*, at p. 56.

[156] *Farmer v. Glyn-Jones* [1903] 2 KB 6.

barrister,[157] ensured that he was prosecuted for selling unstamped a bottle of medicine with a label bearing the words: 'Ammoniated TINCTURE OF QUININE B.P. – A well-known and highly recommended remedy for INFLUENZA AND COLDS. Dose – One teaspoonful in water every four hours until relieved'. Because this was a friendly action, Glyn-Jones corresponded with the revenue authorities before any summons. He forwarded two copies of the label to the board, stating that he intended to sell a bottle of this medicine at his premises, unstamped, to ensure the trade had the question definitely settled by a decision of the courts of law. He did so, and an information was accordingly laid against him for having sold a dutiable medicine without a stamp. The action was heard at the Thames Police Court in May 1902.[158]

There was no doubt that the medicine had been 'recommended' by Glyn-Jones as a remedy for a human ailment, the label saying as much. This appeared unambiguously to breach the words of the exemption, which said that a known, admitted and approved medicine sold by a qualified person would escape the charge as long as it was not secret, proprietary, patent or recommended by the 'owners, proprietors, makers, compounders, original or first vendors thereof'.[159] As the other conditions were clearly satisfied, the vendor being a qualified chemist, the medicine being known and approved through its inclusion in the *British Pharmacopoeia* and no proprietary rights being claimed in it by the vendor, the strict legal point at issue was whether Glyn-Jones was the 'original or first vendor'. If he was, then he would fall outside the terms of the exemption. The magistrate took the view that he was not, and that accordingly he was within the exemption. On appeal by way of case stated, this decision was affirmed. Glyn-Jones' counsel, Mr Asquith, argued that the 'original or first vendor' was the person who first made up and sold the medicine from his original prescription, and the Divisional Court agreed with him. Glyn-Jones had purchased the medicine from the manufacturing chemist without any label recommending the medicine.[160] The only recommendation had been made by Glyn-Jones at the retail stage when he attached a label to that effect. So because no recommendation had been made by the original or first vendor, the medicine was not dutiable when it left his hands,

[157] See generally John A. Hunt, 'Pharmacy in the Modern World, 1841 to 1986,' in Stuart Anderson (ed.), *Making Medicines* (London: Pharmaceutical Press 2005), pp. 77, 79–83.
[158] 'Legal Intelligence, Medicine Stamp Duty Acts', (1902) 68 *Pharmaceutical Journal* (series 4) 443, 523, 525, 561, 562–3. For the report to the profession of the *Farmer* case in the Divisional Court see 'Legal Intelligence, Medicine Stamp Duty Acts', (1903) 70 *Pharmaceutical Journal* (series 4) 503, 630.
[159] 52 Geo. III c. 150 (1812).
[160] Had that person ever advertised his remedy, it would have been liable to duty thereafter.

and the fact that Glyn-Jones subsequently affixed a label recommending it did not make it dutiable. The decision of the Divisional Court, fully explained and justified, effectively affirmed the original 'Chemists' Privilege', which had been introduced in 1785 but ignored by the revenue authorities, namely the exemption from duty of *known, admitted and approved* remedies sold by qualified individuals, even if recommended for human ailments, as long as that recommendation had not been made by the owner, proprietor, maker, compounder, original or first vendor.[161]

The decision that the exemption was, after all, material, was received by the revenue authorities with dismay and by the trade with confusion. The ruling reversed their practice of more than 100 years, a practice that was well settled and understood,[162] but they were obliged to implement the decision. Apparently adopting the view of Sir Henry Primrose, the chairman of the Board of Inland Revenue, they proceeded to give the exemption the widest possible scope.[163] The board set out its practice in a circular in 1904. It laid down only two conditions for claiming the exemption: professional pharmaceutical qualification and a disclosure of the ingredients.[164] A qualified chemist could sell any medicine unstamped, even if it was secret, patent, proprietary or recommended,[165] providing that the label disclosed the principal ingredients or carried a reference to its formula in an approved publication. After 1909 the exemption was expressly limited to remedies in which no proprietary rights were claimed.

On the point of pharmaceutical qualification, the statute stated that the exemption, like that for pure drugs, could be claimed only by qualified individuals who had served a 'regular apprenticeship' as surgeon, apothecary, chemist or druggist, and accordingly the meaning of the phrase had to be determined.[166] The courts adopted a strict construction and decided

---

[161] For contemporary analyses of the *Sanguinetti* and *Farmer* decisions, see 'The Recent Medicine Stamp Duty Decisions', (1903) 71 *Pharmaceutical Journal* (series 4) 75; 'The Scope of the "Special Exemptions" of the Medicine-stamp Acts', (1904) 64 *Chemist and Druggist* 13.

[162] Note that this is reported very briefly, with no comment, in the annual report of the Commissioners of Inland Revenue, and yet was a decision of immense importance: Forty-seventh Report of the Commissioners of Inland Revenue, *House of Commons Parliamentary Papers* (1904) (Cd. 2228) xviii 401 at p. 552.

[163] *Board of Customs and Excise and Predecessor: Private Office Papers, The Medicine Stamp Duties 1783–1936*: TNA CUST 118/366 at p. 88.

[164] *Precedents and Instructions, 1904*: TNA IR 78/60; TNA IR 83/61; *Board of Customs and Excise and Predecessor: Private Office Papers, The Medicine Stamp Duties 1783–1936*: TNA CUST 118/366 at pp. 84–6.

[165] Including those medicines, such as 'cough mixtures', brought into charge by the decision in *Ransom v. Sanguinetti*: (1903) 71 *Pharmaceutical Journal* (series 4) 200.

[166] Or who had served as a surgeon in the navy or army under a commission or appointment duly entered at the War Office or Navy Office: 25 Geo. III c. 79 s. 3.

that the apprenticeship had to be under a contract in writing, and could not be by mere service under an oral contract. So when a chemist who had been working for his father for the full term of a regular apprenticeship claimed the *known, admitted and approved* remedy exemption, it was denied him because his apprenticeship had been under an oral contract with his father and not under any formal written agreement.[167] However, by 1903 this traditional method of qualification was being replaced in practice by qualification by examination and registration, and the board – with a view to keeping the law up to date – allowed the exemption to chemists qualifying in that way.[168] It would not, however, go so far as to allow it to limited companies on the grounds that they could not be 'qualified' within the terms of the exemption,[169] and that limited liability companies did not exist when the medicine stamp duty and the exemption were introduced.[170] This was a real difficulty, as the board felt that it was unjust to deny the exemption to limited companies where a qualified chemist was employed, and yet because the legislation did not permit it, it would need to be formally amended. This difficulty was overcome in 1909 when the Poisons and Pharmacy Act 1908 came into force, expressly permitting a body corporate to carry on the business of a pharmaceutical chemist or chemist and druggist as long as one person on the premises was a registered pharmacist and controlling the sale of the drugs.[171]

Disclosure of the ingredients was less controversial. Immediately after the decision, the board insisted on full and accurate disclosure by a description of the exact quantity of every ingredient on the label itself.[172] On further consideration, the board agreed that it sufficed if the principal active ingredients were disclosed,[173] or alternatively there appeared a clear statement that the medicine had been prepared in accordance with the formula in the *British Pharmacopoeia* or

---

[167] *Kirkby v. Taylor* [1910] 1 KB 529.
[168] 'Liability to Medicine Stamp Duty', (1903) 71 *Pharmaceutical Journal* (series 4) 200.
[169] And that one qualified member of a firm could not qualify the firm itself. See *Board of Customs and Excise and Predecessor: Private Office Papers, The Medicine Stamp Duties 1783–1936*: TNA CUST 118/366 at pp. 82–3. But see *Precedents and Instructions, 1904*: TNA IR 78/60 at p. 123, where the board agrees temporarily to suspend proceedings against limited companies.
[170] For the revenue practice on *known, admitted and approved* medicines after the *Glyn-Jones* decision, see the Circular of 15 August 1903: *Board of Customs and Excise and Predecessor: Private Office Papers, The Medicine Stamp Duties 1783–1936*: TNA CUST 118/366 at pp. 84–6.
[171] Poisons and Pharmacy Act 1908 (8 Edw. VII c. 55) s. 3 (4)(a)(b). See too Pharmacy and Poisons Act 1933 (23 & 24 Geo. V c. 25) s. 9.
[172] 'The Incidence of Medicine Stamp Duty', (1903) 71 *Pharmaceutical Journal* (series 4) 233, 234.
[173] 'Known, Admitted, and Approved', (1903) 71 *Pharmaceutical Journal* (series 4) 293.

other well-known book of reference by simply including the letters 'B.P.'[174] The process was straightforward. Qualified chemists could, for a small fee or none, have the formula of their particular medicine included in books of reference and could thereby claim the exemption from tax even if they recommended the medicine as widely and extravagantly as any quack.[175]

In adopting this wide interpretation of the exemption, the revenue authorities treated the definitive interpretation by the regular courts of law with the same indifference that they had shown towards the original statutory provision. Confident in their implementation of the court's decision, they wryly observed that 'it might appear that an interpretation of a statute sanctioned by a century of practice was that intended by Parliament'.[176] Taking the view that the literal interpretation of the statutory provision that the court had adopted in the *Glyn-Jones* case would have been unworkable in practice,[177] and that the decision itself was probably wrong,[178] they ignored the key point in the court's decision to the effect that the chemist who claimed the exemption had to establish that the original or first vendor had never recommended it. They disregarded it on the basis that it was unrealistic, impractical and indeed impossible in current trading conditions to determine whether a particular chemist was the first vendor of an article. Furthermore, the practice did not insist on the other conditions in the statutory provision. It allowed the medicine to be recommended; it did not limit the exemption to chemists qualified by apprenticeship and allowed those qualified by examination to claim it; and although at first it did not allow the exemption to be claimed by corporate bodies who could clearly not have undergone an apprenticeship,[179] it has been seen that eventually it allowed even that. As a result, the method of the exemption's implementation by the revenue authorities bore little relation to the words of the provision in the statute and disregarded its interpretative case law.

---

[174] *Board of Customs and Excise and Predecessor: Private Office Papers, The Medicine Stamp Duties 1783–1936*: TNA CUST 118/366 at p. 81. As to books of reference, see *Precedents & Instructions*, 1904: TNA IR 78/60 at p. 123. Note that some of these books of reference were compiled by the professional press and so a chemist could submit his or her own formulae for inclusion in them.

[175] The condition added in 1909 that the exemption should be limited to remedies in respect of which no proprietary right was claimed was of little practical effect because the disclosure of the ingredients could legitimately be taken as rebutting any proprietary claim: *Board of Customs and Excise and Predecessor: Private Office Papers, The Medicine Stamp Duties 1783–1936*: TNA CUST 118/366 at pp. 103, 104.

[176] *Ibid.*, p. 77.

[177] *Ibid.*, p. 87.

[178] *Ibid.*

[179] *Taxes, Precedent Book, 1892–1910*, 1904: TNA IR 83/61.

Breaking Bulk

The second example of a board practice that appeared to ignore the statutory provision was that relating to the trade custom of breaking up bulk purchases of medicines. Small shopkeepers and retail chemists usually purchased their medicines in bulk from a manufacturer or wholesaler. The latter – the original vendor – paid the duty according to the value of the medicine so the retailer would obtain the package with stamp affixed and duty paid. The retailer, particularly in poorer districts, would often then open the package and sell the individual contents either as two or three pills in the hand, or in penny doses of powders in a twist or cone of paper. Where the medicine was in the form of a liquid, it was resold as a dose in an open cup or glass brought by the customer and taken at the counter. In 1867, following some queries by both chemists and revenue officers, the solicitor of Inland Revenue took the view that despite the legislative provision that duty was to be paid on every enclosure containing a dutiable medicine, in such cases the resale of individual contents did not need to be restamped,[180] an opinion that formed the basis of revenue practice for the rest of the nineteenth century.[181] The reasoning was twofold: first, that because the full duty had already been paid when the original vendor sold the medicine to the retailer, no further stamp duty needed to be paid when a bulk order was broken up for resale in small quantities, although the retailer was required to hold a medicine vendor's licence. Second, the mode of retail was not such as to involve any enclosure within the meaning of the Act. But whereas two or three pills in the hand were clearly not in any kind of enclosure, powders sold in twists of paper clearly were. Nevertheless the board decided that as long as the paper containers were not sealed in any way, with wax, string or glue, they were not enclosures within the statute and so did not have to pay the tax.

Despite considerable technical problems of statutory interpretation in connection with the interrelationship between loosely worded provisions in the legislation, the long-established practice of breaking bulk continued.[182] The concession resulted in the practice of selling medicines in penny twists becoming very common, notably *Beecham's Pills*, a popular laxative, and *Steedman's Soothing Powders*, widely used in teething powders.[183] Any shopkeeper could

---

[180] *Board of Customs and Excise and Predecessor: Private Office Papers, The Medicine Stamp Duties 1783–1936:* TNA CUST 118/366 at p. 57.

[181] 'The Opening of Packages of Patent Medicines', (1882) 12 *Pharmaceutical Journal* (series 3) 886.

[182] *Precedents and Instructions,*1904: TNA IR 78/60 at pp. 114–15.

[183] See Peter G. Homan, Briony Hudson, Raymond C. Rowe, *Popular Medicines*, (London: Pharmaceutical Press, 2008), p.129.

purchase a medicine vendor's licence for five shillings and take advantage of the concession, a concession that became increasingly attractive after 1915 when the rates of medicine stamp duty doubled. It was this practice that accounted for the rise in the number of medicine vendors' licences issued. Furthermore, although the paper twists originally had to be completely plain, after 1910 they were allowed to bear a recommendation or advertisement and as such were almost identical to normal enclosures that bore the medicine stamp.[184] In the last years of the tax, the sale of articles in broken bulk was said to amount to hundreds of thousands of pounds, that up to eighty per cent of *Steedman's Powders* were sold in this way, and there was a similarly widespread practice in relation to *Aspro* and *Beecham's Pills*.[185]

Even though the practice of breaking bulk potentially caused a loss to the revenue and harm to the public health through the dangers of contamination, it was retained because it benefitted the poor and was commercially significant to manufacturers because it greatly increased the market for their medicines. The solicitor of Customs and Excise observed in 1912 that the practice was 'really a matter of convenience that the Board has never interfered with'.[186] It was officially admitted that this was a 'legal and administrative' interpretation,[187] in other words that it was only partly based on the statutory provision and significantly affected by pragmatic considerations of revenue yield and collection.

The Dispensing Concession

The third example of the board's practice reaching beyond the letter of the law was the dispensing concession. Foreign medicines were expressly chargeable to the medicine stamp duty by their inclusion as such in the schedule.[188] The medicine stamp duty did not apply to medicines sold in Ireland. In 1884 some Irish dealers in medicines supplied British chemists with foreign medicines for use in dispensing. Because the sale took place in Ireland, not England, no

---

[184] *Board of Customs and Excise and Predecessor: Private Office Papers, The Medicine Stamp Duties 1783–1936*: TNA CUST 118/366 at p. 60.

[185] Report and Minutes of Evidence from the Select Committee on Medicine Stamp Duties, *House of Commons Parliamentary Papers* (1937) (Cmd. 54) viii 129 at qq. 523–24 *per* J. Kenningham, Secretary of the Proprietary Association of Great Britain.

[186] Report and Minutes of Evidence from the Select Committee on Patent Medicines, *House of Commons Parliamentary Papers* (1914) (Cd. 414) ix 1, q. 245, *per* Sir Nathaniel Highmore, solicitor to the Customs and Excise.

[187] *Board of Customs and Excise and Predecessor: Private Office Papers, The Medicine Stamp Duties 1783–1936*: TNA CUST 118/366 at p. 60.

[188] 52 Geo. III c. 150 (1812). The provision had existed in the legislation since 1802.

duty was chargeable. The British traders complained to the board that they could not enjoy this same advantage and had to pay the duty when they purchased medicines within Great Britain. The board, wishing to place British dealers in the same favourable position, responded by introducing a concession to the effect that it would not prosecute where an otherwise dutiable medicine was supplied unstamped by a British dealer to a chemist for the purposes of dispensing legitimate prescriptions.[189] This extra-statutory concession was unprinted and not to be found in any official instructions. The board allowed it on a case-by-case basis, and did so on the grounds that it was within the spirit of the legislation, because the duty had never been intended to apply to medicines dispensed by chemists and medical practitioners.

The concession was, however, limited in its scope. It was restricted to retail chemists and so could not be claimed by doctors who purchased medicines to make up their own prescriptions, and it did not apply when a chemist wished to sell, under prescription, an unmixed dutiable medicine. When in 1928 it was found that a dutiable medicine prescribed by doctors to be used unmixed was usually supplied by chemists unstamped, on the popular understanding that if it were prescribed by a medical practitioner it could not be a proprietary medicine, common sense suggested that the concession should be allowed to qualified medical practitioners. As a result the concession was extended to cover the supply of dutiable medicines unstamped to doctors or chemists for dispensing purposes only.[190] The effect of this extended extra-statutory concession was that manufacturers and first vendors could sell, free of duty, medicines that would otherwise be dutiable to medical practitioners or chemists for use in dispensing as part of a medicine or for sale unmixed to a patient, on the basis of a legitimate prescription. However, the manufacturer or first vendor had to apply for permission to the revenue authorities for each preparation in question, the enclosure had to bear a special and distinctive label indicating that it was supplied for dispensing purposes only and not for sale, to carry the words 'Only to be supplied unstamped when prescribed by a duly registered medical practitioner'. Furthermore, no written recommendation of any kind was to accompany the medicine, and an annual return of the total amount of such preparations had to be made to the revenue authorities.[191]

[189] Board of Customs and Excise and Predecessor: Private Office Papers, The Medicine Stamp Duties 1783–1936: TNA CUST 118/366 at pp. 67–9. See too Alpe, Handy Book, p. 110.
[190] Board of Customs and Excise and Predecessor: Private Office Papers, The Medicine Stamp Duties 1783–1936: TNA CUST 118/366 at pp. 69–71.
[191] Report and Minutes of Evidence from the Select Committee on Patent Medicines, House of Commons Parliamentary Papers (1914) (Cd. 414) ix 1, q. 4715 per Cyril Kirby, solicitor for the Chemists' Defence Association.

REASONS FOR REVENUE PRACTICE

The extensive interpretation of the wording of the medicine duty legislation by the revenue authorities was unequivocally founded in necessity. The statutory expression of the tax was flawed in that it was antiquated, obscure, full of lacunae and in many instances hopelessly uncertain. Aware of the impossibility of administering such a code, the board nevertheless was under a statutory duty to implement it, and to do so it had no choice but to undertake itself the interpretation of the legislation.[192] The trade in proprietary medicines was so large and dynamic that a rapid and operationally definitive interpretation of key terms was absolutely essential if the tax were not to collapse completely. With the slowness, unpredictability and paucity of judicial decisions it inevitably fell on the executive to undertake the construction of the legislation. Even the medicine vendors appreciated the difficulties faced by the revenue boards in this respect, understanding the authorities were statutorily bound to administer the law and could only work with what they had – which Francis Spilsbury described as early as 1785 as 'a mutilated manuscript'.[193]

The reasons for the board's practice of simply ignoring some parts of a statutory provision or a judicial decision and thereby granting relief from the tax to certain individuals were less obvious. They were, however, all underpinned by the implicit need to sustain the yield of the tax, and essentially they consisted of pragmatism, fairness and the convenience of the public.

First, and above all, the board acted pragmatically. It had to ensure that an antiquated tax worked in practice in order to collect the revenue.[194] For example, the provision to the effect that if a preparation had ever been subject to tax as a proprietary article, it would continue to be so, was ignored for the simple reason that it was generally impossible for chemists or the board retrospectively to prove the existence or non-existence of a proprietary claim made perhaps many decades before.[195] Similarly, the extraordinary interpretation of the *known, admitted and approved* remedy exemption was adopted to circumvent the administrative difficulties resulting from the court's attempt to revive an out-of-date and hitherto inoperative provision in *Farmer v. Glyn-Jones* and

---

[192] See Sir Maurice Sheldon Amos, 'The Interpretation of Statutes', (1934) 163 *Cambridge Law Journal* 5.

[193] Spilsbury, *Discursory Thoughts*, p. 19.

[194] Report and Minutes of Evidence from the Select Committee on Patent Medicines, *House of Commons Parliamentary Papers* (1914) (Cd. 414) ix 1, qq. 90, 209, *per* Sir Nathaniel Highmore, solicitor to the Customs and Excise.

[195] *Board of Customs and Excise and Predecessor: Private Office Papers, The Medicine Stamp Duties 1783–1936*, TNA CUST 118/366 at p. 41.

to apply it to modern trading conditions.[196] The board immediately saw that it was entirely unrealistic and unworkable to expect a chemist to prove that the original or first vendor had never recommended the medicine.[197] Instead the board developed a working rule that was simple, straightforward and well understood. Similarly, in that context, the relaxation of the statutory provision as to the qualification of the claimant showed a pragmatic understanding that qualification by a regular indentured apprenticeship had effectively died out. Yet another outdated provision was addressed by the concession of 'breaking bulk'.[198] The legislation assumed that packets of medicines would be stamped by the makers and sold to the public, and never contemplated the breaking up of bulk purchases. It was similarly practical considerations that led to a strong reluctance lightly to abolish or even disturb any practice once it was established in the revenue and understood by the taxpayer, for it would disrupt the administrative process of tax.[199] Indeed, the upsetting of a practice was regarded as sufficient reason to ignore a judicial ruling or statutory provision.[200] For example, the board carefully balanced the advantages and disadvantages of the 'breaking bulk' concession, and despite accepting that the revenue advantage was not clear, decided in 1906 not to interfere with the long-established practice. And again, the compromise practice as to the naming of medicines according to organs of the body concerned to some extent ignored the decision in *Ransom v. Sanguinetti*, with the board maintaining that a line had to be drawn somewhere, and that it was 'a reasonable arrangement'.[201] The board also sensibly ignored obsolete provisions. For example, by the twentieth century most of the articles exempted from the duty because they were in the Books of Rates were either no longer in use or of small importance. Only a few, such as opium, were still in use and included

[196] *Ibid.*, p. 81.
[197] *Ibid.*, pp. 82, 87.
[198] Report and Minutes of Evidence from the Select Committee on Patent Medicines, *House of Commons Parliamentary Papers* (1914) (Cd. 414) ix 1 at q. 245, *per* Sir Nathaniel Highmore, solicitor to the Customs and Excise.
[199] Report and Minutes of Evidence from the Select Committee on Medicine Stamp Duties, *House of Commons Parliamentary Papers* (1937) (Cmd. 54) viii 129 at q. 228 *per* C. J. Flynn of the Board of Customs and Excise.
[200] See for example the Bradley Haverstoe case in 1851 where a decision of the Court of Queen's Bench in relation to the land tax was ignored on pragmatic grounds; Letters relative to Judgment of Court of Queen's Bench in Case of *Queen v Commissioners of Land Tax for Bradley Haverstoe, House of Commons Parliamentary Papers* (1851) (528) xxxi 329 at p. 337.
[201] Report and Minutes of Evidence from the Select Committee on Medicine Stamp Duties, *House of Commons Parliamentary Papers* (1937) (Cmd. 54) viii 129 at q. 179 *per* C. J. Flynn of the Board of Customs and Excise.

in the official *Pharmacopoeia*. In practice, therefore, the revenue authorities disregarded this exemption, not mentioning it in the instructions to its officers in 1848. It seems that the chemists and druggists ignored it as well.

Second, where they could, the revenue authorities acted in the interests of fairness, albeit not always entirely altruistically. It is true they argued that in all their practices they were not imposing tax, but legally relieving individuals of it in cases of hardship or injustice on the margins of the tax code,[202] but they knew that only if a tax were perceived by the taxpaying public as fundamentally fair would compliance be ensured. For example, the practice not to tax peppermint lozenges even though they were named in the earliest schedules was to mitigate what the board saw as a clear unfairness in the law, and similarly it did not tax some scheduled perfumes because they had already paid customs duty on perfumed spirits.[203] *Eau de Cologne* and *Arquebusade water* were so treated, apparently under the authority of a Treasury Minute.[204] British *Eau de Cologne* escaped the charge, which somewhat undermined the reasoning.[205] Some beverages containing medicinal drugs benefitted from the same reasoning, with dandelion coffee escaping the charge if the excise duty on coffee substitutes was payable.[206] Again, one of the reasons why small sales of broken bulk medicines in penny twists were not required to be stamped was because the same medicine had already paid the duty when sold by the wholesaler.[207] Commercial fairness was equally valued. So where the schedule

[202] The same justification is used today: 'An Extra-Statutory Concession is a relaxation which gives taxpayers a reduction in tax liability to which they would not be entitled under the strict letter of the law. Most concessions are made to deal with what are, on the whole, minor or transitory anomalies under the legislation and to meet cases of hardship at the margins of the code where a statutory remedy would be difficult to devise or would run to a length out of proportion to the intrinsic importance of the matter': http://www.hmrc.gov.uk/specialist/esc.pdf.

[203] Unless held out as a medicine or beneficial for some human ailment: Report and Minutes of Evidence from the Select Committee on Patent Medicines, *House of Commons Parliamentary Papers* (1914) (Cd. 414) ix 1, q. 37, *per* Sir Nathaniel Highmore, solicitor to the Customs and Excise.

[204] Dowell, *History of Taxation*, vol. 4, p. 370.

[205] Alpe, *Handy Book*, p. 25.

[206] *Board of Customs and Excise and Predecessor: Private Office Papers, The Medicine Stamp Duties 1783–1936*: TNA CUST 118/366 at p. 37. Dandelion root, a common weed, was mixed with coffee and was said to have medicinal qualities. But see Nineteenth Report of the Commissioners of Inland Revenue, *House of Commons Parliamentary Papers* 1876 (C. 1607) xx 457 at pp. 478–9.

[207] Report and Minutes of Evidence from the Select Committee on Medicine Stamp Duties, *House of Commons Parliamentary Papers* (1937) (Cmd. 54) viii 129, Memorandum of C. J. Flynn of the Board of Customs and Excise at p. 165.

to the Act of 1812 provided that 'foreign medicines of all kinds, except drugs' were taxable,[208] the board gave this provision its correct wide interpretation and brought into charge all foreign medicines even if they were not secret, proprietary, formally patented or recommended.[209] In the interests of the accepted policies of free trade, following representations to the Chancellor of the Exchequer, in 1885 the board unilaterally decided to tax foreign medicines according to the criteria that it applied to British medicines,[210] limiting liability to those that satisfied the requirements of the general charge to the medicine stamp duty under British law.[211] The words of the statute clearly did not warrant this more restrictive interpretation and accordingly this concession amounted to a decision by the board not to enforce the law. The reason for the dispensing concession was to put British manufacturers on the same commercial footing as foreign manufacturers, and in a similar way the board felt it was unjust to deny the *known, admitted and approved* remedy exemption to limited companies where a qualified chemist was employed, although the legislation forbade it.

Third, some revenue practices were introduced to help the general public. For example, the original, pre-*Sanguinetti* concession for medicines that were described according to the ailment they purported to relieve was introduced to enable the public to distinguish medicines from each other according to their needs,[212] and the practice of breaking bulk was permitted to enable the poor to buy medicines in small quantities.[213]

---

[208] 52 Geo. III c. 150 (1812).

[209] *Board of Customs and Excise and Predecessor: Private Office Papers, The Medicine Stamp Duties 1783–1936*: TNA CUST 118/366 at p. 67.

[210] Namely if they were secret, proprietary, patented or recommended: Report and Minutes of Evidence from the Select Committee on Patent Medicines, *House of Commons Parliamentary Papers* (1914) (Cd. 414) ix 1 at qq. 174–77, *per* Sir Nathaniel Highmore, solicitor to the Customs and Excise; *Parl. Deb.*, vol. 297, ser. 3, col. 1158, 30 April 1885 (HC), *per* Hugh Childers; Report and Minutes of Evidence from the Select Committee on Medicine Stamp Duties, *House of Commons Parliamentary Papers* (1937) (Cmd. 54) viii 129, Memorandum of C. J. Flynn of the Board of Customs and Excise, pp. 161–2; 'The Sale of Foreign Proprietary Medicines – Prosecution by the Inland Revenue Authorities', (1880) 10 *Pharmaceutical Journal* (series 3) 828.

[211] Report and Minutes of Evidence from the Select Committee on Patent Medicines, *House of Commons Parliamentary Papers* (1914) (Cd. 414) ix 1 at q.4797 *per* Cyril Kirby, solicitor for the Chemists' Defence Association. But see 'The Stamp Act and Proprietary Medicines', (1884) *British Medical Journal* 328.

[212] (1848) 7 *Pharmaceutical Journal* (series 1) 453; Report and Minutes of Evidence from the Select Committee on Patent Medicines, *House of Commons Parliamentary Papers* (1914) (Cd. 414) ix 1 at q. 4709 *per* Cyril Kirby, solicitor for the Chemists' Defence Association.

[213] Report and Minutes of Evidence from the Select Committee on Medicine Stamp Duties, *House of Commons Parliamentary Papers* (1937) (Cmd. 54) viii 129 at p. 139.

THE AUTHORITY OF LAW

Uncertain, excessively complicated, incomplete and out-of-date legislation made bureaucratic interpretation and the growth of extra-statutory concessions inevitable, and – in proportion to the flaws in the legislation – prolific. Indeed, revenue practice dominated the medicine stamp duty more than any other tax and became the main expression of the law. This exceptional degree of bureaucratic lawmaking had a significant and far-reaching impact, going beyond the tax itself and those subject to it. It was an effect that undermined the integrity of tax law in particular and the authority of law in general.

Most of the revenue authorities' interpretation of key terms and the development of concessions were not only necessary to implement the law, but were derived from expert legal advice from their solicitor.[214] Despite this, such revenue practice was constitutionally unsound and, accordingly, fundamentally illegal and, indeed, dangerous.[215] It was stated unequivocally in the Bill of Rights 1689 that no one could be taxed without his or her consent.[216] That consent was parliamentary in nature, meaning that all taxes had to adopt statutory form, ensuring that no one could be taxed other than by express words in an Act of Parliament. That meant that a tax could be imposed only by legislation, and the intention of Parliament expressed in that legislation was paramount. But because the revenue officials had drafted the original provisions in discussion with the Treasury, who regulated the country's finances, they believed they knew what the true intention of the medicine stamp duty legislation was, which commodities had been envisaged as the object of the charge and the reasons for it. They were confident that the object had been to tax proprietary medicines only and to ensure that qualified practitioners could freely sell regular medicines and make up physicians' prescriptions free of duty without the risk of penalty.[217] When this intention was not translated into robust statutory

---

[214] For example, the concession for asthma cigarettes was based on advice given to the board in 1876 by Sir William Melvill, solicitor to the Inland Revenue: Report and Minutes of Evidence from the Select Committee on Patent Medicines, *House of Commons Parliamentary Papers* (1914) (Cd. 414) ix 1 at q. 40, *per* Sir Nathaniel Highmore, solicitor to the Customs and Excise.

[215] See Second Report and Minutes of Evidence before Committee of Public Accounts, *House of Commons Parliamentary Papers* (1897) (C. 196) viii 5, pp. 5–12, qq. 359–463, 878–1006. They would become of particular importance in the twentieth century: see generally Sir Alexander Johnston, *The Inland Revenue* (London: George Allen & Unwin, 1965), pp. 67–8; David W. Williams, 'Extra Statutory Concessions', (1979) *British Tax Review* 137.

[216] Bill of Rights 1689 (1 Will. & M. sess. 2 c. 2), s. 4.

[217] Chamberlaine, *History of the Proceedings*, p. 5; The board was confident, for example, that the 1833 Act repealing the provision in the schedule that charged artificial mineral waters to tax had not intended to release waters recommended for the relief of an ailment from the charge: *Stamp Duty, Law Officers' Opinions*, vol. 1, 1828–1908: TNA IR 98/11 at S. 61.

language, the board attempted to carry it out as best it could. It thus imple-mented the provisions according to its own, extra-parliamentary, view of them.

This revenue practice amounted for all practical purposes to lawmaking. As the central board in London arrived at its decisions on every new situ-ation or commercial development, prompted by inquiries from the trade and their own officers, so it disseminated them throughout the national network of its officers through its published regulations, instructions and circulars.[218] The board insisted on uniform and complete adherence by its staff to these numerous official communications. On a point of law, the board's opinion – whether in a formal circular or expressed in individual correspondence – was conclusive for its officers. This created a robust policy of statutory implemen-tation that left no room for any local or individual divergence. In this way, the rulings of the board were binding in every practical way until taxpayers chal-lenged them. Taxpayers could and did do this, unofficially by writing to the board directly, or waiting upon its members, and there is abundant evidence of this kind of informal appeal.[219] Taxpayers, however, found little flexibility in the revenue authorities. Not only was the dominant concern with a uniform and unambiguous implementation of the law, the administrative departments of government were permeated by professional and conservative civil serv-ants, adhering to established routines, procedures and practices, loyal to their department and with an intensely powerful sense of their duty to raise the public revenue.[220] As a result, once a revenue practice was settled, it was very difficult to change it. The solicitor to the Customs and Excise observed in 1912 that 'once you have settled a practice it is a little difficult to go behind it'.[221]

There was little realistic scope for official challenge. Appeals were permit-ted from the magistrates' decisions to the High Court on a point of law by way of case stated under the Summary Jurisdiction Acts 1857 and 1879,[222] but most individuals drawn into the criminal process through a breach of the legisla-tion were concerned above all with negotiating the reduction of any penalty imposed upon them with the board. Such negotiation would be conducted informally and directly with the board. Even if their circumstances allowed it, and despite the active encouragement of the board to appeal whenever a

[218] See for example, *Precedents and Instructions*, 1903: TNA IR 78/289; TNA IR 78/60.
[219] See, for example, *Board of Inland Revenue decisions on medicine stamp duty, 1892*: TNA DSIR 26/138.
[220] See John Brewer, *The Sinews of Power* (London: Unwin Hyman, 1989), pp. 83–5.
[221] Report and Minutes of Evidence from the Select Committee on Patent Medicines, *House of Commons Parliamentary Papers* (1914) (Cd. 414) ix 1, q. 41, *per* Sir Nathaniel Highmore, solici-tor to the Customs and Excise.
[222] 20 & 21 Vict. c. 43 s. 2; 42 & 43 Vict. c. 49 s. 33.

taxpayer disagreed with its interpretation,[223] nearly all taxpayers decided not to pursue a formal challenge. To do so in the superior courts was inconvenient, expensive and stressful, particularly because it was well known that the board had the determination and the means to pursue appeals to the highest court when it considered the point one of wider importance. Judicial decisions on the meaning of the legislation were scarce. The first was in 1878,[224] and by 1910 there were still only six.

Whatever its motivations and justifications, the actions of the revenue authorities were illegal. Constitutionally, the interpretation of statutory language was not one that the constitution gave to the executive. Only the judges of the regular courts could legitimately and authoritatively interpret the statutory language and assign it a meaning – that meaning reflecting the intention of Parliament. Once a judicial decision had been pronounced on the meaning of a tax provision, that was its definitive meaning, and was to be applied by the tax authorities and relied upon by the taxpaying public. The revenue authorities who administered the tax were constitutionally permitted no discretion. They were bound to adhere to the words of the statute, to tax where the statute instructed and not to relieve from tax where the statute did not allow it. So each time the board interpreted vague or uncertain key words and phrases in the statutory charging provisions, giving a wide interpretation of a charging section or a narrow interpretation of an exemption, it was acting exactly as the judges of the regular courts would, yet without the scrutiny of Parliament. Similarly, when the board chose not to tax certain individuals by granting concessions, it was taking upon itself the right to decide on the chargeability of an individual, which was strictly the right only of Parliament.[225] Revenue practice constituted taxation by the executive and, as such, was contrary to the fundamental constitutional principles of law and taxation.

The revenue authorities could find no help in their parent legislation. Although they were given the widest statutory powers to execute the tax legislation covering virtually any act in the administration of the taxes within their remit, the overarching statutory duty of care and management imposed on them was undefined either in the legislation itself or by the courts of law. Legally, therefore, the board had no support for its disregard of statutory provisions and judicial decisions in the interests of necessity, practicality, common sense or even perceived fairness. Furthermore, it was arguable that the board was illegally using its express and exclusive powers to institute, stay or

---

[223] See for example letter published in (1888) 18 *Pharmaceutical Journal* (series 3) 760.
[224] *Attorney General* v. *Lamplough* (1878) LR 3 Ex D 214.
[225] Bill of Rights 1689 (1 Will. & M. sess. 2 c. 2), s. 4.

mitigate proceedings, or to come to terms with an offender. Although the board maintained that these wide powers were 'carefully administered',[226] they were never intended to be used to enable the board to grant exemption from taxes at its pleasure. Yet, for example, the board determined the scope of the *known, admitted and approved* remedy exemption by deciding not to press for the duty, which was simply 'another way of saying that we do not regard them as liable to duty',[227] and adopted a similar practice in relation to foreign medicines unstamped by a British manufacturer or wholesaler to a retail chemist for the purposes of dispensing legitimate prescriptions.[228] Expert legal opinion held that this wide discretion as to the instigation and management of prosecutions, a practice of long standing, amounted to taxation at the discretion of the board and the assumption of a power to exempt individuals from tax whom Parliament had decreed should be taxed. Indeed, Sir Charles FitzRoy, the solicitor to the Board of Customs and Excise, had no response when he was pressed by the Select Committee on the Medicine Stamp Duties in 1936 to explain the 'curious' and 'very unsatisfactory' practice whereby the revenue authorities took it upon themselves not to press for the duties in certain cases.[229]

From the earliest days of the tax the board fully appreciated the illegality of its practices and the undesirability of dealing with flawed legislation through concessions.[230] When medicine vendors went to clarify the application of the Act with the board in 1785, they replied 'Consult the act – we are no lawyers',[231] a response that, if true, not only showed that the interpretation of statutes was understood to be the responsibility of lawyers, but equally reveals the disingenuousness of the Stamp Commissioners who necessarily, inevitably and knowingly were primarily responsible for interpreting the taxing legislation. In some instances the board acknowledged that the strict rules were

---

[226] Report and Minutes of Evidence from the Select Committee on Patent Medicines, *House of Commons Parliamentary Papers* (1914) (Cd. 414) ix 1 at q. 205, *per* Sir Nathaniel Highmore, solicitor to the Customs and Excise.

[227] Report and Minutes of Evidence from the Select Committee on Medicine Stamp Duties, *House of Commons Parliamentary Papers* (1937) (Cmd. 54) viii 129 at q. 231 *per* C. J. Flynn of the Board of Customs and Excise.

[228] Report and Minutes of Evidence from the Select Committee on Patent Medicines, *House of Commons Parliamentary Papers* (1914) (Cd. 414) ix 1 at q. 4715 *per* Cyril Kirby, solicitor to the Chemists' Defence Association.

[229] Report and Minutes of Evidence from the Select Committee on Medicine Stamp Duties, *House of Commons Parliamentary Papers* (1937) (Cmd. 54) viii 129 at qq. 5–6.

[230] Report and Minutes of Evidence from the Select Committee on Patent Medicines, *House of Commons Parliamentary Papers* (1914) (Cd. 414) ix 1 at q. 252, *per* Sir Nathaniel Highmore, solicitor to the Customs and Excise.

[231] Spilsbury, *Discursory Thoughts*, p. 19.

not always observed, such as where in relation to the provision requiring that once a medicine had been subject to the tax, it would always be subject to it, it admitted that this was 'one of several instances where the rule is relaxed in practice'.[232] Sometimes it even acknowledged it had strayed beyond this. For example, the official interpretation of the *known, admitted and approved* remedy exemption from 1903 was clearly far wider than either the legislation or the interpretative case law warranted, unambiguously ignoring the words of both. When the board sought counsel's opinion in 1935 about this practice, that opinion was uncompromising, condemning its actions as illegal and unconstitutional.[233] The board took care this was not made public, privately admitting that it 'might be represented as a glaring instance of legislation by Executive action and an unauthorised assumption, or usurpation, of the functions of Parliament'.[234] Successive solicitors to the board knew it could not stand in a court of law.[235] Similarly the board privately acknowledged that the 'breaking bulk' concession was a 'legal and administrative' interpretation,[236] namely one only partly based on the statutory provision and significantly affected by pragmatic considerations of revenue yield and collection. Here too the board's solicitor in 1904 understood that the concession contravened the statute, as did the professional bodies who pressed for its abolition on those grounds.[237] In relation to the board's practice as to the naming of medicines developed after the decision in *Ransom v. Sanguinetti*, Sir Arnold Wilson called it 'a private bargain between the trade and the Commissioners of Excise without any reference either to law or the Courts'.[238] He asked a representative of the board: 'You would regard it as being almost unique in the history of Government Departments to be compelled by a dubiety of the law to exercise their discretion on such a scale?' to which was replied: 'No, I think we always have to exercise our discretion, in a sense, in interpreting Statutes'.[239] One of the rare public admissions of the illegality of its practice by the board was in

[232] *Board of Customs and Excise and Predecessor: Private Office Papers, The Medicine Stamp Duties 1783–1936*: TNA CUST 118/366 at p. 41.
[233] See Chapter 5.
[234] *Board of Customs and Excise and Predecessor: Private Office Papers, The Medicine Stamp Duties 1783–1936*: TNA CUST 118/366 at p. 86.
[235] *Medicine Stamp Duty, 1936*: TNA T 172/1844.
[236] *Board of Customs and Excise and Predecessor: Private Office Papers, The Medicine Stamp Duties 1783–1936*, TNA CUST 118/366 at p. 60.
[237] *Ibid.*, p. 61. However, counsel's opinion in 1926 on the legality of the concession was inconclusive: *ibid.*, pp. 61–2.
[238] Report and Minutes of Evidence from the Select Committee on Medicine Stamp Duties, *House of Commons Parliamentary Papers* (1937) (Cmd. 54) viii 129 at q. 178.
[239] *Ibid.*, q. 180 *per* C. J. Flynn, member of the Board of Customs and Excise.

relation to its concession for asthma cigarettes, which its solicitor acknowledged in 1914 was 'perhaps ... not quite legal'.[240]

CONCLUSION

The very particular nature of the administration of the medicine stamp duty was almost entirely due to the nature of its parent legislation. Loose drafting coloured the entire practical administration of the medicine stamp duty because it was difficult to implement such legislation with confidence. It encouraged evasion and avoidance. With the object of charge and the scope of the exemptions unclear, taxpayers and their representatives were able to put forward arguments that they fell outside the charge, arguments that were difficult to refute with certainty. Similarly, evasion, unless of the most obvious kind such as using a stamp twice, was more difficult to identify, because without a certain charge the fact of evasion was fluid. The outcome of imprecise drafting of the legislation was thus profoundly damaging in the first instance to the tax as a revenue-raising instrument. With a potent fiscal imperative, the only practical solution was bureaucratic lawmaking, but that led to the total domination of the tax by the revenue authorities through their development of an extensive code of revenue practice. This brought with it profound theoretical difficulties as to the authority of Parliament and the function of the judiciary, and severe practical problems of illegality that the need for public revenue was allowed to dominate.

---

[240] Report and Minutes of Evidence from the Select Committee on Patent Medicines, *House of Commons Parliamentary Papers* (1914) (Cd. 414) ix 1 at q. 38, *per* Sir Nathaniel Highmore, solicitor to the Customs and Excise.

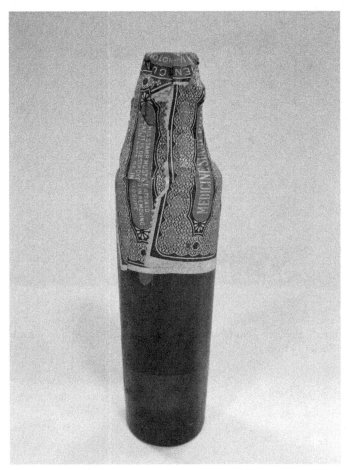

FIGURE 3 Wrapped medicine bottle, by kind permission of the Royal Pharmaceutical Society Museum.

FIGURE 4 Wrapped medicine container, by kind permission of the Royal Pharmaceutical Society Museum.

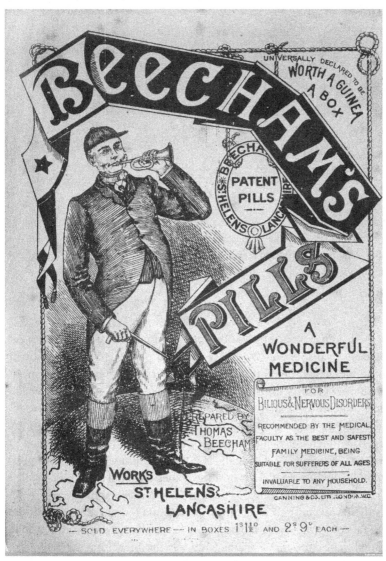

FIGURE 5 Advertisement for Beecham's Pills, ca. 1900, Wellcome Library, London.

3

The Tax and the Profession of Pharmacy

"No other class of retailers is taxed for revenue purposes in the same way as the chemist. His brains are taxed, his name is taxed, his preparations, if properly described, are taxed, the directions for use are taxed, the apostrophe "s" is taxed, and, last but not least, his nerves are taxed."[1]

INTRODUCTION

One of the leading characteristics of proprietary medicines was that they were commercially available, sold over the counter or purchased by post, without prior professional consultation and with no prescription from a regular medical practitioner. They were available from a wide range of vendors, which included surgeons and apothecaries, but generally from grocers, booksellers, individual medicine vendors and, increasingly as the nineteenth century progressed, from chemists and druggists. Chemists and druggists emerged in England as a distinct class during the eighteenth century, although the presence of individuals making their own medicines for retail sale and of skilled wholesale manufacturing druggists was already discernible.[2] By the end of the century their work had developed into a discrete and recognisable occupation. This was a slow process and although the factors that drove it are not fully understood, it is clear that a major force was the increasing concentration on medical practice by the apothecaries at the expense of their own shop-based pharmaceutical practice. At the end of the eighteenth century it was the apothecaries who, being medically qualified, dispensed the prescriptions of

---

[1] 'Letter to the Editor', (1903) 70 *Pharmaceutical Journal* (series 4) 879.
[2] Roy Porter and Dorothy Porter, 'The Rise of the English Drugs Industry: The role of Thomas Corbyn' (1989) 33 *Medical History* 277.

physicians and prescribed remedies for minor ailments.[3] It seems that they also made up and sold medicines according to old prescriptions. Possibly because they left their shops unattended in order to attend patients, or because their prices became too high, it was clear that the pharmaceutical service that the apothecaries provided was no longer adequate for the public's needs and desires.[4] A gap emerged that needed to be filled.[5] So the chemists and druggists began to take on the original apothecaries' work of pharmacy, namely preparing and compounding vegetable, mineral or animal substances to create medicines and their supply to the public. The apothecaries, observed W.J. Reader, 'had left their shops and become doctors. The druggists had stayed in them and become pharmaceutical chemists'.[6] They were small in number. Chemists, who prepared and sold chemical substances, were very few compared with the far more numerous druggists. The latter were concerned with the sale of galenicals, namely drugs of vegetable rather than mineral or chemical origin, and were characterised as essentially shopkeepers who dealt in medicines at wholesale and retail. They often were herbalists and grocers too. The distinction between chemists and druggists was fluid, however, and by the eighteenth century they were largely indistinguishable. They constituted a 'rising class', and from the latter part of the century they emerged as important providers of pharmaceutical services.[7] Their entitlement to this work was expressly confirmed in the Apothecaries Act 1815, in terms of their right to buy, prepare, compound, dispense and sell drugs and medicines, wholesale or

---

3 Surgeons, apothecaries and physicians constituted the historic tripartite structure of the medical profession. Boundaries between the three branches were necessarily fluid and increasingly obsolete, though physicians, the oldest and most senior branch of the medical profession, did not provide medicines directly to their patients or members of the public. Apothecaries and surgeons did. See Anne Digby, *Making a Medical Living* (Cambridge: Cambridge University Press, 1994), pp. 28–9.

4 Porter and Porter 'Thomas Corbyn', 281.

5 'The Origins of the Society', (1941) 146 *Pharmaceutical Journal* (series 4) 124.

6 W. J. Reader, *Professional Men*, (London: Weidenfeld and Nicolson, 1966), p. 41. See too W. A. Jackson, *The Victorian Chemist and Druggist*, (Oxford: Shire Publications Ltd, 1981), p. 3; J. K. Crellin, 'The Growth of Professionalism in Nineteenth-Century British Pharmacy', (1967) 11 *Medical History* 215, 215–6.

7 Glenn Sonnedecker (ed.), *Kremers and Urdang's History of Pharmacy*, 4th edn, (Philadelphia: J. B. Lippincott Company, 1976), p. 104; Jacob Bell, 'A Concise Historical Sketch of the Progress of Pharmacy in Great Britain' (1842) 1 *Pharmaceutical Journal* (series 1) 3–32; Jackson, *Victorian Chemist and Druggist*, p. 3; Crellin, 'The Growth of Professionalism', 215–16. See also Porter and Porter 'Thomas Corbyn', 277; J. Burnby, 'The Origins of the Chemist and Druggist', (2001) 31 *Pharmaceutical Historian* 27; Peter M. Worling, 'Pharmacy in the Early Modern World', 1617 to 1841 AD', in Stuart Anderson (ed.), *Making Medicines* (London: Pharmaceutical Press

retail,[8] and the chemist and druggist – a conjunctive title – was established.[9] The practice of pharmacy ostensibly became their province. It was important work, providing the principal source of advice to customers, who came into their shop seeking a medicine to relieve various minor ailments such as coughs or indigestion, when access to the regular medical profession was an expense that many families could not meet. It was also highly skilled and responsible work. A chemist and druggist needed to be able to identify the hundreds of plants and chemicals that formed the basis of the medicines, to master often complex techniques to convert the active ingredients – the drugs – into useable medicines for the public.

Despite the specialist expertise of chemists and druggists, they were not perceived as professionals in the same way as physicians, surgeons or apothecaries in the late eighteenth and throughout the nineteenth century. Professionalism was never an absolute social construct, and its meaning evolved and changed according to the historical period.[10] A profession, according to Dr Johnson in 1755, could be applied to any 'calling, vocation, known employment',[11] but in

2005), p. 57. John A. Hunt, 'The Evolution of Pharmacy in Britain (1428–1913)' (2006) 48 *Pharmacy in History*, 35. See too 'The Closing Century', (1900) 56 *Chemist and Druggist* 142.

[8] Apothecaries Act 1815 (55 Geo. III c. 194) s. 28.

[9] See generally Burnby, 'The Origins of the Chemist and Druggist', 27; Hunt, 'The Evolution of Pharmacy', 35; Irvine Loudon, 'The Vile Race of Quacks with which this Country is Infested', in W. F. Bynum and Roy Porter (eds.), *Medical Fringe & Medical Orthodoxy 1750–1850* (London: Croom Helm, 1987), pp. 106–28.

[10] Gregory J. Higby, 'Professionalism and the Nineteenth-Century American Pharmacist', (1986) 28 *Pharmacy in History* 115; Hannes Siegrist, 'Professionalization as a Process: Patterns, Progression and Discontinuity', in Michael Burrage and Rolf Torstendahl (eds.), *Professions in Theory and History* (London: SAGE Publications, 1990), pp. 178–9. See generally Andrew Abbott, *The System of Professions*, (Chicago: University of Chicago Press, 1998); Lori Loeb, 'Doctors and Patent Medicines in Modern Britain: Professionalism and Consumerism', (2001) 33 *Albion: A Quarterly Journal Concerned with British Studies* 404, 404–9; Matthew Ramsey, 'The Politics of Professional Monopoly in Nineteenth-Century Medicine: The French Model and Its Rivals', in Gerald L. Geison (ed.), *Professions and the French State, 1700–1900* (Philadelphia: University of Pennsylvania Press, 1984), p. 225; Matthew Ramsey, *Professional and Popular Medicine in France 1770–1830* (Cambridge: Cambridge University Press, 1988), pp.1–13; J.A. Jackson (ed.), *Professions and Professionalization* (Cambridge: Cambridge University Press, 1970); Rolf Torstendahl and Michael Burrage (eds.), *The Formation of Professions: Knowledge, State and Strategy* (London: Sage, 1990); Terence J. Johnson, *Professions and Power* (London: Macmillan Press, 1972); Robert Dingwall and Philip Lewis (eds.), *The Sociology of the Professions: Lawyers, Doctors and Others* (London: Macmillan Press Ltd, 1983).

[11] Samuel Johnson, A *Dictionary of the English Language*, reprint of the edition first published London: Kapton, 1755) (New York: AMS Press, 1967).

the early nineteenth century it was usually applied to the three learned professions, namely the church, medicine and the law, entry to which required a liberal education based in the classics.[12] Later in the nineteenth century, qualification by formal instruction and examination came to be regarded as satisfying the standard expected of a professional, but a constant was that one of the key features of professional status was the requirement for a demonstrably high level of education.

At the beginning of the nineteenth century, chemists and druggists constituted a heterogeneous group drawn from a number of different occupational backgrounds and included both trained and untrained individuals, some apothecaries, grocers and assistants in physicians' dispensaries. The occupation was entirely unregulated and no formal specialist education and training requirement was prescribed as it was, for example, for the apothecaries in their pharmacy work.[13] A qualified chemist and druggist would be trained in the traditional way by an apprenticeship of some seven years to an established practitioner and thereafter would gain further experience before seeking to become established on his or her own account.[14] Even when qualification by examination and registration was introduced, the wording of the Pharmacy Act 1868 allowed unexamined and unregistered individuals to practise as chemists and druggists as long as they did not use that title, and so medicines continued to be sold by barbers, booksellers, hairdressers, stationers, tobacconists and many other shopkeepers.[15] As a result, for much of the nineteenth century, chemists and druggists were not regarded as professionals.[16] Only when pharmacy was legally permitted to be practised solely by qualified individuals would 'the trade become an honourable profession'.[17] And in the absence of mandatory educational achievement, the other features affirming professional status, such as self-government, exclusivity, prestige and social standing, were lacking.

---

[12] Reader, *Professional Men*, pp. 1–24.
[13] See Report and Minutes of Evidence from the Select Committee on the Pharmacy Bill, *House of Commons Parliamentary Papers* (1852) (387) xiii 275 at qq.462–78; 784–89 *per* John Savory, chemist; Peter Squire, chemist.
[14] Any chemist seeking a rigorous education in pharmacy before the later years of the nineteenth century had to study abroad, at the School of Pharmacy in Paris for example: Report and Minutes of Evidence from the Select Committee on the Pharmacy Bill, *House of Commons Parliamentary Papers* (1852) (387) xiii 275 at qq. 457–66 *per* John Savory, chemist.
[15] John Attfield, *Introductory Address: The Future Supply of Drugs to the Public, Delivered to the British Pharmaceutical Conference 20th Annual Meeting, Southport*, (LSE Selected Pamphlets, 1883), p. 5. But see Porter and Porter, 'The Rise of the English Drugs Industry', 294.
[16] Reader, *Professional Men*, pp. 32–43; Crellin, 'The Growth of Professionalism', 217.
[17] 'The Progress of Pharmacy in Great Britain', (1844) 4 *Pharmaceutical Journal* (series 1) 1, 4.

There were, however, factors other than mandatory qualification that played a part in the process of professionalisation. Chemists and druggists not only dispensed medicines, that is, made up physicians' prescriptions, but also sold their own nostrums made to their own formulae, labelled, for example, *The Tonic* or *The Mixture*,[18] and a wide range of commercial proprietary medicines. Everything about the sale of the latter suggested trade rather than professional activity because all those involved in the promotion and sale of these articles did so with commercial intentions. They were above all businessmen and women whose activities were governed by a robust profit motive and many of them were strikingly successful. Qualified and unqualified chemists and druggists, individual proprietors marketing their own nostrums, booksellers, grocers and other shopkeepers selling a range of proprietary medicines were all traders in status and public perception. The substance and form of taxes, and the way they were administered, however, had potentially profound social effects that were often entirely unforeseen by the legislators who introduced them into the fiscal regime. The role of a tax in the social process of professionalisation in the long nineteenth century was one such effect, and this chapter explores the impact of the medicine stamp duty on the transformation of chemists and druggists from a mere occupation into a recognised profession.

CHEMISTS AND DRUGGISTS IN THE MEDICINE
STAMP DUTY LEGISLATION

When the medicine stamp duty was first introduced in 1783, the charge to tax was laid on all persons selling medicines in Great Britain.[19] Such individuals had to purchase an annual licence and pay duty on the container of every medicine they sold. The Act, however, contained a major exception. It exempted from its operation anyone who had served a regular apprenticeship to any surgeon, apothecary, druggist or chemist, or who had kept a shop for three years before the passing of the Act for the purpose of selling drugs and medicines only, not being drugs or medicines sold by virtue

---

[18]   Stuart Anderson, 'From "Bespoke" to "Off-the-Peg": Community Pharmacists and the Retailing of Medicines in Great Britain 1900–1970', in Louise Hill Curth (ed.), *From Physick to Pharmacology: Five Hundred Years of British Drug Retailing* (Aldershot: Ashgate, 2006), p. 105 at pp. 123–5.

[19]   23 Geo. III c. 62 (1783).

of His Majesty's letters patent.[20] In addition, and by separate provision, it exempted any individual who had served as a surgeon in the navy or army under a commission duly recorded at the war office or navy office.[21] This particular exemption had not appeared in the original proposals first put to Parliament, but it simply reflected another path to qualification, and was probably merely correcting an oversight. Chemists and druggists, therefore, could sell any medicine whatever its nature, except, some argued, medicines sold under letters patent, without the need for a licence and free from any duty.

Accepting that it was not possible to lay down precisely which medicines were to bear the duty, the legislators instead adopted a test they believed would result in the same outcome: they attempted to tax proprietary medicines by targeting the quality of the individual vendor. They did so on the understanding that the kind of medicines the Act wished to tax would be sold only by medically unqualified vendors, never by qualified individuals, indeed that if an unqualified vendor sold a medicine it must be a 'quack' preparation. Accordingly, to require unqualified individuals to be licensed and then to tax their stock was an effective way of ensuring proprietary medicines were subjected to the charge and would leave qualified individuals to sell their regular medicines free of duty. A distinction of professional status and expertise thus lay at the very heart of the charge, which suggests, as Stephen Dowell observed in 1884, that the tax of 1783 was imposed, in part at least, in the interests of the qualified practitioners.[22] Certainly an unambiguous decision to afford special treatment to 'regular traders' and protect them from the tax was admitted by the revenue authorities when the Act was passed.[23]

In 1785, however, the basis of liability was fundamentally changed. The charge was now imposed on every preparation used as a medicine to prevent, cure or relieve any human ailment, if the maker or seller made or sold it under letters patent, or claimed a secret art, or an exclusive right in doing so, or recommended it to the public as an effective remedy or if it was expressly

---

[20] *Ibid.*, s. 1.

[21] *Ibid.*, s. 2.

[22] Stephen Dowell, *A History of Taxation and Taxes*, 4 vols. (London: Longmans, Green and Co., 1884), vol. 4, p. 366.

[23] *Stamp Office: Report of Several Defects in the present law affecting duties*, 15 February 1785: The National Archives (TNA): T1/624/504.

named in the schedule to the Act.[24] It was clear that the fact that a vendor of a proprietary medicine was medically qualified should and would have no effect on the charge to tax if they sold such a preparation. The legislature, however, wanted to ensure that this deliberately widely drawn charge to tax did not inadvertently attach to the sale or provision of legitimate medicines within orthodox medical and pharmaceutical practice. The intention was to protect the regular practitioner insofar as he did not step 'out of the line of his Profession to sanction the use of Compositions of which he knows not certainly, either the quality or the quantity of the Ingredients',[25] in other words, to sell dubious proprietary medicines. This protection was effected through the three exemptions included in the Act, all applying to medicines sold by their ordinary or scientific names, with no proprietary claims, no secret formulae and most certainly no element of advertising.[26]

The first exemption applied to imported medicines subject to customs duties, essentially natural drugs and certain chemicals, which were in general use by chemists and druggists and apothecaries to make up their medicines. The second exemption, even more clearly directed to protect legitimate medical practice, exempted medicines that were 'entire', namely pure and unmixed, and were sold by surgeons, apothecaries, chemists and druggists who had served regular apprenticeships, and surgeons serving in the navy or army. Again these were pure and crude drugs needed to make up their medicines. The third exemption similarly protected regular medicines, in this case composite medicines that were *known, admitted and approved* remedies for illnesses sold by a qualified person with no element of secrecy, exclusivity, or recommendation.[27] It allowed the sale unstamped of medicines supplied by the chemist and doctor and the everyday remedies purchased by the public for the treatment of minor ailments.

Legally, the three exemptions were to a greater or lesser extent futile – the medicines comprised in the first two would not fall within the charge to tax because they would not normally be secret, patented, exclusive or recommended, and the third exemption was entirely nugatory because a preparation that was not secret, proprietary, patent nor recommended, as the provision required, would not have been subject to duty anyway. The legal form of the

---

[24] Medicine Stamp Duty Act 1785 (25 Geo. III c. 79) ss. 2, 16.
[25] *Stamp Office: Observations upon the present Medicine Act and Proposals for an Improvement of that Duty*, 21 May 1785: TNA: T1/624/514.
[26] See Chapter 1.
[27] See *Board of Customs and Excise and Predecessor: Private Office Papers, Medicine Stamp Duty 1783–1936*: TNA CUST 118/366 at pp. 132–4.

exemptions thus confirm that they were introduced to ensure that there could be no doubt that medicines used in regular medical and pharmaceutical practice were not within the charge. Indeed, the *known, admitted and approved* remedy exemption was later recognised as a declaratory enactment confirming to a wary medical profession that the normal medicines of regular medical practitioners sold in the normal way would remain unaffected by the new duty.[28]

It was not only through the express statutory provision that chemists and druggists were protected from any inadvertent encroachment of the tax into their regular pharmaceutical practice. It has been seen that the central revenue boards played a key role through their implementation of the formal legal rules and the development of revenue practice.[29] The outstanding example of this was their interpretation of the exemption for *known, approved and admitted* remedies sold by qualified chemists. Having treated it as insignificant for more than 100 years, and therefore of no benefit to chemists and druggists, following the test case of *Farmer v. Glyn-Jones* in 1903[30] the board was forced to accept that it was material. As a result, qualified chemists and druggists were permitted to sell proprietary medicines free of duty as long as the formula was disclosed, and the process of disclosure was made particularly easy.[31] The board allowed chemists qualified by examination to claim the exemption, where the statute did not allow it, and eventually even allowed corporate bodies the privilege.[32] The 'Chemists' Privilege' was of immense importance to chemists and druggists. It gave them for the first time a material advantage over other retailers in selling proprietary medicines. They could sell them free of duty whereas unqualified retailers, namely grocers and department stores, had to sell the identical medicine with the duty.

PROFESSIONAL REACTIONS TO THE TAX

Objections to the Principle of the Tax

Objections to the principle of a tax are generally raised at certain clear points in its life: its introduction above all, any reform of its substance, the

---

[28] *Ibid.*, at pp. 9–10; Dowell, *History of Taxation*, vol. 4, p. 367.
[29] See Chapter 2.
[30] *Farmer* v. *Glyn-Jones* [1903] 2 KB 6.
[31] See Chapter 4.
[32] See Chapter 2.

increase in its rates, or its repeal. Because of the legislative inertia surround-
ing the medicine stamp duty, and its extraordinarily long duration, its desirability in principle was rarely discussed. When it was first introduced in
1783, despite being a new impost on a previously untaxed commodity, it was
met with remarkably little popular opposition. It had of course been selected
by the government as an unobtrusive tax that would slip quietly into the
stamp duty regime with the public hardly noticing it, and to a large extent
the qualities of this form of indirect taxation ensured that was the case, for
the public had become accustomed to indirect taxation in the form of the
excise and other stamp duties. It is also likely that opposition to certain other
contemporaneous taxes, namely those on windows and shops, masked any
resentment of the medicine stamp duty.[33] Indeed, the *Morning Chronicle
and London Advertiser* merely observed that the medicine stamp duty 'was
defective in nothing but extent'.[34] The licence, it said, should be at least five
or ten guineas, and it called for a tax on every handbill or advertisement
for any proprietary medicine, and on every wrapper. Most contemporary
newspapers reported the tax only as part of their daily parliamentary reports,
and no discussion of the measure was included. The tax's formal legislative passage was similarly smooth. Parliament agreed to all of Lord John
Cavendish's proposals, with virtually no comment on any of the individual
imposts,[35] the debate consisting almost entirely of an exchange of sarcastic
invective between Fox and Pitt on financial policy more generally.[36] The
popular and parliamentary reaction to the Act of 1785 was equally muted.
It raised little comment from the consuming public, mainly because the
measure was nothing more than a revision, albeit a major one, of an existing
impost. Furthermore, the recast medicine stamp duty was at least not perceived as breaching the accepted canons of taxation as the income tax was
to do nearly fifteen years later.

Within the trade, however, there was significant disquiet, indeed, 'general
alarm'.[37] There were predictable objections from chemists and druggists, who

---

[33] *St James's Chronicle* or *British Evening-Post*, 25–27 November 1784; John Cannon, *The Fox-North Coalition* (Cambridge: Cambridge University Press, 1969), pp. 88–9.

[34] *Morning Chronicle and London Advertiser*, May 30, 1783.

[35] The only concern raised was that the tax on carts and wagons could be oppressive to farm-ers: *Parliamentary Register 1780–1796*, vol. 10, 26 May 1783, p. 85 *per* Sir Edward Astley.

[36] *Ibid.*, pp. 76–86.

[37] Francis Spilsbury, *Discursory Thoughts Disputing the Construction of His Majesty's Hon. Commissioners and Crown Lawyers, relative to the Medicine and Horse Acts…with Remarks on the Late Trials Concerning the Medicine Act*, 2nd edn, (London; Dispensary, Soho Square, 1785), p. 6.

feared they would have to raise their prices and that their businesses would suffer. Of the two elements – the duty on the container of the medicine and the licence to sell dutiable medicines – it was the latter that was objected to in material and enduring terms. Well into the nineteenth century it was felt that the licence was 'a great nuisance' and 'a very absurd thing'.[38] The original rates for the licence set in the early nineteenth century became unfair in their operation. They were considerably higher in London and Edinburgh, and yet it was increasingly the case that the trade in proprietary medicines became greater in provincial towns such as Brighton.[39] Although many chemists and druggists complained frequently of this inequality to the Chancellor of the Exchequer, others were prepared to pay the higher duty to retain the trade in their exclusive hands. Later, however, the prevailing feeling was that chemists and druggists should be exempt from the licence fee because they were required by the state to become professionally qualified to provide a public service and so should not then have to pay to perform that function.[40]

Other chemists and druggists, such as Francis Spilsbury – proprietor of a celebrated medicine and tenacious strident critic of the tax – expressed humanitarian concerns. Just as the window tax was portrayed as a tax on fresh air and light, and the newspaper and paper duties as taxes on knowledge, so the medicine stamp duty was condemned as a tax on illness, 'an impost on misery and disease'.[41] Spilsbury argued that the imposition of tax on those medicines that were provided to the public in an easily accessible and useable form would disadvantage the public by raising their price. 'Endure your pains – suffer death – or pay the King's duty' he cried.[42] This was the usual eighteenth-century rhetoric against unpopular taxes, but it was one that inevitably gave rise to the most emotive language. Spilsbury used all his literary

---

[38] Report and Minutes of Evidence, Select Committee to inquire into Adulteration of Food, Drinks and Drugs, *House of Commons Parliamentary Papers* (1856) (379) viii 1 at q. 2376 *per* Jacob Bell.

[39] Dowell, *History of Taxation*, vol. 4, p. 371.

[40] Report and Minutes of Evidence from the Select Committee on Medicine Stamp Duties, *House of Commons Parliamentary Papers* (1937) (Cmd. 54) viii 129 at q. 427 *per* H. N. Linstead, Secretary of the Royal Pharmaceutical Society of Great Britain.

[41] Francis Spilsbury, *The Power of Gold Displayed in the Humane Proposal of the Rt Hon William Pitt, Chancellor of the Exchequer, to bring forward an Act to put His Majesty into the disagreeable situation of signing a decree, that no sick or lame person, or diseased cattle, in Great Britain, shall have a medicine of repute without paying tribute; which the writer contends, is not justifiable either by the Law of God, or Man, and is a disgraceful impost, as it places the life of a human being in competition with a three-penny or six-penny stamp*, 3rd edn, (London: Dispensary, Soho Square, 1788), p. v.

[42] Spilsbury, *Discursory Thoughts*, p. 11.

skills to show that the tax was falling on the vulnerable, on those in pain and distress and, most of all, on the poor, who had no other recourse to medical care. He illustrated his objections to this 'merciless impost'[43] with servants and apprentices becoming ill, and ordinary people suffering accidents and contracting such serious illnesses as fevers, cancer, dropsy and consumption. '[I]s an infant dying with disease, an object of taxation?' he asked.[44] 'Is the life of a Briton to be put in competition with a three-penny, six-penny, or a one shilling stamp?'[45] The tax, he said, was imposed on every person 'stretched on the rack of nature's ills in the solemn chamber, divided by a thin partition from the grave … chained in the agonies of pain, terrified by death …'[46] He accused the government of 'warring against its own subjects' by extorting a tax upon the sick members of society, and maintained that the medicine stamp duty was 'a bribe to screen the [quacks'] illicit practices'.[47] To tax medicines was 'opposite to all prudential measures, respecting the public welfare',[48] a 'preposterous motion'.[49] The tax was, in short, 'contrary to the dictates of reason, justice, and humanity'.[50]

Spilsbury also saw the medicine stamp duty as militating against the accepted eighteenth-century canons of taxation. Adam Smith had observed that all commodities that were not necessaries and yet were 'objects of almost universal consumption' were 'extremely proper subjects of taxation'.[51] He defined as necessaries those commodities that either nature rendered indispensable for the support of life, or that the 'established rules of decency … rendered necessary to the lowest rank of people'. Everything else, he said, was a luxury.[52] What distinguished medicines from other taxed commodities was that they were purchased by the sick in the hope that they would constitute

---

[43] *Ibid.*, p. 7.
[44] Francis Spilsbury, *The Power of Gold Displayed in the Humane Proposal of the Right Hon. William Pitt, Chancellor of the Exchequer, to bring forward an Act to put his Majesty into the disagreeable situation of signing a decree, that no sick or lame person, or diseased cattle, in Great Britain, shall have a medicine of repute without paying tribute; which the writer contends, is not justifiable either by the law of God, or man, and is a disgraceful impost, as it places the life of a human being in competition with a three-penny or six-penny stamp*, 1st edn, (London: Dispensary, Soho Square, 1785), p. 3
[45] *Ibid.*, p. 6.
[46] Spilsbury, *Discursory Thoughts*, p. 12.
[47] *Ibid.*, p. 2.
[48] *Ibid.*, p. 1.
[49] *Ibid.*, p. 2.
[50] Spilsbury, *The Power of Gold Displayed* (1785), p. 2.
[51] Adam Smith, *An Inquiry into the Nature and Causes of the Wealth of Nations* (R. H. Campbell, A. S. Skinner, W. B. Todd (eds.), 2 vols. (Oxford: Clarendon Press, 1976), vol. 2, p. 936.
[52] *Ibid.*, p. 870.

a cure for their ailment. In that sense they could not be regarded a luxury. As Spilsbury argued, whether one kept horses, servants or a house was a matter of personal choice, but 'no man can command health'.[53] The first medicine stamp Act was, he said, 'a brutal act …',[54] one that '[bartered] Honour and Humanity for gold'.[55] His opposition was unabated when the recast Act of 1785 came into force, for he condemned it as 'impolitic', 'impious' and 'brutal'.[56] Three years after the recast Act of 1785 had come into force, Spilsbury was still publicly opposing its provisions.[57]

Once the medicine stamp duty had settled into its place within the fiscal system and the world of proprietary medicines, its desirability in principle was discussed only occasionally. When it was raised, however, the argument, sentiment, language and a degree of cynicism hardly changed. In a speech to the Royal College of Surgeons in Ireland in 1839, in which the speaker maintained there was no political will to improve the health of the people, he complained that any government interference was limited to taking advantage of the sick by, among other things, imposing taxes on proprietary medicines.[58] 'Every one must admit', it was said in 1909,

> that few things can be more cruel than to trade upon the hopes and fears of sick people or to sell them worthless remedies with the positive assurance of cure. Yet this is what is done by the sellers of quack remedies, and the Inland Revenue pockets the patent medicine duty without a blush.[59]

In 1926 it was argued that proprietary medicines were often the only option for large poor families who did not have the means to seek specialised medical advice, and the point was made that the government should not be taxing a commodity without knowing whether it was harmful or beneficial.[60] Others condemned it as 'another method of indirect taxation of the poor which is really indefensible'.[61] When in the mid-1930s a select committee proposed recasting and broadening the medicine stamp duty, the same arguments were

---

[53] Spilsbury, *The Power of Gold Displayed* (1788), p. v; Spilsbury, *Discursory Thoughts*, p. 11.

[54] Spilsbury, *The Power of Gold Displayed* (1785), p. 4.

[55] *Ibid.*, p. 7.

[56] Spilsbury, *The Power of Gold Displayed* (1788), p. 22.

[57] *Ibid.*

[58] 'Review', (1839) 32 *The Lancet* 88, 89.

[59] British Medical Association, *Secret Remedies: What they Cost and What they Contain*, (London: British Medical Association, 1909), p. 76. See too 'Liability to Medicine Stamp Duty', (1903) 71 *Pharmaceutical Journal* (series 4) 33.

[60] *Parliamentary Debates* [hereafter *Parl. Deb.*], vol. 205, ser 5, cols. 753–54, 26 April 1927 (HC) *per* George Hardie.

[61] *Ibid*, col. 755 *per* Ernest Thurtle.

voiced: that it would result in a tax on everyday medicines used by the public, which was unjustifiable because these were articles of necessity not luxury;[62] that these medicines, being needed by the sick, were 'not fit subjects for taxation'.[63] In short, that it was 'wrong in principle'.[64]

Inaccessibility of the Law to the Profession

The objections of the chemists and druggists were not, however, primarily directed towards the principle of the tax, or even to any commercial effect on their businesses. They were far more concerned, and with very good reason, by the inaccessibility of its substance and administration. Indeed, the relationship between chemists and druggists and the medicine stamp duty was one of breadth and intensity, but it was based on a lack of understanding and an absence of transparency. In both form and substance, the legislation itself was utterly inaccessible to all vendors of medicines.

Because constitutionally an individual could only be taxed by express and clear words in an Act of Parliament, parliamentary draftsmen tried to leave nothing to chance and strove to be precise and explicit in casting a charge to tax in statutory language. This made the medicine stamp duty legislation, and indeed all tax Acts, difficult to read. The clauses were long, detailed and complex, the language was archaic and the punctuation was minimal. Moreover, following the normal and enduring legislative practice in tax law, the administrative and management provisions of the stamp duties in general were incorporated into the medicine stamp duty regime.[65] So, for example, the Stamp Duties Management Act 1891[66] and the Stamp Act 1891,[67] applying to all stamp duties, were added to those addressing the medicine stamp duty specifically. Furthermore, within the medicine stamp duty legislation itself there were impenetrable elements. Not only was the overall structure of comprehensive charge, refinement and exemption excessively complicated, there were inaccessible details, even if medicine vendors were able to obtain copies

---

[62] *Board of Customs and Excise and Predecessor: Private Office Papers, The Medicine Stamp Duties 1936–39*: TNA CUST 118/391 at p. 43. In this instance the view was expressed by the Cambridge and District Branch of the Pharmaceutical Society, and is one of many examples of this view expressed in the aftermath of the select committee report.

[63] Report and Minutes of Evidence from the Select Committee on Medicine Stamp Duties, *House of Commons Parliamentary Papers* (1937) (Cmd. 54) viii 129 at q. 544 *per* J. Kenningham, Secretary of the Proprietary Association of Great Britain.

[64] *Ibid.*, Memorandum of F. W. Woolworth & Co Ltd at p. 312.

[65] 42 Geo. III c. 56 s. 21 (1802).

[66] 54 & 55 Vict c. 38.

[67] 54 & 55 Vict c. 39.

of the Acts.[68] To take a specific example, the Books of Rates laying down the customs duties and forming the basis of the first exemption to the tax from 1785 were available only in parliamentary libraries, and were scarcely accessible to the ordinary chemist and druggist. Even lawyers would not have reason to have a copy, and so it was highly problematic for any medicine vendors to know whether a particular medicine they were selling fell within that particular exemption. Ordinary chemists and druggists struggled comprehensively to identify and access the body of legislation dating from 1694, let alone acquire sufficient technical knowledge to understand it.

The new medicine stamp duty left the trade confused. The 1783 Act was condemned as 'monstrous',[69] an 'ambiguous, ill-shapen act',[70] 'incomprehensible' and 'a perplexed act that must be revised'.[71] Uncertainty as to its application was rife and the confusion was clear to see in the editorials and correspondence of the national newspapers. One correspondent observed that there was not a chemist in London who did not compound and sell medicines under his own name, such as dentifrices, tinctures and lozenges, 'and which, nevertheless, do not properly come under the idea of quack medicines, seeing that they are the common prescriptions of physicians ready made up'. He asked whether the Act applied to such articles and to remedies, considered as 'simples', such as *Turner's Cerate*, which had been sold under particular names for years.[72] The situation was no better in the provinces. Another correspondent observed that 'the greatest part of the Country Venders are thrown into the greatest Difficulties and Confusion by the different Constructions put on the Medicine Act' and called for an official explanation of its application.[73] His first query concerned the meaning of the term 'medicines'. He was unsure whether the duty attached only to those remedies commonly called 'quack' medicines, such as *Daffy's Elixir, Scots Pills, Godfrey's Cordial*, and sold in packets, or whether it included articles sold by chemists and druggists such as *Spirit of Hartshorn* and *Tincture of Myrrh*, which were sold by the penny or the ounce. He wished to know whether roots such as ginger and gentian were

---

[68] As Chamberlaine assumed they would: William Chamberlaine, *History of the Proceedings of the Committee appointed by the General Meeting of Apothecaries, Chemists, and Druggists, in London, for the Purpose of obtaining Relief from the Hardships imposed on the Dealers in Medicine, by certain Clauses and Provisions contained in the new Medicine Act, passed June 3, 1802 etc*, (London: Highley, 1804), p. 44.

[69] Spilsbury, *The Power of Gold Displayed* (1785), p. 2.

[70] *Ibid.*

[71] Spilsbury, *Discursory Thoughts*, p. 50.

[72] *Morning Chronicle and London Advertiser*, 19 August 1783.

[73] *St. James's Chronicle* or *British Evening-Post*, 2–4 September 2, 1783.

medicines for the purpose of the Act and whether articles that were medicines and colours, such as *Factitious Cinnabar*, needed to be stamped.[74] The chemists and druggists were even more baffled by the obscurity of the scope of the exemptions in the 1783 Act, principally and unsurprisingly by the ill-drawn provision for established shopkeepers, but also by the exemptions for the medically qualified. In particular they were unclear whether patent medicines properly so called were liable to the duty when sold by medically qualified individuals, and there was no agreement on the point.[75]

When the new wide general charge was introduced in 1785, the consensus among chemists and druggists was that it constituted an improvement.[76] Even Francis Spilsbury accepted that the new Act successfully extended the duty to all medicines other than 'pharmaceutical' ones and that the charging sections were firmly grounded in a popular understanding of the nature of proprietary medicines.[77] Indeed, when the 1785 Act was passed, Francis Newbery, proprietor of the celebrated *Dr James's Fever Powder*, inserted advertisements in the *Morning Post* and other newspapers explaining that the new Act imposed a duty on all proprietary medicines, whoever sold them, and accordingly published a list of those he sold and their prices, duty included.[78] He clearly thought the tax would affect his business, because he proposed certain discounts to attract sales, notably offering a reduced rate on the purchase of six or more packets of a proprietary medicine, and keeping *Dr James's Fever Powder* at the old price.[79]

Nevertheless, a rare and acute editorial comment on the 1785 Act at the very time it came into force said that the statute was 'still clogged with two or three of the old blunders, that were a great plague to the traders in general, as well as the Board of Commissioners for Stamp Duties',[80] namely the lack of clarity in defining the key terms in the legislation. The exceptional difficulties of statutory definition peculiar to proprietary medicines that had led legislators to turn in 1785 to description rather than definition, resulted in a statutory regime characterised by incomprehensible language, overlapping

---

74 *Ibid.*
75 Spilsbury, *Discursory Thoughts* p. 5; Anon, *A Concise Abstract of the Most Important Clauses in the following Interesting Acts of Parliament'* (London: J. Walker, 1785), p. 89; *Morning Chronicle and London Advertiser*, May 30, 1783.
76 *Morning Chronicle and London Advertiser*, 26 September 1785.
77 Spilsbury, *The Power of Gold Displayed* (1785), p. 7.
78 See for example *London Chronicle*, 25–27 December 1788.
79 *Morning Post and Daily Advertiser*, 6 January 1786. See too E. *Johnson's British Gazette and Sunday Monitor*, 24 January 1802.
80 *Morning Chronicle and London Advertiser*, 26 September 1785.

and sometimes redundant provisions, express contradictions and incompatible clauses. The observation in *The Lancet* of 1829 that the legislation was
'loose and vilely-written', 'defective' and a 'piece of tom-foolery'[81] remained
true for the entire life of the tax. Nearly a century later it was condemned in
Parliament as a 'pettyfogging tax',[82] and, most famously, Rowlatt J described
it as a 'mass of confused and obsolete verbiage'.[83] The Select Committee on
Patent Medicines reported in 1914 that it had 'found much difficulty in arriv-
ing at a clear appreciation of the law and its administration',[84] despite examin-
ing 42 witnesses, through 14,000 questions, and representing revenue officials,
lawyers, chemists and medical practitioners. As a representative of the board
observed in 1936, '[t]he law is very old and very archaic, and it is very difficult
to construe. That being so, it is possible to take different views as to what its
precise meaning is. I think the Courts have almost despaired of construing
it'.[85] If judges quailed, there was little hope for the ordinary chemist and druggist. Attempts to rationalise or classify the provisions of the law resulted in
an erroneous understanding of its provisions and scope or a misunderstanding of its emphasis or objectives. As a result, many if not most chemists and
druggists did not feel they understood the legislation. They were puzzled by
it, and found it perplexing and embarrassing.[86] 'The fact is', said one chemist, 'that no one understands it; not even those who have to administer it'.[87]
Dowell's comment in 1884 that following the consolidation of 1870 the law
relating to stamp duties was 'well arranged, easy to find, and within the com-
prehension of the most moderate intellect',[88] and that of E. N. Alpe, writing
on the medicine stamp duty with practical experience from his position as an
assistant solicitor in the Inland Revenue, that the law relating to the medicine
stamp duty specifically was 'very simple and comprehensible',[89] would have
been greeted with utter incredulity by the great body of chemists and druggists

---

[81] 'Editorial', (1829) 13 *The Lancet*, 377, 379–80.

[82] *Parl. Deb.*, vol. 205, ser. 5, col. 747, 26 April 1927 (HC) *per* Lieutenant Commander Kenworthy.

[83] *Attorney General* v. *Lewis and Burrows Ltd.* [1932] KB 538, 543.

[84] Report and Minutes of Evidence from the Select Committee on Patent Medicines, *House of Commons Parliamentary Papers* (1914) (Cd. 414) ix 1 at p. v.

[85] Report and Minutes of Evidence from the Select Committee on Medicine Stamp Duties, *House of Commons Parliamentary Papers* (1937) (Cmd. 54) viii 129 at q. 112 *per* C. J. Flynn of the Board of Customs and Excise.

[86] 'The Patent Medicine Stamp Acts – Deputation to the Board of Inland Revenue, (1886) 16 *Pharmaceutical Journal* (series 3) 907; *Board of Customs and Excise and Predecessor: Private Office Papers, The Medicine Stamp Duties 1783–1936*: TNA CUST 118/366 at p.71.

[87] 'The Medicine Stamp Act', (1889) 20 *Pharmaceutical Journal* (series 3) 479.

[88] Dowell, *History of Taxation*, vol. 3, p. 344.

[89] E. N. Alpe, *Handy Book of Medicine Stamp Duty*, (London: Offices of 'The Chemist and Druggist', ca. 1888), Preface.

whose professional lives were materially affected by a duty they struggled to understand.

The inaccessibility and obscurity of the legislative provisions, in both form and substance, constituted a major cause of complaint for the chemists and druggists, but it was compounded and indeed subsumed by their resentment of the administration of the tax by the central revenue boards. Taxation by administrative act, which the vagueness of the statutory language and the lack of reform rendered necessary, made the law even more inaccessible and impenetrable to the chemists and druggists. The revenue boards interpreted the legislation so as to decide which medicines were liable to the tax and which were not.[90] These interpretations were not available to the public as of right, as the legislation and interpretative case law in the regular courts were, however inaccessible the latter were in practical terms. And when the revenue boards began to develop practices that allowed relief from the charge to tax quite distinct from the statutory code, practices that again were not available to the public as of right, the medicine stamp duty code was striking in its lack of transparency. The impenetrability of the primary legislation and the prevalence of unpublished revenue practice available only to revenue officials made it impossible for individual vendors to know with any kind of certainty whether they were liable to the tax.

Objection to the Administration of the Tax by the Central Boards

Because the revenue practices that governed the administration of the medicine stamp duty were inherently informal and based on usage, they lacked any kind of coherence or objective rigour. This, just as much as their physical and intellectual inaccessibility, was resented by the chemists and druggists. As far as they were concerned, these practices resulted in baffling incongruences from the very inception of the tax. Examples abounded: under the Act of 1783 a medically qualified person selling a patent medicine was held to be liable to the duty even though the Act exempted him; a druggist selling a proprietary medicine, and other items such as tobacco, was held not to be liable to the duty, whereas a bookseller selling a proprietary medicine and books was liable;[91] and again, the Stamp Commissioners said that all proprietary medicines were liable to the tax even if not strictly patent medicines because they were of the kind the legislature intended to tax.[92] Even the Stamp Commissioners

---

[90] See Chapter 2.
[91] Spilsbury, *Discursory Thoughts*, p. 9.
[92] *Ibid.*, pp. 5–6.

themselves later admitted that the administration of the new duty had been 'partial and oppressive'[93] and that the inconsistent treatment of various dealers in medicines was 'contrary to the most common Principles of Trade or Taxation'.[94] The interpretation of the word 'only' within the exemptions to the 1783 Act was an early issue of particularly intense criticism. Francis Spilsbury argued the 'only' related to patent medicines, not other items, and that the Act was 'twisted', that 'half a sentence left out in the reading, and the rest is supplied by imagination!' to raise revenue.[95] He accused the commissioners of inconsistency in their reading of the Act and of the effect of the word 'only', so as arbitrarily to include some groups and exclude others from the exemption, to the public harm.[96] It was an approach that, he said, deserved 'universal censure'.[97] So strained and inconsistent were many such constructions that they were perceived as 'ridiculous', 'arbitrary', 'unjustifiable' and 'mistaken'.[98] 'Will his Majesty patronize such constructions?' demanded Spilsbury.

Inconsistencies also arose from the subjective nature of many of the board's decisions when those depended, as they often did, on the view taken by the individuals in office at any particular time. An inquiry of 1826 revealed that decisions that should have been made by a quorum of four commissioners were often made by one alone. Even when such unacceptable practices were addressed, it was still the case that interpretations accepted by the commissioners came from the board's solicitor, and when both the commissioners and the solicitor changed, the holding of different views was to some extent inevitable. For example, there were allegations of inconsistent decisions relating to mineral and aerated waters,[99] and to orange quinine wine.[100] Inconsistencies and uncertainty could also arise where the revenue authorities had difficulty in settling their practice. A striking example was the attempt of the board throughout 1903 and 1904 to work out how the decisions in *Ransom* v. *Sanguinetti* and *Farmer* v. *Glyn-Jones* affected their practice, and how it could be implemented so as not to inconvenience the trade or the revenue. The board is seen to

---

[93] *Stamp Office: Observations upon the present Medicine Act and Proposals for an Improvement of that Duty*, 21 May 1785: TNA: T1/624/514.

[94] *Ibid.*

[95] Spilsbury, *Discursory Thoughts*, p. 7.

[96] *Ibid.*, pp. 7–8.

[97] *Ibid.*, p. 8.

[98] *Ibid.*, p. 9.

[99] See the case of Thomas Binge reported in 'Editorial', (1829) 13 *The Lancet* 377.

[100] 'The Medicine Stamp and Licence Acts', (1865) 7 *Pharmaceutical Journal* (series 2) 296; See too Report and Minutes of Evidence from the Select Committee on Patent Medicines, *House of Commons Parliamentary Papers* (1914) (Cd.414) ix 1 at qq. 11, 714–16 *per* Ernest John Parry, analytical chemist.

change its mind as it gradually refined its practice throughout that period.[101] Some chemists believed that 'the judgments of the Board of Inland Revenue as to liability to medicine stamp duty were uncertain and contradictory', that the board was 'unable clearly to define the law, but seem to be guided in their interpretation by expediency rather than by principle'.[102] In defence of the board, however, a correspondent to the *Pharmaceutical Journal* said that in his experience 'the Board have never exacted a penalty when one could satisfy them there had been a conflict of official opinion'.[103]

The chemists and druggists found some of the interpretations by the revenue boards inexplicable. A prime example was the fine distinctions, the 'hair-splitting technicalities',[104] the board drew when deciding on the chargeability of medicines described by reference to the ailment or the organ of the body during the nineteenth century.[105] With 'thin'[106] and 'absurd'[107] distinctions, vendors could not be certain what was dutiable and what was not. Even the opinions of the experienced solicitor employed by the Chemists and Druggists' Trade Association in the late nineteenth century did not always tally with those of the board. The exemptions to the medicine stamp duty were equally obscure to manufacturers and chemists. One firm in Margate, for example, had been carbonating *Lithia Water* since the mid-nineteenth century and it had been free of the duty as being within the artificial mineral water exemption, but they were told in 1905 that if they added two other salts to the water it would come within the charge, a decision that they were 'quite at a loss to understand'.[108]

In allowing their concessions the board was being 'lenient' and 'indulgent' in the interpretation of the letter of the law, but it was alive to any taxpayer taking advantage of this and thereby evading the spirit of the legislation. Were this to happen, the board would 'act as might seem advisable in accordance with the power it possesses'.[109] Chemists and other vendors who not only were often uncertain whether the medicines they were selling had to be stamped,

---

[101] 'The Medicine Stamp Duty Difficulty', (1903) 71 *Pharmaceutical Journal* (series 4) 837.

[102] 'The Medicine Stamp Act', (1889) 20 *Pharmaceutical Journal* (series 3) 405.

[103] 'Liability to Medicine Stamp Duty', (1903) 71 *Pharmaceutical Journal* (series 4) 33.

[104] 'The Medicine Stamp Duty Act', (1903) 71 *Pharmaceutical Journal* (series 4) 579.

[105] *Board of Customs and Excise and Predecessor: Private Office Papers, The Medicine Stamp Duties 1783–1936*: TNA CUST 118/366 at pp. 50–1. See Chapter 2.

[106] Report and Minutes of Evidence from the Select Committee on Patent Medicines, *House of Commons Parliamentary Papers* (1914) (Cd. 414) ix 1 at q. 4928 *per* Cyril Kirby, solicitor for the Chemists' Defence Association.

[107] *Ibid.*, q. 4932 *per* Charles Bathurst, member of the committee.

[108] TNA IR 40/2276.

[109] (1848) 7 *Pharmaceutical Journal* (series 1) 453.

were also ignorant as to how far they could rely on the board's practice, and so were in a constant state of uncertainty. What was clear was that whether a medicine was dutiable was not a question of whether it was legally dutiable, but whether the members of the board regarded it as such,[110] and whether they chose to prosecute for a breach of the enacted law. For example, the board mitigated the problems caused by the ill-considered schedule of 1802 by issuing instructions to its officers to enforce the law but not to prosecute for offences relating to the articles in the schedule that were clearly not meant to be there and promised that in general the authorities would not encourage any vexatious suits, nor strain the meaning of the Act,[111] nor prosecute 'on every trifling and unintentional offence against the act'.[112]

Uncertain legislation and inconsistent revenue practice inevitably resulted in unpredictability. Sellers of medicines could rarely be certain whether any particular medicine was dutiable or not, and this lack of confidence in the law was keenly felt. As a medical practitioner observed in 1912, '[I] believe I am right in saying that outside the Customs and Excise Department, there is no man living who can give a definite pronouncement as to whether the wording on a label renders the preparation to which it is attached liable or not liable to the stamp duty'.[113]

It was not only the inaccessibility and impenetrability – and therefore the unpredictability – of revenue practice that raised the ire of chemists and druggists. They also understood from the inception of the tax that the practice of the revenue boards was of questionable legality. It has been seen that through necessity, or simply in order to be fair, the boards implemented the provisions according to their own extra-parliamentary view on them.[114] The medicine vendors who were the first to experience the new tax in the 1780s complained from its earliest days as to its administration by the revenue authorities. In the years before the development of modern taxation resulted in the immense growth and power of the government departments responsible for the administration of the duties, the exercise of legislative power by the executive was strongly resented. The public accepted that taxation was necessary for the proper functioning of the state, but condemned as arbitrary the interpretation of the law

---

[110] Report and Minutes of Evidence from the Select Committee on Patent Medicines, *House of Commons Parliamentary Papers* (1914) (Cd. 414) ix 1 at q. 4715 *per* Cyril Kirby, solicitor for the Chemists' Defence Association.

[111] Chamberlaine, *History of the Proceedings*, pp. 5, 34–5.

[112] *Ibid.*, p. 22.

[113] Eric Pritchard, 'The Regulation of the Sale of Proprietary and Secret Drugs' (1911–12) 9 *Transactions of the Medico-Legal Society* 87, 90.

[114] See Chapter 2.

by the executive and their administration of the law on that basis. As early as 1785 it was understood that this amounted to unconstitutional lawmaking. In a strikingly perceptive, indeed prescient, reflection, Francis Spilsbury observed that 'the people do not like to be governed by the Commissioners instead of their King'.[115] '[H]as the Legislature', he asked, 'transferred such discretionary powers to any officers of the crown?'[116] Even though the Act was poorly drafted, the commissioners should not be permitted to assign a meaning to the words that could not be supported 'by precedent, reason, or justice'.[117] Chemists and druggists perfectly understood that the board interpreted the legislation itself and introduced concessions as it thought fit, and as far as they were concerned it was making law, and its actions were of doubtful legitimacy. One trade deputation of chemists and druggists to the board in 1886 stated that they were 'aware that the work of [the board] was administrative only, and that they had nothing to do with the construction of the Acts of Parliament ...'[118] and the Western Chemists' Association of London were told in 1902 that '[i]t was all very well to talk about concessions, but no Government department should have the right to make a concession which meant that duty which ought to be paid to the Government was not paid'.[119] In 1903 a chemist said:

> It does seem a unique application of an Act of Parliament that, like a camera obscura, it can be turned in so many directions, bringing within its sphere such variety of moods and tenses, phrases or facts, till it has become perfectly bewildering – and all this by the Board of Inland Revenue, composed of irresponsible and unknown personages, who are supposed to possess the power of affirming, modifying, and applying an Act with an elasticity so different from other British laws, so that the business of a fully qualified chemist has become of recent years oppressed beyond measure.[120]

Objections to Methods of Enforcement

The resentment by chemists and druggists of the illegality, uncertainty and, above all, unpredictability of the revenue practice that governed the medicine stamp duty found expression in the trade's attitude to the methods of the law's

---

[115] Spilsbury, *Discursory Thoughts*, p. 25.
[116] *Ibid.*, p. 9.
[117] *Ibid.*, p. 19.
[118] 'The Patent Medicine Stamp Acts – Deputation to the Board of Inland Revenue', (1886) 16 *Pharmaceutical Journal* (series 3) 907, 908.
[119] 'The Stamp Act and its Difficulties', (1902) 68 *Pharmaceutical Journal* (series 4) 247.
[120] 'Medicine Stamp Duty', (1903) 71 *Pharmaceutical Journal* (series 4) 470.

enforcement. All the problems with the revenue board's control of the tax came to a head when the decision was made to prosecute a trader for breach of the law, and the board would prosecute, or threaten to prosecute, all breaches of the law by any vendor, whether a small shopkeeper, market stall holder or more substantial enterprise. Indiscriminate prosecutions founded on unclear words in the legislation or the personal views of revenue officials, the use of common informers to institute prosecutions and the role of the board in mitigating penalties combined to create a bitter and abrasive relationship between the revenue authorities and the chemists and druggists. Periodic changes in policy by the board led to waves of prosecutions against often respectable and honest, although mistaken, chemists and druggists. The consequences for vendors if they sold dutiable medicines unstamped or unlicensed were severe: a criminal prosecution with disproportionately high financial penalties if a guilty verdict were found, bringing with it damage to the businesses and reputations of respectable vendors of medicines and a very real danger of personal ruin.

The relationship between the revenue board and chemists and druggists began most unfortunately due to the method of enforcement prescribed by the legislation when the medicine stamp duty was introduced, namely that of common informers.[121] This was the system whereby any individual could initiate proceedings against a person he or she suspected of selling dutiable medicine unstamped or without a licence, and potentially profit financially from that action. The process, which began with the individual posing as a customer to purchase medicines believed to be sold in breach of the legislation, permitted the informer to make a secret oath which accordingly preserved his or her anonymity, and sufficed for the writ to issue against the trader who could not, therefore, answer the accusations of the informer face to face.[122] If the prosecution was successful, the informer was entitled to a share – usually half – of the heavy penalty imposed on the seller of the medicine.

The alliance between such persons and the legal establishment, described as a 'marriage of justice with malice or avarice'[123] was distrusted and condemned by all those subject to it, and profoundly objectionable to the chemists and druggists.[124] Complaints were frequent from the tax's earliest days, the

[121] See generally M. W. Beresford, 'The Common Informer, the Penal Statutes and Economic Regulation', (1957) 10 *Economic History Review* (NS) 221. See pp. 51–3.

[122] Editorial', (1829) 13 *The Lancet* 377, 380–1. The oath was described as 'a dicer's oath', namely worthless and untrustworthy: *ibid.*, 380.

[123] Beresford, 'Common Informer', 221.

[124] So unpopular were informers under the Spirit Duties Act 1735 (9 Geo. II c. 23) that they were attacked by the people: Dowell, *History of Taxation*, vol. 4, pp. 107–8.

Morning Herald in 1788 describing it as 'a lamentable instance of state necessity' and informers themselves as 'miscreants', 'reptiles' and 'unprincipled
wretches'.[125] It was believed that unscrupulous greedy informers deliberately
provoked inadvertent sales of unstamped articles or sales in the grey areas in
the legislation. Certainly there was evidence elsewhere to support this: it was
said that in the 1820s most of the informations on breach of the receipts duty
were 'grounded in malice ... used to administer to the very worst passions ...
[and] frequently obtained by trick'.[126] It was maintained that there should be
some other method devised to ensure the collection of taxes for the support
of the state that did not involve 'the infamous assistance of perjurers, and the
exploitation of social confidence'.[127] The chemists and druggists maintained
they were 'harassed and persecuted' to the point of 'utter ruin of themselves
and their families'[128] as they exposed the considerable problems resulting from
the activities of the 'swarms'[129] of professional informers. They viewed it as
a 'system of *espionage*'[130] and condemned informers as 'persons of a certain
class, not distinguished for high moral feeling or delicacy in swearing' and
the chemists believed that the commissioners themselves could be deceived.[131]
The Lancet was equally strident, calling the informers 'abandoned wretches'[132]
and said that the system of medicine tax informers was 'a disgrace to the country'.[133] Indiscriminate prosecutions caused 'the greatest alarm'[134] throughout
the profession and amounted to nothing short of oppression.

Extant reports of proceedings revealed the problem. In a case tried before
the Lord Mayor, Sir John Eamer, in 1802, the 'informer's affidavit man' entered
the courtroom carrying a large bag full of articles purchased unstamped from
dealers, each one marked with the dealer's name, the date and place of the

[125] The newspaper was quoted by Spilsbury, *The Power of Gold Displayed* (1788), p. vii.
[126] Fourteenth Report of the Commissioners of Inquiry into the Collection and Management
    of the Revenue arising in Ireland, Scotland; etc. Board of Stamps, *House of Commons
    Parliamentary Papers* (1826) (436) x 69 at p. 481, *per* Godfrey Sykes, solicitor to the Stamp
    Department.
[127] Quoted by Spilsbury, *The Power of Gold Displayed* (1788), p. vii.
[128] *Journals of the House of Commons*, vol. 58, 7 December 1802, p. 60, in a petition by the chem-
    ists and druggists of Tavistock in Devon. Nevertheless, the threat of prosecution to obtain
    money was one that a 'firm and prudent man' would be expected to resist, and as such the
    making of such a threat was held not to be an indictable offence: R v. *Southerton* (1805) 6 East
    126 at 140 *per* Lord Ellenborough CJ.
[129] Chamberlaine, *History of the Proceedings*, p. 2.
[130] 'The Medicine Stamp Act – Fraud and Attempt at Extortion', (1848) 8 *Pharmaceutical Journal*
    (series 1) 409.
[131] *Ibid.*
[132] Editorial', (1829) 13 *The Lancet* 377, 381.
[133] *Ibid.*
[134] *Ibid.*, 378.

purchase, and the circumstances of the purchase.[135] The dealers in question were grocers, confectioners and widows of apothecaries. No apothecaries or druggists were prosecuted, it being understood that informers tended to attack the most vulnerable, who were ignorant of the law and unlikely to contend the prosecution. Because if successful the penalties would be lucrative for the informers, they were able to afford professional counsel to prosecute the case. In the first case, where one ounce of refined liquorice had been sold unstamped by a grocer, an eminent barrister prosecuted, and the solicitor of the Stamp Office, Mr Estcourt, defended, aiming to demonstrate that the grocer had been acting with the sanction of the Stamp Commissioners, who had informed a deputation of confectioners that they would not be prosecuted for selling articles that were not medicines. As counsel for the prosecution observed, it was irrelevant whether the law was mistakenly drawn or not; the law was stated, could not be ignored, and the grocer had breached it. Conviction seemed inevitable, but for the fortuitous noting of a mistake in the information. The information did not contain the essential words of the Act in the allegation of the crime alleged, and this technical omission sufficed to undermine the validity of the information. The information, and all the others, was immediately quashed.

It was believed that common informers routinely exploited the uncertainty of the law, *Tolu Lozenges* being a favourite article for informers in this respect. It was believed that under the Acts of 1785 and 1802 common informers made more out of them than all other medicines put together. The reason, it was said, was that there was no consensus among the magistrates, with some saying that the composition was not secret and therefore not dutiable; others recalled it had once been a patent medicine and convicted on that basis. Informers knew which magistrates held the latter view, and laid their informations accordingly.[136] Furthermore, the poor drafting of the Act gave rise to confusion and opportunities for dishonest informers. For example, one section provided the stamped label must be fixed so that it could not be used again, on penalty of £10 for each offence. This could allow a corrupt informer to purchase hundreds of bottles of soda water, soak off the labels without damaging them, and proceed to prosecute the seller for fines of many thousands of pounds.[137]

To the relief of medicine vendors, the system of lay informers was abolished in 1803.[138] Although the laying of an information remained the method of

---

[135] Chamberlaine, *History of the Proceedings*, pp. 7–10.
[136] *Ibid.*, pp. 31–2.
[137] Editorial', (1829) 13 *The Lancet* 377, 380.
[138] 43 Geo. III c. 73 s. 4.

enforcement, it was now at the instigation of officers of the board who were
sent out across the country to enforce the law, and had no interest, pecuniary
or otherwise, in the outcome of the proceedings beyond ensuring the law was
being observed:

> The object of the proceedings is not to raise money by penalties but, to pro-
> tect the revenue, and at the same time, to protect the honest tradesman, who
> complies with the requirements of the Stamp Acts, against the unfair compe-
> tition of his less scrupulous neighbours, who either designedly or from cul-
> pable ignorance, evade the tax which in justice should be paid by all alike.[139]

Indeed, the revenue officers were often alerted to breaches in the law by
chemists whose business was being undermined by colleagues evading the
duties.[140]

The objection to private profit abated, but resentment continued to grow.
Chemists and druggists simply did not, and could not, know which articles
were liable to the duty. In their ignorance or carelessness, they were coupled
with those traders who deliberately defrauded the revenue authorities[141] and
suffered the 'unpleasantness and injustice of any imputation upon their char-
acters as respectable and upright tradesmen'.[142] Individuals caught by the wide
scope of the Act complained to their members of Parliament of the 'great
hardship' caused by prosecutions.[143] In a decade of widespread, organised and
formal discontent with the 'vexatious and injurious operation and ruinous
effects of the Medicine Stamp Act on their retail trade',[144] the 1830s saw petitions presented to the House of Commons by associations of chemists and
druggists from all over the country, including London, Manchester, Norwich,
King's Lynn, Newcastle upon Tyne, Bristol, Bridgwater and Exeter. Statistics
presented to the House of Commons in 1830 showed that most individuals
on whom Exchequer writs had been served did not appear before the Court
of Exchequer at all but were dealt with directly by the revenue boards and
that there was no consistency in how they were treated.[145] Some paid the full

[139] (1854) 14 *Pharmaceutical Journal* (series 1) 146.
[140] *Ibid.*
[141] *Parl. Deb.*, vol. 25, ser 2, col. 91, 8 June 1830 (HC) *per* Mr Hobhouse.
[142] In a petition by the chemists and druggists of Norwich: *Journals of the House of Commons*, vol. 85, 4 June 1830, p. 512.
[143] For example, the prosecution of a perfumer who had invented a vegetable soap to promote hair growth: *Parl. Deb.*, vol. 23, ser 2, col. 1402, 6 April 1830 (HC).
[144] In a petition by the chemists and druggists of King's Lynn: *Journals of the House of Commons*, vol. 85, 21 May 1830, p. 456.
[145] *Parl. Deb.*, vol. 25, ser 2, cols. 89–90, 8 June 1830 (HC) *per* Mr Hobhouse.

penalty, some engaged in negotiation with the board and were charged varying amounts and some resisted firmly and successfully avoided paying anything.

The Relationship with the Revenue Authorities

The unpopularity of the system of informers, the readiness of the central revenue board to prosecute and the uncertain legal grounds upon which the prosecutions were based gave rise to the most intense dislike of the revenue authorities themselves. The extent of the considerable power they exercised in relation to the medicine stamp duty was perfectly understood in the first half of the nineteenth century. The trade knew that liability depended on the interpretation of the legislation adopted by the commissioners or, rather, their solicitor.[146] With little public confidence in such interpretation and even less in the methods of enforcement, the administration of the tax was perceived as oppressive and bullying. Adding to that the discretionary powers of the board in relation to both prosecution and penalties, the system was a mixture of 'compromise and intimidation'.[147] In the 1780s the threat to 'exchequer' vendors who did not purchase a licence was likened to that of a common highwayman,[148] and it was believed that many vendors bought licences through fear rather than a genuine belief that they were legally required to.[149] They were, said Francis Spilsbury, 'helpless men, terrified by threats, by advertisements, by constructions …'[150] The word 'exchequer' was 'cousin to Inquisition',[151] and descriptions such as 'the Exchequer cudgel', '[flagellation] with the Exchequer scourge' were commonplace.[152] Spilsbury railed, '[t]o refuse a woman in labour a cheap medicine to ease her pains without paying for a stamp. Let her die first, is the language of the Stamp Office; or, We'll exchequer you'.[153]

Resentment continued to be directed against the board and its officers personally well into the next century. The editor of *The Lancet* complained in 1829 that '… the feelings and pockets of the members of an entire profession are to be sacrificed, in order to satiate the greedy and morbid appetites of some

---

[146] 'Editorial', (1829) 13 *The Lancet* 377, 378–79.
[147] Fourteenth Report of the Commissioners of Inquiry into the Collection and Management of the Revenue arising in Ireland, Scotland; etc. Board of Stamps, *House of Commons Parliamentary Papers* (1826) (436) x 69 at p. 78.
[148] Spilsbury, *Discursory Thoughts*, p. 20.
[149] *Ibid.*, pp. 6, 21.
[150] *Ibid.*, p. 7.
[151] *Ibid.*, p. 20.
[152] Spilsbury, *The Power of Gold Displayed* (1785), pp. 2, 3.
[153] *Ibid.*, p. 2.

two or three hungry commissioners and their satellites.'[154] He condemned this practice by the board as the 'whims and caprices of the senseless and heartless creatures, who may be appointed to carry its provisions, or rather its *no*-provisions, into effect'.[155] Prosecutions caused a feeling of 'universal disgust' against the revenue commissioners themselves.[156]

This perception of the Stamp Commissioners in particular was exacerbated by the findings of an official inquiry into the collection and management of the stamp duties in 1826. The report was highly critical of the inefficiency of the board, finding 'laxity and defectiveness of system ... in almost every branch of the Stamp department in England'[157] causing unacceptable delays and inconvenience to the public. The commissioners were personally criticised for sloth, ineptitude, a lack of commitment, absence of leadership, internal dissentions, and conflicts of interest.[158] It found a process of administration and management to be 'neither regular nor effectual'[159] and designed for the convenience of the commissioners rather than any inherent efficiency and security.

By the middle years of the nineteenth century, professional and commercial objections to the administration of the medicine stamp duty by the revenue boards lessened. The reasons were various. Certainly the bureaucratic practices that benefitted chemists and druggists were positive factors, as with the wide interpretation of the *known, admitted and approved* remedies exemption after 1903, the development of extra-statutory concessions such as that for dispensing and breaking bulk, and the availability – at a price – of appropriated stamps,[160] whereby the medicine stamp could be used for advertising purposes. There was also a growing understanding that the interpretation of the statutes by the board was necessary in view of the nature

[154] Editorial', (1829) 13 *The Lancet* 377, 378.
[155] *Ibid.*, 380.
[156] *Ibid.*, 378.
[157] Fourteenth Report of the Commissioners of Inquiry into the Collection and Management of the Revenue arising in Ireland, Scotland; etc. Board of Stamps, *House of Commons Parliamentary Papers* (1826) (436) x 69 at p. 200.
[158] Thirteenth Report of the Commissioners of Inquiry into the Collection and Management of the Revenue arising in Ireland, Scotland; etc., *House of Commons Parliamentary Papers* (1826) (435) x 1 at pp. 6–14. Note that the merger of the Stamp Office with the Board of Taxes in 1834 was the result of the damning findings of this inquiry: Fourteenth Report of the Commissioners of Inquiry into the Collection and Management of the Revenue arising in Ireland, Scotland; etc. Board of Stamps, *House of Commons Parliamentary Papers* (1826) (436) x 69.
[159] Thirteenth Report of the Commissioners of Inquiry into the Collection and Management of the Revenue arising in Ireland, Scotland; etc., *House of Commons Parliamentary Papers* (1826) (435) x 1 at p. 7.
[160] See Chapter 4.

of the legislation. The obsolescence of the legislation came to be universally recognised,[161] and with it an understanding that the poor drafting of the Act made it impossible – and pointless – to administer it according to its terms. The chemists and druggists, while recognising the illegality of bureaucratic lawmaking, came to see that the commissioners, obliged to administer the law, simply did their best with what they had. Furthermore, there developed a wider understanding of the revenue practices as they became established and as the burgeoning professional press explained them to its readers.[162] Indeed, by the time of the repeal of the tax, the revenue practice was 'more or less settled and understood by the trade'.[163] Moreover, the more moderate among the chemists and druggists appreciated that in the implementation of the legislation's many doubtful points the board had not always prosecuted when it could legitimately have done so, and that the revenue authorities 'do not take advantage of the full powers they possess, but in general exercise considerable leniency, never knowingly commence proceedings in any doubtful case, and suspend them whenever an explanation or plea is put in which, in their opinion, appears to claim indulgence'.[164] Some chemists and druggists recognised in 1886 that the board 'had much greater powers than was generally thought to be the case, and they exercised them with moderation and discretion:'[165] indeed, the board could 'harass the trade very considerably if they chose to enforce the Acts with harshness'.[166] Even F. W. Woolworth's, frustrated by their inability to access the privileges accorded to qualified chemists in the early twentieth century, said they could 'fully appreciate, and sympathise with, the difficulties experienced by [the board] in administering the Acts',[167] and the Company Chemists Association, representing corporate chemists such as Boots and Timothy Whites, paid 'just tribute' to the revenue authorities in their task of administering out-of-date

---

[161] Including by the board itself: Report and Minutes of Evidence from the Select Committee on Patent Medicines, *House of Commons Parliamentary Papers* (1914) (Cd. 414) ix 1 at q. 90 *per* Sir Nathaniel Highmore, solicitor to the Board of Customs and Excise.

[162] See for example the explanation of the board's understanding of 'recommendations' in (1848) 7 *Pharmaceutical Journal* (series 1) 453.

[163] *Board of Customs and Excise and Predecessor: Private Office Papers, The Medicine Stamp Duties 1783–1936*: TNA CUST 118/366 at p. 122.

[164] 'The Medicine Stamp Act – Fraud and Attempt at Extortion', (1848) 8 *Pharmaceutical Journal* (series 1) 409; 'The Medicine Stamp Act', (1848) 8 *Pharmaceutical Journal* (series 1) 212, 213.

[165] (1886) 16 *Pharmaceutical Journal* (series 3) 908.

[166] *Ibid*.

[167] Report and Minutes of Evidence from the Select Committee on Medicine Stamp Duties, *House of Commons Parliamentary Papers* (1937) (Cmd. 54) viii 129, Memorandum of F. W. Woolworth & Co Ltd at p. 313.

legislation.[168] In the same vein, the Proprietary Association of Great Britain felt that the revenue authorities had 'always … been guided by the dictates of common sense'.[169]

The revenue authorities themselves contributed to the improvement in relations with the trade. They appreciated the inaccessibility of the legislation – acutely so, as they struggled to implement it – and attempted to rectify this as far as they could by giving printed rules and regulations to vendors when they applied for their licences. The board went even further when in 1847 proceedings were taken against a number of chemists and druggists for breach of the medicine stamp duty legislation, and as a result the Pharmaceutical Society made representations to the board. These representations were successful to the extent that the board took the highly unusual step of making available the generally confidential official *Instructions* relating to the duty that the board issued to its own officers. These were published in the *Pharmaceutical Journal*.[170]

The revenue officials also ensured they were accessible to the public. Confounded by the grounds of liability, chemists and druggists could turn only to the officials of the revenue authorities for advice to ensure they complied with the law, or when they faced a prosecution they deemed unjust. The revenue staff could be contacted by post or by personal attendance at their head office in London, and sometimes the commissioners themselves would meet members of the public in person to hear complaints or concerns and to advise accordingly.[171] In the 1820s members of the public frequently attended the office of the board's solicitor for advice and information, primarily as the channel of communication to the board, and to make suggestions and put forward cases of hardship.[172] For example, Thomas Binge, prosecuted for selling soda powders in the 1820s, immediately consulted the board's solicitor, Joseph Timm.[173]

[168] *Ibid.*, Precis of Evidence of the Company Chemists Association at p. 339.
[169] *Ibid.*, Memorandum of the Proprietary Association of Great Britain at p. 220.
[170] 'The Medicine Stamp Act', (1848) 8 *Pharmaceutical Journal* (series 1) 153. The instructions are reproduced at *Board of Customs and Excise and Predecessor: Private Office Papers, The Medicine Stamp Duties 1783–1936*: TNA CUST 118/366 at pp. 150–6.
[171] Thirteenth Report of the Commissioners of Inquiry into the Collection and Management of the Revenue arising in Ireland, Scotland; etc., *House of Commons Parliamentary Papers* (1826) (435) x 1 at p. 35 *per* William Kappen, Secretary to the Board.
[172] Fourteenth Report of the Commissioners of Inquiry into the Collection and Management of the Revenue arising in Ireland, Scotland; etc. Board of Stamps, *House of Commons Parliamentary Papers* (1826) (436) x 69 at p. 757, *per* Godfrey Sykes, solicitor to the Stamp Department.
[173] 'Editorial', (1829) 13 *The Lancet* 377, 378.

Throughout the nineteenth century and indeed right up to the abolition of the tax, chemists and druggists in their hundreds sent medicine labels and other printed matter in for the opinion of the board. The board, although not obliged to, responded accordingly, and the professional journals carried reports of these decisions in all their editions. One typical example among hundreds is the correspondence between A. P. Towle, proprietor of *Towle's Chlorodyne*, and the revenue authorities, represented by Stephen Dowell in 1865 and 1866, prompted by an article in the *Pharmaceutical Journal* and seeking advice as to the fiscal impact of information included with the medicine as supplied to the general public and to the medical profession.[174] There was a limit to this, however. The revenue authorities were not prepared to give a definitive ruling on all doubtful points in the administration of the law and explain how they would exercise their 'discretionary forbearance',[175] nor to give individual rulings on the applicability of the *known, admitted and approved* remedies exemption. They invariably responded with a statement of the terms of the exemption and an instruction to judge for themselves whether they came within those terms.[176]

There are many instances where revenue officials are seen to treat taxpayers with courtesy and, often, immense patience. The campaigners against the tax of 1802, for example, were treated with impeccable professional respect by the Stamp Commissioners and their officials, who took great pains fully to discuss their demands and suggestions.[177] In the early twentieth century, the board was regularly praised for its 'extreme fairness and courtesy' in dealing with border-line cases, and its adherence to 'the dictates of common sense'.[178] Woolworth's, whose threatened action against the revenue to establish the illegality of their practices ultimately brought about the end of the tax,[179] said they had 'the highest regard for the Department from whom they have always received the most fair and courteous consideration'.[180] The consensus among chemists and

---

[174] TNA IR 40/2008.

[175] 'The Medicine Stamp Act', (1848) 8 *Pharmaceutical Journal* (series 1) 212.

[176] *Precedents & Instructions*, 1904: TNA IR 78/60 at p. 123; 'The Medicine Stamp Duty Act', (1903) 71 *Pharmaceutical Journal* (series 4) 579; 'The New Interpretation of the Medicine Stamp Acts', *ibid.*, 594.

[177] Chamberlaine, *History of the Proceedings*, p. 36.

[178] Report and Minutes of Evidence from the Select Committee on Medicine Stamp Duties, *House of Commons Parliamentary Papers* (1937) (Cmd. 54) viii 129 at p. 220; 'Somerset House Courtesy', (1903) 63 *Chemist and Druggist* 784; 'A Visit to Somerset House', (1903) 71 *Pharmaceutical Journal* (series 4) 265.

[179] See Chapter 5.

[180] Report and Minutes of Evidence from the Select Committee on Medicine Stamp Duties, *House of Commons Parliamentary Papers* (1937) (Cmd. 54) viii 129, Memorandum of F. W. Woolworth & Co Ltd at p. 313.

druggists was expressed by 'Xrayser' in the *Chemist and Druggist* in 1903: '[t]he Board has long lived down its sinister reputation, and in the matter of the medicine stamp-duty at least its fairness and courtesy are universally known, admitted, and approved'.[181]

TAX AND PROFESSIONALISATION

In its express general charge and its exemptions, the medicine stamp duty was unequivocally designed to ensure that regular medical and pharmaceutical practice was protected. When the medicine stamp duty was first introduced in the latter years of the eighteenth century, chemists and druggists, while emerging as a distinct occupation in the provision of pharmaceutical services, namely the preparation and compounding of vegetable, mineral or animal substances to create medicines and supplying them to the public, did not yet constitute a profession in the accepted sense of the term. The medicine stamp duty, however, had a twofold effect on chemists and druggists that contributed materially to their transformation from a mere occupation to a recognisable profession. By affirming the occupation as such, and by constituting a cause behind which individuals could unify, the medicine stamp duty recognised, supported and promoted the professional pharmaceutical practice of chemists and druggists.

Occupational Affirmation

Individuals could only be made subject to a tax as a class, or indeed exempted from it, if the delineation of the class was clearly understood by both the taxing authorities of government and the taxpaying public. Limiting the scope of the medicine stamp duty by exemptions that all aimed to protect regular pharmacy, and expressly referring to chemists and druggists as such, constituted an unambiguous legislative recognition of chemists and druggists as a coherent occupational group and shows they were established in the official mind as a discrete occupation. Moreover, because the legislation defined them by reference to qualification and training, however fragile that was in reality, it recognised them as a skilled group in a category that included the ancient and well-established professions of apothecary and surgeon. As a correspondent to the *Pharmaceutical Journal* observed in 1903, '[t]he best thing possible to chemists from a business point of view is to have their qualification recognised

---

[181] Xrayser, 'Observations and Reflections, Somerset House', (1903) 63 *Chemist and Druggist* 691.

by a great public department'.[182] Furthermore, the very fact that the exemptions were designed to ensure that the tax did not impinge on their legitimate pharmaceutical practice by inadvertently taxing regular medicines sold by the medical profession as part of their normal stock in trade and intended for legitimate use in regular medical and pharmaceutical practice, supported chemists and druggists as part of the regular medical establishment and as the guardians of legitimate pharmacy. In plainly aiming to protect qualified individuals from all aspects of the tax, these statutory provisions also sent an implicit but clear signal that the duty was directed towards unqualified vendors of medicines by leaving them to bear the burden of it and, implicitly, to be excluded from orthodox pharmacy. The legislation thereby drew a very stark distinction between chemists and druggists on the one hand, and quacks on the other. The practice of the revenue authorities equally affirmed chemists and druggists as a privileged class within their occupational cadre. This was particularly noticeable in the 'Chemists' Privilege', namely the generous post-1903 interpretation of the *known, admitted and approved* remedies exemption.[183] This new interpretation undoubtedly reflected the reality of pharmaceutical practice, recognising that skilled chemists and druggists made their own remedies, which would otherwise be caught by the legislation. If not encouraging professionalisation, it undoubtedly recognised the skill of pharmacy and extended a favourable treatment beyond the context of regular pharmaceutical practice.

Professional Unity

The response of the chemists and druggists to the introduction of the medicine stamp duty was perhaps the most powerful formative factor that the tax contributed to the evolution of the profession. Their objections to the tax, above all to its administration, drew them together as never before.[184] In the latter years of the eighteenth century the chemists and druggists were not a sufficiently powerful group effectively to voice any objections, and in the same vein there was no presence or focus of opposition. Respect for the King and a desire to maintain the status quo as far as possible in a turbulent political climate encouraged this quiescence. Resistance was limited to ad hoc action by groups of individuals, as with the campaign of non-cooperation in 1784, which led the Stamp Office to publish a notice in the newspapers stating that any

---

[182] 'Liability to Medicine Stamp Duty', (1903) 71 *Pharmaceutical Journal* (series 4) 125.

[183] See Chapter 2.

[184] See generally J. G. L Burnby, 'The Professionalisation of British Pharmacy' (1988) 18 *Pharmaceutical Historian* 3.

medicine vendors coming within the meaning of the Act and not complying
with it would face immediate prosecution. The period, however, marked a
gathering momentum of dissatisfaction with the tax, and in 1802, when the tax
was nearly two decades old, objections to the content of the new schedule of
chargeable medicines acted as a catalyst for the first united action of chemists
and druggists as an occupational group.

The third Medicine Stamp Act 1802 had introduced a new and considerably enlarged schedule of expressly dutiable articles.[185] Many of the new
preparations in the list should have been exempt as being outside the spirit of
the tax,[186] but being expressly named they were brought into charge whether
or not they were sold with labels recommending them. They included some
single unmixed drugs such as Spanish juice, refined liquorice, India arrowroot and Turkey rhubarb, and some regular compounded medicines such as
Huxham's Tincture of Bark, *Goulard's Extract* and *Syrup of Tolu*. The new
schedule also included items that were broadly or indefinitely described, such
as all dentifrices, items of confectionary such as ginger and peppermint lozenges and many toilet articles, such as perfumes and cosmetics. The chargeability of lozenges was especially contentious. Lozenges were consumed in
large quantities in the early nineteenth century. It was said that some 170 tons
of the best double-refined sugar was used annually in Great Britain in their
manufacture.[187] Although they were essentially confectionary, they were partly
medicinal and as such were widely sold by druggists and apothecaries. All
those that bore a name, such as *Ching's*, *Dawson's* or *Steer's* lozenges were
clearly within the charge. However, lozenges such as peppermint lozenges,
which were not secret as to their composition and were widely consumed by
the public and sold by chemists by weight with no medicine stamp, were now
subject to the tax.

Chemists and druggists argued that this new schedule was scientifically
and professionally incorrect, because, through a lack of consultation by the
central revenue board with skilled practitioners in pharmacy, it failed to draw
a realistic and informed distinction between the preparations of the regular
practitioner and the 'pretended arcana of charlatans and nostrum-mongers'.[188]
So alarmed were they by the extension of the schedule in this way that they

[185] 42 Geo. III c. 56 (1802).
[186] See the petition of Sheffield druggists, *Journals of the House of Commons*, vol. 58, 10 December
1802, p. 79. See too the petitions of Ashburton, *ibid.*, 13 December 1802, p. 84 and Exeter, *ibid.*,
17 December 1802, p. 103.
[187] Chamberlaine, *History of the Proceedings*, p. 13.
[188] *Ibid.*, p. 17.

united in an unprecedented and vigorous campaign for the reform of the legislation to make it workable,[189] revealing a depth of feeling far greater than that following the introduction of the duty nearly twenty years before. They had to fight the campaign alone with little support from the apothecaries and surgeons, despite a common vulnerability to the defects of the legislation,[190] primarily because at the dawn of the nineteenth century it was the druggists who were principally involved in the sale of proprietary medicines, often in both the retail and export trades with significant turnovers. An exception to this professional apathy was a London surgeon, William Chamberlaine, who led the opposition to the extension of the tax with energy and vision.[191] He took a leading role in forming a new Association of Apothecaries and Chemists and Druggists in 1802, the proceedings of which he published in 1804.[192] The formation of an occupational association specifically created to oppose the tax, whether local or national, temporary or permanent, was a typical nineteenth century social and cultural response seen in relation to most unpopular taxation initiatives.

Objecting to the new schedule, as well as the lack of consultation, bureaucratic lawmaking by the revenue board and methods of enforcement, the association adopted a familiar and robust strategy of opposition. Campaigning swiftly and strongly, it held meetings, printed circulars, advertised, employed a solicitor, took the opinion of counsel, lobbied members of Parliament, held regular meetings with the Lord Mayor and other members for the City of London and challenged the taxing decisions of the revenue boards by correspondence and personal meetings.[193] Three tactics were central to the campaign. First, the association urged the immediate submission of petitions to Parliament from all over the country praying for relief from the medicine duty, or calling for its abolition.[194] Adopting a common form, the chemists and druggists complained that the Act had subjected them to 'grievous burthens,

---

[189] They quickly understood that the total repeal of the 1802 Act could never be obtained: Chamberlaine, *History of the Proceedings*, p. 11.

[190] Only thirty apothecaries and fewer than a dozen surgeons subscribed to the fund set up by the association to fund the campaign for the reform of the 1802 Act: *ibid.*

[191] 'The Origins of the Society', (1941) 146 *Pharmaceutical Journal* (series 4) 124.

[192] The *Proceedings* were published to assist retail druggists and apothecaries, country dealers in the drug trade, merchants exporting drugs abroad and magistrates before whom informations for breach of the medicine stamp duty legislation were brought: Chamberlaine, *History of the Proceedings*, pp. iv–v.

[193] *Ibid.*, pp. 10–11.

[194] See examples at *Journals of the House of Commons*, vol. 58, 10, 13, 17 December 1802, pp. 79, 84, 103.

inconveniences, and losses'[195] and that it 'bore severely' on them.[196] Second, Chamberlaine himself met with an official from the central tax board and, with the active encouragement of the Stamp Commissioners, drafted a new schedule in which the offending articles were removed. He concentrated almost exclusively on those articles that were in the *Pharmacopoeia* rather than those that were essentially confectionary and perfumery.[197] Third, the association prepared a memorial to the Lords of the Treasury calling for an end to the prosecution of chemists and druggists for selling articles that were included in the schedule but did not otherwise come within the proper meaning of the Act, and met the Secretary to the Treasury.[198]

The association of 1802 was created solely to provide a united opposition to changes in the tax regime applicable to medicines to protect the trade of chemists and druggists. Although it was temporary, enduring only as long as it took to resolve the particular grievance, and did not promote any agenda of educational reform or professional regulation, it was more than just an 'ephemeral' association merely marking the growing political power of the chemists and druggists.[199] It constituted an unambiguous and early expression of occupational cohesion.

The association of 1802 enjoyed a measure of success, obtaining concessions and amendments to the legislation, with a revised schedule of dutiable medicines being adopted in an Act of 1803.[200] The new schedule contained some 450 articles, and so was considerably shorter than that in the 1802 Act.[201] It no longer included articles from the *Pharmacopoeia*, notably any single unmixed drugs, and articles that had been indefinitely described were deleted.

---

[195] This was included in a typical example of such petitions, by the chemists and druggists of Plymouth in November 1802. They complained that by the Act of 1785 they were subjected to 'grievous burthens, inconveniences, and losses, arising not only from the many doubts and difficulties in which the construction of several of the clauses in the Act is involved, but also from the mode by which the Duties thereby granted are directed to be collected and paid': *ibid.*, 29 November 1802, p. 35.

[196] *Monthly Review*, August 1804, p. 423.

[197] Chamberlaine, *History of the Proceedings*, pp. 2–3.

[198] *Ibid.*, p. 3.

[199] S. W. F. Holloway, 'The Orthodox Fringe: The Origins of the Pharmaceutical Society of Great Britain', in W. F. Bynum and Roy Porter (eds.), *Medical Fringe and Medical Orthodoxy 1750–1850* (London: Croom Helm, 1987), p. 130.

[200] 43 Geo. III c.73 (1803). For a comparison of the 1802 and 1803 schedules, making it clear which articles had been removed in the latter, see Chamberlaine, *History of the Proceedings*, pp. 44–45.

[201] In one of the very few treatises on the medicine stamp duty, E. N. Alpe says he could not understand why some eighty products should be removed from the charge. He suggested that either the new schedule was 'carelessly drawn' or it was compiled from the lists of medicines that the earlier Acts had required sellers to submit and that were, through want of enforcement, irregular and incomplete: Alpe, *Handy Book*, p. 18.

For example lip salves and tooth powders 'of all sorts', were removed from the charge and could be sold providing they were not claimed as proprietary or secret, or held out to the public by printed advertisement. Arrowroot was removed, being a food rather than a medicine, as were articles such as candied ginger, more properly confectionary than medicine.[202] Despite having pressed very hard for their removal, however, lozenges were retained in the schedule, although this was probably simply an oversight of detail in the press of parliamentary business and national affairs. In 1815, the matter was partly resolved by an Act of that year, when ginger and peppermint lozenges and other confectionary were exempt from the duty as long as they were not sold as medicines, and confirmed that no medicine licence was required for selling the exempt lozenges.[203] In the same way, tinctures for the teeth and gums were accidentally retained in 1802. *Arquebusade water*, too, remained subject to the charge.[204] This preparation for washing wounds already bore a heavy duty. It was understood that the duty would act as a prohibition, and that a cheaper substitute would be found for the same purpose, and that anyway it was not a secret nostrum, the recipe being widely known, but still it remained within the charge.

In the matter of prosecutions, too, the association of 1802 was effective, being largely responsible for the legislation in 1803 which provided that only persons acting under the authority of the central revenue boards or the Attorney General could now bring a prosecution.[205] This was welcomed by the profession as affording protection from unscrupulous lay informers motivated by personal pecuniary profit. As the *Pharmaceutical Journal* pointed out,

> the object ... is not to raise money by penalties, but to protect the revenue and at the same time to protect the honest tradesman who complies with the requirements [of the Act], against the unfair competition of his less scrupulous neighbours, who, either designedly, or from culpable ignorance, evade the tax which in justice should be paid by all alike.[206]

---

[202] The members of the association had success beyond the tax field, in successfully opposing bills concerning the sale of poisons in 1813 and 1819 which they believed threatened their business and ensured their exemption from the Apothecaries Act 1815.

[203] Stamp Act 1815 (55 Geo. III c.184) s. 54.

[204] *Eau d'Arquebusade*, also known as musket shot water, was a preparation of agrimony leaves and seeds and other plant extracts, used since the Middle Ages as a herbal cure for gunshot wounds.

[205] 43 Geo. III c. 73 s. 4 (1803).

[206] 'The Medicine Stamp and Licence Acts', (1854–55) 14 *Pharmaceutical Journal* (series 1) 146, 147.

The association achieved other concessions. In response to the complaint that a medicine vendor could be ruined by the latitude given to informers in bringing their informations, the informer was obliged to bring any action within three months of the offence being committed instead of six, and the association also achieved the award of greater powers of mitigation of penalties by magistrates.[207]

Such early and relatively minor successes, essentially reforms of detail, marked the high point of effective collective action. The next major campaign of opposition occurred in 1829, and at its centre was the issue of the uncertainty of the law and, it followed, unjust prosecutions. So common were such instances, reaching some hundreds according to *The Lancet* and constituting a harassing and frightful evil,[208] and so intense was the public resentment of informers, that the chemists and druggists in the 1820s again began to unite in opposition to the tax and its administration. In 1829 there was an attempt to mobilise the medicine traders, when a circular signed under the name of 'Amicus Justitiae' suggested a public meeting of members of the trade be called to form a society to petition the Treasury and Parliament, to protect members against unjust prosecutions and to protect the public against higher prices caused by chemists and druggists charging the duty on preparations that were not legally subject to it rather than risk the expense of challenging the issue in the courts of law.[209] The first step was the formation of a new society, the General Association of Chemists and Druggists of Great Britain, with a wider membership and the fresh formation of numerous local associations. The cause of the chemists and druggists was championed by John Hobhouse in Parliament. Although he lacked a full grasp of the tax, misunderstanding its original objective, mistaking some of its detail and not entirely appreciating that the chemists and druggists were strictly at fault, he correctly asserted that the revenue boards exercised a power that went far beyond the authority conferred by the legislation.[210] He also brought the difficulties of the medicine stamp duty to an audience beyond the specialist world of pharmaceutical practice.[211]

---

[207] 43 Geo. III c. 73 s. 5 (1803). The association had, however, pressed for a period of just one month: Chamberlaine, *History of the Proceedings*, pp. 4–5.

[208] 'Editorial', (1829) 13 *The Lancet* 377, 379.

[209] *Ibid.*

[210] *Parl. Deb.*, vol. 25, ser 2, col. 90, 8 June 1830 (HC) *per* Mr Hobhouse. For example, he argued that the policy of the original legislation had been 'to protect Patent Medicines from the fraudulent substitution of quack compounds': *ibid.*, col. 89.

[211] *Ibid.*, cols. 90–1.

The campaign of 1829, like that of 1802, was strong, but in terms of any material change in the legislation it succeeded only in obtaining an assurance from the Chancellor of the Exchequer that the much-resented duty on soda water would be repealed, which it eventually was in 1833.[212] In opposing the imposition of the charge through the interpretation of the legislation by the revenue authorities, with its evident injustices and anomalies, the chemists and druggists faced an intractable challenge. The only solution to such bureaucratic lawmaking was a complete recasting of the legislation itself to render it as unambiguous as possible and thus minimise the revenue authorities' need to exercise discretion. That was as unlikely as the abolition of the tax itself. Although they were urged to petition Parliament for the repeal of the legislation as the only realistic option, they constituted an insufficiently powerful sector of society and there were no other sufficiently powerful interests campaigning in their support. The pressure for repeal of the various stamp duties on knowledge, namely on newspapers, advertisements and paper, was ideologically inspired, led by middle-class and working-class radicals united by a desire to educate the working classes but with different political objectives.[213] Pressure for the repeal of the medicine stamp duty, on the other hand, had no ideological basis. It stemmed entirely from the vested professional interests of chemists and druggists and the manufacturers of the proprietary medicines. They were not supported in their fiscal opposition by their powerful colleagues in the regular medical professions, did not create dedicated abolition committees and had insufficient representation in Parliament.[214] In this environment, the financial imperatives underlying the introduction of the tax and the isolationist culture of the central revenue boards proved too powerful.

Whatever the limits of the achievements of the two associations of 1802 and 1829, they were pioneering instances of professional unity, created solely to oppose the medicine stamp duty. Having served to unite the chemists and druggists, albeit for discrete and immediate purposes which, once fulfilled or frustrated, led to the disbanding of the associations, tax remained a significant and unifying issue for chemists and druggists but one that became subsumed

---

[212] Stamps, etc. Act 1833 (3 & 4 Will. IV c. 97) s. 20.

[213] Lynne Oats and Pauline Sadler, 'The Abolition of the Taxes on Knowledge', in John Tiley (ed.), *Studies in the History of Tax Law*, vol. 2, (Oxford: Hart Publishing, 2007), p. 292.

[214] This was understood by the pioneers of professional pharmacy, as it was by the regular medical profession. Accordingly Jacob Bell, one of the founding members of the Pharmaceutical Society and the founder and first editor of the *Pharmaceutical Journal* in 1841 became member of Parliament for St Albans in 1850, and William Glyn-Jones, another of the great names in pharmacy, became the member for Stepney in 1910.

by other concerns regarded as more clearly material to obtaining professional status. Unlike its predecessors in 1802 and 1829, the Pharmaceutical Society of 1841 – an acknowledged landmark in the process of professionalisation within pharmacy – was not formed to secure the reform of the medicine stamp duty, but to improve the education of chemists and druggists and its underpinning in science, to raise the status of the occupation and to safeguard the business interests of chemists and druggists.[215] So although its principal raison d'être did not lie in the medicine stamp duty, this last objective naturally encompassed the impact of taxation on its members. This was all the more so because of the strongly commercial nature of the calling of chemists and druggists, and the business background of the society's founders. They were among the most successful, wealthy and powerful chemists and druggists in London, a position arrived at only through the exercise of an acute mercantile sense, commercial awareness and a highly developed spirit of enterprise.[216] It was thus in this context that the Pharmaceutical Society kept a very close and informed eye on the substance and administration of the medicine stamp duty. Although it did not engage in campaigns for the abolition or even the substantive reform of the tax, accepting that it was there to stay, its watching brief ensured that chemists and druggists could understand an obscure legal regime and effectively manage their tax liability, and their targeted actions in relation to specific issues the tax threw up ensured that in substance and administration it was kept within professionally acceptable bounds.[217]

---

[215] See generally Leslie G. Matthews, *History of Pharmacy in Britain* (Edinburgh: E. & S. Livingstone, 1962), pp. 120–48; S. W. F. Holloway, *Royal Pharmaceutical Society of Great Britain 1841–1991, A Political and Social History* (London: The Pharmaceutical Press, 1991); S. W. F. Holloway, 'The Orthodox Fringe: The Origins of the Pharmaceutical Society of Great Britain', in W. F. Bynum and Roy Porter (eds.), *Medical Fringe and Medical Orthodoxy 1750–1850* (London: Croom Helm, 1987), pp. 129–57; 'The Progress of Pharmacy in Great Britain', (1844) 4 *Pharmaceutical Journal* (series 1) 1; Report and Minutes of Evidence from the Select Committee on the Pharmacy Bill, *House of Commons Parliamentary Papers* (1852) (387) xiii 275 at qq. 492–533; 796–818; 944; Crellin, 'The Growth of Professionalism', 217–18; Royal Charter of Incorporation of the Pharmaceutical Society of Great Britain, *House of Commons Parliamentary Papers* (1851) (474) xliii 397. See the evidence of the Royal Pharmaceutical Society to the Select Committee on the Medicine Stamp Duties in 1936, which strongly promoted the interests of chemists: Report and Minutes of Evidence from the Select Committee on Medicine Stamp Duties, *House of Commons Parliamentary Papers* (1937) (Cmd. 54) viii 129, Memorandum of H. N. Linstead, Secretary of the Royal Pharmaceutical Society of Great Britain at p. 195.

[216] Holloway, 'The Orthodox Fringe', 147–53.

[217] Although various trade associations of chemists and druggists throughout the nineteenth century continued to campaign for its revision. See for example 'The Patent Medicine Stamp Acts – Deputation to the Board of Inland Revenue', (1886) 16 *Pharmaceutical Journal* (series 3) 907.

The emphasis of the Pharmaceutical Society and its journal was primarily on professional pharmacy, specifically education, training, registration and discipline.[218] As a result, other societies came to be formed exclusively to address commercial pharmacy. Local associations were often very active. For example, in 1894 the Edinburgh chemists and druggists, along with other Scottish chemists' trade associations, felt themselves particularly badly affected by denial of the *known, admitted and approved* remedies exemption to medicines labelled in the possessive case, and they petitioned the Board of Inland Revenue, albeit unsuccessfully.[219] New national associations were formed, such as the Chemists' and Druggists' Defence Association, founded in 1876 to represent the trade nationally, and the National Pharmaceutical Union, founded to safeguard the trade interest of retail chemists in private practice. The case of *The Pharmaceutical Society* v. *London Provincial Supply Association* in 1880 established that limited companies could carry on the business of chemist and druggist,[220] and this practice, exemplified by the pioneering Jesse Boot, led to the widespread availability of proprietary medicines at cheaper prices than an independent chemist and druggist could match, primarily through bulk buying. This tendency was curbed only by the formation in 1896 of the Proprietary Articles Trade Association, led by William Glyn-Jones, to manage relations between the manufacturer and the wholesale and retail distributors of proprietary medicines and which mobilised the resistance of the chemist and druggist and led to the maintenance of an established retail price.[221]

All these associations engaged with the medicine stamp duty. In 1886 the Chemists' and Druggists' Defence Association sent a deputation to the Board

---

[218] It was the Pharmaceutical Society that first addressed the crucial issue of education and training, recognizing that improved and more consistent educational standards were essential in the context of rapid developments in pharmaceutical chemistry in the early years of the nineteenth century and to raise the status of chemists and druggists. This dominated its work throughout the nineteenth century, but through its activities, the position of the chemist and druggist was 'exalted from that of a mere trader to a member of an educated and scientific profession': (1876) 18 *Chemist and Druggist* 238; Matthews, *History of Pharmacy*, pp. 134–7. By 1870 the term 'chemist' suggested a degree of scientific education, and accordingly distinguished them from general medicine vendors: A Poor Country Practitioner, 'Letters to the Editor', (1870) 96 *The Lancet* 592.

[219] See A. W. Patterson, 'The Edinburgh District Chemists' Trade Association: A Centenary Review' (1993) 23 *Pharmaceutical Historian* 7. See too Holloway, *Royal Pharmaceutical Society*, pp. 313–20.

[220] *Pharmaceutical Society* v. *London Provincial Supply Association* (1880) 5 App Cas 857.

[221] See for example the deputation from the Association to the Chancellor of the Exchequer in 1920: *Board of Customs and Excise and predecessor: Private Office Papers*: TNA CUST 118/63.

of Inland Revenue to suggest modifications to the system of administering the medicine stamp duty. This association then had between three and four thousand members, and its executive was agitated as to the large number of prosecutions for breach of the legislation caused by ignorance of its provisions. It sought to induce the board 'to so modify the working or administration of the Acts as to bring the trade more into harmony with the Inland Revenue officials'.[222] The deputation asked that the board issue a letter of caution for the first offence rather than threatening immediate prosecution in relation, particularly, to chemists and druggists selling very small quantities of preparations of everyday use.[223] The revenue authorities were not sympathetic in their response, balancing the need to protect those chemists and druggists who adhered to the law, but agreed that if they were satisfied as to the individual offender's good faith and that the offender could show that the breach of the law was reasonable, then they would consider the case on its merits.[224] In fact, they were making no new concession, as this reflected their current practice.

All these associations founded publications for the benefit of their members. The supervisory engagement of the Pharmaceutical Society was clearly seen in its official organ, the *Pharmaceutical Journal*, founded by Jacob Bell in 1841, whereas the commercial side of the trade found its principal voice in the *Chemist and Druggist*. Both reveal an astonishingly extensive and sustained engagement by chemists and druggists with the medicine stamp duty. There is scarcely one weekly edition of either the *Pharmaceutical Journal* or the *Chemist and Druggist* from the time they were established in the middle years of the nineteenth century until the abolition of the medicine stamp duty in 1941 that did not mention the tax, and generally each edition saw dozens of entries. The editors of the *Pharmaceutical Journal* advised their readers as to the law on the medicine stamp duty fully, conscientiously, accurately and regularly.[225] Although the editors of the *Journal* had no sympathy with individuals who deliberately evaded the tax, they published an extensive body of correspondence and replies to thousands of individual queries relating to the tax status of specific preparations. Regular editorials and articles explained the law and its method of implementation by the revenue authorities, separate copies of which the editors were willing to send to any individual asking for information on the tax.[226] A review of the legislation published in 1854

---

[222] 'The Patent Medicine Stamp Acts – Deputation to the Board of Inland Revenue', (1886) 16 *Pharmaceutical Journal* (series 3) 907, 908.

[223] *Ibid.*, 910.

[224] *Ibid.*, 910–11.

[225] See the summary in (1854–55) 14 *Pharmaceutical Journal* (series 1) 146.

[226] See for example 'The Medicine Stamp and Licence Acts', (1851) 11 *Pharmaceutical Journal* (series 1) 197.

was used as a guide by chemists and druggists until nearly the end of the century.[227] This advice and instruction on the tax was given to the reader in the clearest and simplest terms possible. Chemists and druggists frequently sent their labels to the professional journals for their opinion as to liability, but the editors repeatedly stressed that their opinion could not be authoritative and advised direct inquiry to the board itself. On behalf of the members of the society, therefore, the *Pharmaceutical Journal* created a dialogue with the revenue authorities. The 'Legal Queries' published weekly in the *Chemist and Druggist* were almost exclusively on medicine stamp duty matters, and the journal regularly carried a section entitled 'Stamped-medicine Notes'. There were longer articles and editorials on specific aspects of the tax, regular reports of prosecutions for breach of the law, a detailed examination of the history and practice of the duty[228] and extensive reporting and analysis of major judicial decisions such as *Ransom v. Sanguinetti* and *Farmer v. Glyn-Jones*.[229] Furthermore, every year the *Chemist and Druggist* published a Diary entitled 'The Medicine Stamp-Duty Acts. A Concise Exposition of the Law Respecting the Manufacture and Sale of Dutiable Medicines in Great Britain'. It explained the origins of the law, and explained which medicines were liable to duty, when duty was not payable, the grounds of liability, including an analysis of all relevant case law, the exemptions from the duty and communications from the revenue authorities. It was invaluable to the practising chemist and druggist.

This constant professional debate and thread of discussion on the tax so visible in the literature engendered a strong sense of occupational unity, but despite the best efforts of the professional and trade journals to raise awareness of the medicine stamp duty and provide accurate information to their readers about it, many chemists and druggists either did not understand, or wilfully did not adhere to, this guidance. They broke the law and were prosecuted for it by the central tax authorities. The editors had little patience with the ignorance displayed by some chemists and druggists: uncertainty as to the doubtful matters of interpretation was one thing; a lack of awareness of the main features of the legislation was inexcusable. Nevertheless, the level of ignorance and misunderstanding as to the medicine stamp duty was high even in the later years of the nineteenth century; many chemists and druggists were

---

[227] (1854–55) 14 *Pharmaceutical Journal* (series 1) 146.

[228] 'Now and Then', (1904) 64 *Chemist and Druggist* 86, 163, 236.

[229] These two decisions occupied hundreds of pages in both journals throughout the summer of 1903, and it is clear from the retrospective article at Christmas 1903 in the *Chemist and Druggist* how important the year was to chemists as result of the decisions: 'A Glance Back', (1903) 63 *Chemist and Druggist* 1051.

simply unaware that they were in breach of the law.[230] Part of the reason for such ignorance, it was suggested, was the pressure of business leaving insufficient time to study the subject, but the problem lay in the uncertainty of the provisions.[231]

THE STIGMA OF COMMERCE

From the end of the eighteenth century the practice of pharmacy comprised both professional and commercial activity. The professional work of chemists and druggists consisted of dispensing, namely the making up and sale of medicines on the instruction of a physician's prescription. But with their roots in the trade of grocer and the retailing arm of the apothecaries, chemists and druggists had a strongly commercial background. Their business activities consisted of the sale of a wide range of general commodities, more or less connected with pharmacy. Drugs and oils, such as castor and cod liver oil, lozenges, paints and colours for artists, dyes, groceries, mineral and aerated waters, wines and spirits, veterinary medicines and, increasingly, toiletries such as soaps and perfumes were all, by custom, sold by chemists and druggists.[232] By the end of the nineteenth century such sidelines increased considerably, and a very common one was photography. Although it seems that chemists and druggists had relatively little concern with the dutiable proprietary medicines in the early part of the nineteenth century, by the middle of the century intense commercial pressures ensured that they had to supply these commodities and their other sidelines to satisfy their customers and ensure a thriving business. They became major suppliers of hundreds of such medicines, both those that were produced commercially and their own preparations made and retailed under their own names.[233] So chemists and druggists would sell their own rheumatic mixture, cough remedy, liver pills and so on, and some, such as *Phospherine* and *Lamplough's Pyretic Saline*, became household

---

[230] See for example an inquiry to the board in 1860 revealing the belief that liability depended on obtaining a patent for the medicine: TNA IR 40/781.

[231] (1886) 16 *Pharmaceutical Journal* (series 3) 908.

[232] 'On the Professional Character of the Pharmaceutical Chemist' (1842) 2 *Pharmaceutical Journal* (series 1) 1; Hilary Marland, 'The 'Doctor's Shop': The Rise of the Chemist and Druggist in Nineteenth-Century Manufacturing Districts' in Louise Hill Curth (ed.), *From Physic to Pharmacology, Five Hundred Years of British Drug Retailing*, (Aldershot: Ashgate, 2006) 79, 87–8. See Figure 6.

[233] Report and Minutes of Evidence from the Select Committee on the Pharmacy Bill, *House of Commons Parliamentary Papers* (1852) (387) xiii 275 at qq. 2400, 2403 *per* J. R. Cormack, physician; Marland, 'The Doctor's Shop,' 98. Sales rose from £600,000 in 1860 to £5 million in 1914: Holloway, *Royal Pharmaceutical Society*, p. 308.

names. The remarkable breadth and nature of the stock of nineteenth-century pharmacies are revealed by the inventories drawn up on their closure, showing them to be little short of general stores.[234]

The commercial nature of the duties of chemists and druggists came to be embodied in the term 'retail pharmacy', which described the work of most chemists and druggists throughout the nineteenth century and beyond, when they were entirely reliant on their trading activities rather than on dispensing physicians' prescriptions.[235] As a result, they were increasingly and legitimately perceived as traders in medicines, and they well understood that their extensive and more lucrative trade in sidelines and proprietary medicines detracted from the respectability of their pharmaceutical work and indeed obscured it.[236] The trade journals made it clear which trading activities were regarded as profitable and not too damaging to the chemists' somewhat fragile professional image, namely the trade in ready-made spectacles, tea, wine, petroleum-based oils, aerated waters, photographic chemicals, scientific apparatus and homoeopathic pharmacy.[237] Nevertheless this tension between the business and professional sides of the work of pharmacists continued well into the twentieth century, when the need for highly skilled qualified chemists to enter the retail trade, and for it to form such a large part of their work, was regarded as 'a regrettable economic necessity'.[238]

[234] J. K. Crellin, 'Pharmacies as General Stores in the 19th Century', (1979) 9 *Pharmaceutical Historian*, [unpaginated].

[235] For a brief history of retail pharmacy in the nineteenth century, see 'Retail Pharmacy over One Hundred Years', (1941) 146 *Pharmaceutical Journal* (series 4) 130. Note that English chemists and druggists undertook relatively little dispensing work: Holloway, 'The Orthodox Fringe', 154–55; Hunt, 'The Evolution of Pharmacy', 39; John Hunt, '15th January 1913 – The Day Pharmacy in Britain Entered a New Era', (2001) 31 *Pharmaceutical Historian*, 10–12.

[236] Attfield, *The Future Supply of Drugs to the Public*, p. 12. See too 'On the Professional Character of the Pharmaceutical Chemist', (1842) 2 *Pharmaceutical Journal* (series 1) 1; 'How do we Stand? A Brief Review of the Chemists' Position', (1904) 72 *Pharmaceutical Journal* (series 4) 165.

[237] See generally, Peter G. Homan, 'Auxiliary Trades: Added Income for the Pharmacy', (2014) 44(2) *Pharmaceutical Historian*, 32.

[238] Report and Minutes of Evidence from the Select Committee on Medicine Stamp Duties, *House of Commons Parliamentary Papers* (1937) (Cmd. 54) viii 129 at q. 520 *per* H. N. Linstead, Secretary of the Royal Pharmaceutical Society of Great Britain. See too Stephen Wilson, 'Pharmacists Can Be Both Good Businessmen and Good Professional Men', in Paul A. Doyle (ed.), *Readings in Pharmacy* (New York: Interscience Publishers, John Wiley & Sons, 1962), p. 325; Glenn Sonnedecker 'To Be or Not to Be – Professional', (1961) 133 *American Journal of Pharmacy*, 243. American pharmacists faced problems of equal magnitude to their British counterparts, stemming from the tensions between professionalism and commercialism: Robert A. Buerki, 'The Public Image of the American Pharmacist in the Popular Press' (1996) 38 *Pharmacy in History*, 62.

With regard to obtaining professional status, the stigma[239] of commerce was potentially fatal. Retail pharmacy undermined professional status in four specific ways. First, it confirmed chemists and druggists as shop-bound, making their living not by charging for attendance and advice, as physicians, surgeons and, to some degree, apothecaries did, but from selling medicines from their shop and conducting their occupation entirely from there.[240] Certainly regular medical practitioners believed that keeping an open shop would undermine their position and dignity.[241] Second, the sale of proprietary medicines in particular detracted from the respectability of their skilled and responsible pharmaceutical work, partly because such remedies were based on unsound medical knowledge but also because the chemist and druggist would not necessarily know their composition or be able to advise on their use.[242] They merely sold them as a commodity, an activity that undermined the notion of a special skill, which chemists and druggists were so anxious to promote.[243] It was a departure 'from the ideal professional position'.[244]

Third, chemists and druggists were defined by their product and much of that product was commercially dealt in. This connection was of long standing. As Dorothy Porter and Roy Porter observed in the context of the seventeenth century, '[t]he business of medicine should not be seen ... simply as a matter of the sale of skills. For most branches of medicine also dealt more and more in an increasingly significant commodity: drugs'.[245] This was still the case well into the nineteenth century. As the leading surgeon Sir Astley Cooper observed in 1834, a man going to a druggist 'goes to buy drugs, as he goes to a grocer's shop, to buy tea and sugar'.[246] It was clear that chemists and druggists had a direct interest in the quantity of medicines they sold, promoting a commercial morality rather than a professional one in which a strong profit motive was inherent, inevitably giving rise to a suspicion of doubtful ethics, and entailing non-professional customs such as the increasingly important

[239] The term used by Crellin, 'The Growth of Professionalism', 222.
[240] For the prescribing activity of chemists and druggists see Marland, 'Doctor's Shop', 79–104.
[241] 'Editorial', (1840) 33 *The Lancet* 588.
[242] 'On the Professional Character of the Pharmaceutical Chemist', (1842) 2 *Pharmaceutical Journal* (series 1) 1.
[243] Higby, 'Professionalism', 119.
[244] 'Liability to Medicine Stamp Duty', (1903) 71 *Pharmaceutical Journal* (series 4) 200, 202. For a modern expression of such concerns, see Sonnedecker, 'To Be or Not to Be', 243, 249.
[245] Porter and Porter, 'Thomas Corbyn', 279.
[246] Report from the Select Committee on Medical Education with Minutes of Evidence, *House of Commons Parliamentary Papers* (1834) (602) xiii 1 at q. 5584.

practice of advertising.[247] Pharmacists were permitted to advertise, for '[h]e is a shopkeeper and he observes the customs of shopkeepers'.[248] But advertising was understood to be incompatible with professional status, and indeed members of the newly formed Pharmaceutical Society were warned to restrain any display of their membership of the society in public advertisements, especially where those advertisements referred to the general retail side of the work.[249]

Fourth – and most importantly – practising pharmacy primarily as a retail business created and perpetuated a widespread public perception of chemists and druggists as mere traders. This perception was exacerbated by the widespread involvement of such unqualified individuals as grocers, barbers, booksellers, hairdressers, stationers and tobacconists in the sale of proprietary medicines.[250]

These factors combined to obscure the line between general shopkeepers and chemists and druggists, to create a strongly commercial ethos of chemists and druggists, and to construct a public perception of trade rather than the provision of a skilled service. In the 1850s chemists and druggists could even be referred to as 'the drudges of trade'.[251] This perception was shared to varying degrees by the chemists and druggists themselves. 'In pharmacy', observed the president of the British Pharmaceutical Conference in 1883, 'we are on the border line of the commercial and the professional. Pharmacy is partly a trade, partly a profession'.[252] He continued: '[t]rade and profession form the warp and woof of pharmacy, interwoven in every part of the fabric'.[253] 'Pharmacy', wrote a correspondent to the editor of the *Pharmaceutical Journal* in 1878, 'dwells on the border land between professions and trades, partaking ... more or less of the character of both'.[254] Acutely conscious of this ambiguity, chemists and druggists reflected it in their nomenclature.

[247] Frederick Stearns, 'The Pharmaceutist as a Merchant', (1865) *American Journal of Pharmacy* 198; See Marland, 'Doctor's Shop', 96–7, 102.
[248] A. M. Carr-Saunders and P. A. Wilson, *The Professions*, (Oxford: Clarendon Press, 1933), pp. 435–6.
[249] 'On the Professional Character of the Pharmaceutical Chemist', (1842) 2 *Pharmaceutical Journal* (series 1) 1, 5.
[250] They could also dispense medicines, due to the flawed wording of the Pharmacy Act 1868 (31 & 32 Vict. c. 121) s. 1, which allowed such individuals to practise as chemists and druggists as long as they did not use that title, nor sell certain poisons.
[251] Referring to the importance of chemical analysis in combatting cholera and the lack of resources afforded to chemists and druggists to undertake it: 'Letters to the Editor', *The Times*, 17 August 1854, 10.
[252] Attfield, *The Future Supply of Drugs to the Public*, p. 7.
[253] *Ibid.*
[254] 'The Trade Side of Pharmacy', (1878) 8 *Pharmaceutical Journal* (series 3) 882.

They regularly referred to their work as a calling, craft, occupation or trade[255] and themselves as 'respectable and upright tradesmen',[256] as tradesmen and professionals in the same breath and occasionally as 'semi-professional'.[257] Officially too chemists and druggists were consistently referred to as tradesmen in formal government reports and returns,[258] and legislative practice in this regard was particularly revealing. The Apothecaries Act 1815 described the work of chemists and druggists as a 'trade or business',[259] a form of words supplied by the chemists and druggists themselves, and later legislation called it a 'business or calling'.[260] Indeed, the legislature had continued difficulty in classifying chemists and druggists: the problem, which was never resolved, was that pharmacy fell between the professions and commerce, with chemists receiving a high level of scientific training and yet most spending their lives as salesmen.[261]

CONCLUSION

The medicine stamp duty brought chemists and druggists as such into a relationship with the central revenue boards for the first time in their history. A number of factors made it a challenging relationship, but primarily the difficulties were the consequences of the flawed nature of the taxing legislation itself and the absence of the executive will to remedy it. This reveals the apathy of government in taxing matters, an acceptance of the status quo, an abdication by the legislature to the revenue boards of ensuring a tax was workable and a disregard for the inevitable theoretical and legal weaknesses that ensued. In this context, the chemists and druggists were ill-equipped to assert themselves within the fiscal regime. When the medicine stamp duty was first introduced in 1783, chemists and druggists were no more than an occupational group, emergent and unformed. As a fledgling profession, it had no

[255] See for example 'The Future of Pharmacy as a Trade', (1904) 72 *Pharmaceutical Journal* (series 4) 337, 338.
[256] *Journals of the House of Commons*, vol. 85, 4 June 1830, p. 512.
[257] (1886) 16 *Pharmaceutical Journal* (series 3) 908.
[258] See for example, Report and Minutes of Evidence from the Select Committee on the Pharmacy Bill, *House of Commons Parliamentary Papers* (1852) (387) xiii 275 at q. 780 *per* Jacob Bell.
[259] 55 Geo. III c. 194 s. 28.
[260] Pharmacy Act 1852 (15 & 16 Vict. c. 56) s. 8.
[261] 'The Future of Pharmacy' (1942) 239 *The Lancet* 119.

coherent representative body to protect its interests and to assert itself in the face of the power of central government. It had no collective knowledge or expertise in tax matters and – as with all taxpayers in the nineteenth century – could not meet the revenue boards in technical understanding of the law and practice of tax. Chemists and druggists were, in this, even more unequal than most taxpayers.

Paradoxically, the existence and implementation of the medicine stamp duty brought its own solutions. The tax was no minor matter for chemists and druggists. It was a feature of their work that they had to address on a daily basis. It demanded their engagement and constant attention. Proprietary medicines formed an increasingly important part of their business, both those that were clearly within the charge – the ubiquitous commercial remedies – and the preparations they made and sold themselves which business methods and commercial imperatives brought so easily within the charge to tax. They had to be meticulous in their attention to their sale to the public. The reality of unpredictable prosecution with severe financial consequences drew chemists and druggists together as never before. The intractability of the legislation raised the need to build a technical resource outside central government, and the various professional and trade journals strove to provide it. And underlying these developments was the fundamental principle of occupational recognition in formal tax legislation and express protection for regular pharmaceutical practice.

Ultimately, however, despite two positive effects of the tax on the occupational coherence of chemists and druggists – legislative recognition and a catalyst for unity – the most powerful effect of the tax was a negative one. The medicine stamp duty, being unambiguously a tax on a commodity, increased the commercial character of chemists and druggists that was proving the most potent obstacle to full professionalisation, and served to reinforce the general perception of chemists and druggists as mere traders rather than skilled professionals. It highlighted and affirmed the central role of medicine as a commercial commodity. By intensifying the focus on the product rather than the service, and by attaching to all proprietary medicines by whomsoever they were sold – chemist and druggist or general trader[262], the tax contributed to the

---

[262] It will be recalled that the only exception, namely the permission given to qualified chemists and druggists to sell *known, admitted and approved* remedies free of the duty after 1903, was, in its scope, merely an extra-statutory bureaucratic concession introduced to make the tax workable in practice.

public view of pharmacy as – at most – a mere occupation, exacerbated the inherent ambiguity within pharmacy practice[263] and exerted a negative influence on the perceptions of professional status as that social phenomenon was perceived in the Victorian era and, indeed, beyond.[264]

---

[263] This ambiguity continued, and still exists: J. Burnby, 'Pharmacy in the Mid-Nineteenth Century' (1992) 22 *Pharmaceutical Historian*, 3; Wilson, 'Pharmacists', p. 325; Sonnedecker, 'To Be or Not to Be', 243.

[264] Norman K. Denzin and Curtis J. Mettlin, 'Incomplete Professionalization: The Case of Pharmacy' (1968) 46 *Social Forces*, 375.

FIGURE 6 March the Chemist, Market Place, Newark, ca. 1880s. Image courtesy of T. Healey and www.picturethepast.org.uk.

FIGURE 7 Reilly & Co., Pharmaceutical Chemists, Nice, France, 1927.

4

The Tax and the Integrity of Medicines

"Quackery is rampant, and now the poison of quack medicines is spreading desolation around, with a virulence and a fatality not exceeded, probably, by that of the plague or the cholera."[1]

INTRODUCTION

The medicine stamp duty was introduced to raise money for a government in a period of acute financial need. The economic imperatives that drove it, its nature as a fiscal response of the state to the phenomenon of proprietary medicines and the dominant perception of quackery as a thriving commercial enterprise are all revealed by the evidence. Its role in ensuring the integrity of the medicines to which it applied is more complex to discern. The policy of any taxing legislation beyond the simply financial is rarely evident, particularly that of the eighteenth century, because of the strength of orthodox thinking that the purpose of a tax was purely to raise money. That is not to say that other motives were absent, but they were rarely articulated and they emerge, if at all, by close examination of contemporary sources, particularly extra-statutory ones, and educated guesses. This is in contrast to modern taxes, where governments are quite open about using taxation to achieve non-fiscal aims and to shape social and environmental policy. Certainly the deliberate protection of regular medicines from any unintended application of the tax, evidenced by the exemptions and the wording of the charge, suggests it was understood that the imposition of tax on them would have had an undesirable effect and that it was accordingly important to ensure they were unambiguously excluded.[2] A primarily financial

---

[1]   'Editorial', 25 *The Lancet* 948, 12 March 1836.
[2]   The Stamp Commissioners expressly confirmed it in 1785: *Stamp Office: Observations upon the present Medicine Act and Proposals for an Improvement of that Duty*, 21 May 1785: The National Archives (TNA): T1/624/514.

reason for introducing the medicine stamp duty was thus not necessarily the whole story. Lord John Cavendish's description of proprietary medicines as 'very proper objects of taxation'[3] was tantalisingly ambiguous. It could reflect an exclusively financial motive for the tax or, indeed, import a regulatory dimension. After all, the social dangers of proprietary medicines were as evident as the financial exigencies of late-eighteenth-century governments, and the need or desirability of some kind of state regulation was an issue of some moment. Although official expression was muted in the eighteenth century, the government was alive to the evils of the trade in proprietary medicines and had a clear interest in controlling them in the interests of the public. It is possible, therefore, that in levying a tax on proprietary medicines, the government intended to impose some kind of control on a trade it understood was both dangerous and undesirable. Any social policy underlying taxing legislation, however, is rarely self-evident, tempting as it is retrospectively to find a social agenda in a tax imposed on a commodity or activity that is understood to be harmful to a section of the public.

Whatever the intention of the original legislators, the tax was retained for nearly 160 years. Its application to proprietary medicines and the exemption for regular medicines sustained over that long period could have given rise to a number of regulatory effects, no less powerful because they were originally unintended. This chapter addresses two issues in this respect: whether there was any intended regulatory objective at all in the imposition and retention of the tax and whether the tax had any unintended impact on ensuring the quality and integrity of the medicines within the charge.

THE DANGERS OF PROPRIETARY MEDICINES

The trade in proprietary medicines was undoubtedly an attractive proposition as an object of taxation in financially straitened times, but the widespread use of these remedies constituted a considerable hazard to public health. The principal danger arose from the composition of the medicines themselves. Many were merely benign, useless and unpleasant, containing harmless substances, or ingredients such as bread, brick dust or sheep dung,[4] but many were highly dangerous. From the middle of the eighteenth century there were

---

3   *Parliamentary Register 1780–1796*, vol. 10, 26 May 1783, p. 71.
4   James Makittrick Adair, 'Essay on Empiricism, or Quackery', *Medical Cautions for the Consideration of Invalids* (Bath: R. Cruttwell, 1786), p. 141.

bitter attacks on quacks by regular practitioners of orthodox medicine in the course of which the dangerous nature of some proprietary remedies and the deception of patients were revealed.[5] It was a real concern, and not entirely a self-interested one, that the practice of self-medication with proprietary medicines bypassed the regular medical professions, and, therefore, the safeguards of medical training and experience. The medicines were sold to the general public with no individual consultation with a trained practitioner, were easily available and were affordable. As Francis Spilsbury observed, they were 'unwholesome medicines, unskilfully applied, and administered merely to extort a few shillings'.[6] Furthermore, many of these medicines were increasingly perceived as morally undesirable. Quite apart from the medicines thinly disguised as abortifacients,[7] those who sold medicines with exaggerated claims to cure diseases that were at that time invariably fatal preyed on the gullibility of the ignorant, the foolish, the worried and the despairing.

Even rudimentary analysis in the eighteenth century showed that many proprietary medicines contained powerful and often harmful ingredients in unregulated amounts and concentrations. Mercury and antimony, the most common mineral constituents of both regular and proprietary medicines, were toxic, yet routinely used.[8] Mercury was the favoured remedy for venereal disease and antimony was employed to reduce fevers, as in the famous *Dr James's Fever Powder*. It is believed that such popular febrifuge powders may well have been responsible for the deaths of Oliver Goldsmith and Laurence Sterne.[9] When *The Lancet* exposed the composition of a number of proprietary medicines in 1823, it revealed that Spilsbury's *Antiscorbutic Drops* consisted of '[c]orrosive sublimate, gentian root, dried orange-peel, of each two drachms; crude antimony, red saunders, of each one drachm; rectified spirits of wine, water, of each eight ounces'.[10] Furthermore, proprietary medicines

---

[5] See for example the dispute between John Coakley Lettsom and Theodor Myersbach discussed by Roy Porter: Roy Porter, *Quacks* (Stroud: Tempus Publishing Ltd, 2000), pp. 180–92.

[6] Francis Spilsbury, *Discursory Thoughts Disputing the Construction of His Majesty's Hon. Commissioners and Crown Lawyers, relative to the Medicine and Horse Acts…with Remarks on the Late Trials Concerning the Medicine Act*, 2nd edn, (London; Dispensary, Soho Square, 1785), p. 2.

[7] As where a handbill would state '[p]regnant women must not take more at a dose than five drops, as a greater quantity will infallibly procure abortion'. These were condemned as 'wickedness in the extreme': *Gazetteer and New Daily Advertiser*, January 31, 1784.

[8] *St James's Chronicle* or the *British Evening-Post*, 25–27 November 1784. See generally R. I. McCallum, *Antimony in Medical History: An Account of the Medical Uses of Antimony and Its Compounds Since Early Times to the Present* (Edinburgh: Pentland Press 1999).

[9] Porter, *Quacks*, p. 21.

[10] 'Compositions of Quack Medicines', (1823) 1 *The Lancet* 30. See too Peter Isaac, 'Charles Elliot and Spilsbury's Antiscorbutic Drops' (1997) 27 *Pharmaceutical Historian* 47.

often contained alcohol and opium, routinely used as analgesics and sedatives and bringing with them the very real dangers of addiction.[11] *Daffy's Elixir*, for example, contained predominantly alcohol. *Godfrey's Cordial* contained opium, as did *Dalby's Carminative*, a preparation to soothe gripe and stomach ailments in infants.

The nineteenth century saw a rising number of deaths, intentional, as in murder or suicide, accidental or negligent, caused by the easy accessibility of toxic proprietary medicines and poisons. The dangers of such preparations were widely publicised in the professional press from the early nineteenth century, a typical early example being an article entitled 'Inflammation of the Bowels Caused by Morison's Pills', which appeared in 1836.[12] The principal concern was with regard to proprietary medicines containing poisons, and the substantial increase in deaths from poisons in the middle years of the nineteenth century ultimately led to their statutory control.[13] The Pharmacy Act 1868[14] regulated the sale of some twenty common poisons, including opium and strychnine, to the public, by providing that only registered pharmaceutical chemists or chemists and druggists could sell them, and then only in certain circumstances under special regulations, notably that the bottles should be clearly labelled to indicate poison and that purchasers should sign the Poisons Book.[15] Section 16 of the Act, however, expressly provided that nothing in the statute should 'extend to or interfere with ... the making or dealings in patent medicines'.[16] This provision had been enacted

[11] (1734) 4 *Gentleman's Magazine* 616–18.
[12] 'Inflammation of the Bowels Caused by Morison's Pills', (1836) 26 *The Lancet* 109; 'Cooling Powders', (1897) 150 *The Lancet* 235
[13] See generally, Gordon E. Appelbe, 'From Arsenic to Thalidomide: A Brief History of Medicine Safety', in Stuart Anderson (ed.), *Making Medicines* (London: Pharmaceutical Press 2005), p. 243; Stuart Anderson, 'From "Bespoke" to "Off-the-Peg": Community Pharmacists and the Retailing of Medicines in Great Britain 1900–1970', in Louise Hill Curth (ed.), *From Physick to Pharmacology: Five Hundred Years of British Drug Retailing*, (Aldershot: Ashgate, 2006), p. 105 at pp. 108–10; Michael H. Jepson, 'From Secret Remedies to Prescription Medicines: A Brief History of Medicine Quality', in Stuart Anderson (ed.), *Making Medicines* (London: Pharmaceutical Press 2005), p. 223; Ernst W. Stieb, 'Drug Control in Britain, 1850–1914', in Blake (ed.), *Safeguarding the Public*, pp. 15–26; Stuart Anderson, 'Drug Regulation and the Welfare State', in Virginia Berridge and Kelly Loughlin (eds.), *Medicine, the Market and the Mass Media* (Abingdon: Routledge, 2005), pp. 193–217.
[14] 31 & 32 Vict. c. 121.
[15] Regulation of dangerous substances continued into the twentieth century with the Poisons and Pharmacy Act 1908 (8 Edw. VII c. 55) and the Dangerous Drugs Act 1920 (10 & 11 Geo. V c. 46) marking the beginning of more general medical regulation of medicines by means of prescriptions. The Pharmacy and Poisons Act 1933 (23 & 24 Geo. V c. 25) listed a number of poisons that could be sold only under prescription.
[16] Pharmacy Act 1868 (31 & 32 Vict. c. 121) s. 16.

to protect the interests of medicine manufacturers and vendors, but, as the member of Parliament for Bridport, Charles Warton, warned the House of Commons in 1882, governments 'ought to be jealous of vested interests affecting the public health'.[17] It enabled proprietary medicines containing poisons to be widely sold by unqualified grocers or in general stores, without the protection afforded other poisons under the Act.[18] So 'anyone could, by putting a Government stamp on the bottle, sell any farrago of poisonous stuff'.[19] The provision was particularly concerning because vendors adopted the popular usage of the phrase 'patent medicines' to mean any proprietary medicine. Had the term been given its legal meaning, namely medicines holding a valid legal patent, the exemption would have been of such limited effect that it would have been virtually nugatory. Furthermore, the unqualified vendors' perception of the medicine stamp went further than merely thinking that 'patent' meant 'proprietary'; many believed that the presence of the stamp and the official approval perceived to be inherent in it gave the medicines the character of formally patented medicines. Although the leading writer on the medicine stamp duty believed that sales of poisons circumventing the controls of the 1868 Act by bearing a medicine stamp were rare and limited to the Fens, where the taking of laudanum was common, it seems that the practice was widespread.[20] Medicines such as *Hunter's Solution of Chloral*, containing a very strong amount of chloral, *Kay's Compound Essence of Linseed*, containing a large quantity of morphia, *Holt's Specific for Whooping Cough* containing antimony,[21] *Indian Tincture* containing methylated spirits and *Bromidia* containing Indian hemp, bromide of potassium, sodium bromide and chloral hydrate, were sold with no indication on the bottle that they contained poison and by unqualified individuals who simply possessed a licence.[22]

[17] *Parliamentary Debates* [hereafter *Parl. Deb.*], vol. 269, ser 3, col. 596, 12 May 1882 (HC). He brought in a patent medicines bill in 1882 in an unsuccessful attempt to restrict the sale of such medicines.
[18] 'The Sale of Patent Medicines containing Poison', (1880) 10 *Pharmaceutical Journal* (series 3), 919; 'The Sale of Poison in the Form of Patent Medicines' Poison', (1881) 12 *Pharmaceutical Journal* (series 3), 319; 'The Sale of Poisons as Patent Medicines', (1882) 12 *Pharmaceutical Journal* (series 3), 841.
[19] *Parl. Deb.*, vol. 286, ser 3, col. 804, 26 March 1884 (HC) *per* Dr Farquharson.
[20] E. N. Alpe, *Handy Book of Medicine Stamp Duty*, (London: Offices of 'The Chemist and Druggist', ca. 1888), p. 21.
[21] A seven-month-old baby died after treatment with *Holt's Specific for Whooping Cough*, and the coroner found that death was accelerated by the antimony contained in the mixture: 'Poisoning by a Patent Medicine', (1884) 14 *Pharmaceutical Journal* (series 3) 539.
[22] 'Poisonous Proprietary Medicines', (1902) 159 *The Lancet* 1268.

Such proprietary medicines were known to be causing injury and death.[23] The professional journals abounded with reports of coroners' inquests into deaths, often of children, through taking proprietary medicines. The extraordinary effectiveness of opiates to relieve severe pain, and their soothing effect on a sufferer's mood, made opium a popular ingredient of proprietary medicines.[24] A four-year-old child died after being given *Budden's Compound Balsam of Horehound* for whooping cough, and the cause of death was inflammation of the lung probably accelerated by narcotic poisoning.[25] Another child was given *Kay's Compound Essence of Linseed* for a cough and died the following day of opium poisoning,[26] and a four-month-old baby died after ingesting a dose of a 'soothing syrup' for a cough; the cause of death was given as narcotic poisoning from the morphia in the medicine.[27] In the mid-nineteenth century there developed a fashion for the use of *Chlorodyne*, a medicine containing principally morphine and chloroform used to treat cholera and diarrhoea and also taken for sleeplessness, which was notorious in professional medical circles. There were a number of *Chlorodynes* on the market, but the most famous was that of the original inventor, Dr John Collis Browne.[28] It was responsible for a large number of deaths, from accidental or deliberate overdose, and these were regularly reported.[29] For example, the *Pharmaceutical Journal* reported the finding of a Gloucestershire coroner's inquest that the death of an elderly woman was due to her having ingested ten drops of *Dr Collis Browne's Chlorodyne*.[30]

In 1882 Charles Warton led a vigorous but unsuccessful parliamentary campaign to have the legislation amended to restrict the sale of proprietary medicines containing poisons.[31] His private member's bill of 1884 failed when the

[23]   *Parl. Deb.*, vol. 269, ser 3, col. 598, 12 May 1882 (HC); *ibid.*, vol. 284, col. 176, 7 February 1884; *ibid.*, vol. 286, cols. 801–5, 26 March 1884.
[24]   See generally, Virginia Berridge, *Opium and the People: Opiate Use and Drug Control Policy in Nineteenth and Early Twentieth Century England*, (London: Free Association Books, 1999).
[25]   'Alleged Acceleration of the Death of a Child by a Patent Medicine', (1881) 12 *Pharmaceutical Journal* (series 3) 532.
[26]   'Alleged Poisoning by a Proprietary Medicine', (1872) 2 *Pharmaceutical Journal* (series 3) 837.
[27]   'The Sale of Patent Medicines containing Poisons', (1882) 13 *Pharmaceutical Journal* (series 3) 339.
[28]   Henri C. Silberman, 'The Many Aspects of Chlorodyne' (2006) 36 *Pharmaceutical Historian*, 27; 'Is Chlorodyne Subject to a Medicine Stamp?', (1866) 7 *Pharmaceutical Journal* (series 2) 385.
[29]   'The Sale of Patent Medicines containing Poison', (1880) 10 *Pharmaceutical Journal* (series 3) 919; 'Death from an Overdose of Chlorodyne', (1884) 14 *Pharmaceutical Journal* (series 3) 735.
[30]   (1865) 6 *Pharmaceutical Journal* (series 2) 39; 'Chlorodyne', (1892) 139 *The Lancet* 1042; 'Proprietary Medicines' (1892) 140 *The Lancet* 1411.
[31]   *Parl. Deb.*, vol. 269, ser 3, col. 595, 12 May 1882 (HC); *ibid.*, vol. 286, cols. 801–4, 26 March 1884; *ibid.*, vol. 290, cols. 968–71, 14 July 1884.

vested interests of the trade proved too strong and the government deemed
the bill unworkable. The problem was ultimately overcome by a number of
judicial decisions in which the statutory language was given its correct meaning.[32] It was held in the case of *Pharmaceutical Society* v. *Piper* in 1893 that
the expression 'patent medicine' in section 16 of the Pharmacy and Poisons
Act 1868 meant a medicine protected by formal letters patent, and not merely
a medicine subject to the tax popularly called the patent medicine duty.[33]
And in *Pharmaceutical Society* v. *Fox* in 1896 the court held that the patent
had to be in force for the medicine to come within the exemption in section
16.[34] Thereafter it was settled that the only medicines containing poison that
unqualified persons were permitted to sell were those subject to a valid patent.

Although the physical dangers of proprietary medicines were known in the
early nineteenth century,[35] they were only fully understood and demonstrated
with the development of scientific analysis from the early twentieth century.
The British Medical Association arranged for expert analysis of many of the
most common proprietary medicines representing the whole range of preparations from those fraudulently claiming to cure the most serious diseases to
ordinary domestic remedies. It published the results in two celebrated volumes, *Secret Remedies: What They Cost and What They Contain* and *More
Secret Remedies*, the first volume appearing in 1909.[36] It was found that most
proprietary medicines were directed towards diseases that were common and
serious enough to cause very real suffering. The medicines were classified
according to the ailment they sought to cure. The analysis was 'tedious and
often difficult',[37] but was undertaken with painstaking care by a skilled analytical chemist. Catarrh and cold cures were the cheapest remedies, but constituted a good example of 'barefaced pretensions in which nostrum-mongers
indulge'.[38] *Dr Lane's Catarrh Cure* was shown to consist of carbolic acid and
common salt in solution, sold at the price of one shilling. Its accompanying
literature portrayed catarrh as a serious, indeed potentially fatal, chronic condition causing consumption, and promised a complete cure. Coughs were

[32] That there was a distinction between patent and proprietary medicines had been clear within
the legislation since the Sale of Food and Drugs Act 1875 (38 & 39 Vict. c.63) s.6(2) expressly
distinguished the two.
[33] *Pharmaceutical Society* v. *Piper & Co.* [1893] 1 QB 686,691, 697–99.
[34] *Pharmaceutical Society* v. *Fox* (1896) 12 TLR 471.
[35] See for example, 'Compositions of Quack Medicines', (1823) 1 *The Lancet* 30, 62, 89, 138.
[36] British Medical Association, *Secret Remedies: What They Cost and What They Contain*,
(London: British Medical Association, 1909).
[37] *Ibid.*, p. v.
[38] *Ibid.*, p. vi and pp. 1–9.

among the most common ailments treated without medical advice through proprietary medicines.[39] Although the British Medical Association considered cough treatment to be a legitimate use of such medicines, most were mainly sugar, alcohol and chloroform, and some contained morphine. *Beecham's Cough Pills* stated on an accompanying circular that they did not contain opium, but analysis showed that they contained morphine. *Owbridge's Lung Tonic* was found to contain chloroform, alcohol, honey and oils of aniseed and peppermint, whereas *Veno's Lightning Cough Cure* contained glycerine, alcohol and a trace of chloroform. All the cough and cold remedies were sold with guarantees of safe, speedy and effective cure for all manner of respiratory diseases from colds to asthma and, in some cases, consumption.

Sales of headache powders were huge, and one of the most celebrated was *Daisy Powders*. The association's analysis showed that the powders consisted of acetanilide alone, and as a single unmixed drug it was not liable to stamp duty.[40] Nearly all headache powders, despite each claiming a unique cure, contained acetanilide or phenacetin, or both.

Blood purifiers such as *Clarke's World-Famed Blood Mixture* and *Harvey's Blood Pills* claimed to cure the widest range of diseases, including cancer, syphilis, rheumatism, ringworm and skin diseases of every description.[41] Most were found to contain principally potassium iodide, although one – *Munyon's Blood Curb* – contained only sugar. Medicines for the cure or relief of rheumatism, gout and sciatica, such as *Baring Gould's Anti-Rheumatic Pearls* and *Oquit* almost invariably consisted of aspirin.[42] Kidney medicines such as *Bodd's Kidney Pills* were usually composed of potassium nitrate,[43] although *Munyon's Kidney Cure*, like its *Blood Curb*, contained only sugar. The contents of a bottle of *Munyon's Kidney Cure* were calculated to cost one thirty-fifth of a penny. Remedies for piles (haemorrhoids) included substances commonly used by the medical profession, but some, such as *Muco-Food Cones*, were found to consist of flour and cocoa butter.[44]

Obesity cures were very popular.[45] Lemons and seaweed were commonly believed to promote weight loss, and accordingly remedies such as *Antipon* and *Russell's Anti-Corpulent Preparation* were composed of citric acid and *Hargreave's Reducing Wafers* contained bladderwrack. These were harmless if

---

[39] *Ibid.*, pp. 9–20.
[40] *Ibid.*, p. 37 and pp. 37–42.
[41] *Ibid.*, pp. 42–60.
[42] *Ibid.*, pp. 54–65.
[43] *Ibid.*, pp. 65–75.
[44] *Ibid.*, p. 148.
[45] *Ibid.*, pp. 83–104.

exploitatively priced. One of the most popular cures for baldness, *Capsuloids*, was found to consist of dried haemoglobin.[46] Proprietary remedies for skin diseases were among the most widely advertised but consisted essentially of a treatment of soap and ointment composed of the simplest ingredients.[47] Cures for deafness consisted principally of some form of fat or oil – paraffin, beeswax or Vaseline, for example.[48] As for eye diseases, the famous *Singleton's Eye Ointment* consisted principally of red mercuric oxide in a fatty base, and the British Medical Association said that the manufacturer's assertion that the ointment required 'great skill in the making' was 'absurd'.[49] It put the cost of the ingredients in a pot at one ninth of a penny while the medicine was being sold at two shillings a pot.

Most concerning were medicines sold as cures for such incurable diseases as consumption, diabetes and cancer.[50] *Congreve's Balsamic Elixir* claimed to cure consumption but was found to contain primarily coloured alcohol; *Dill's Diabetic Mixture* contained alcohol, sodium bicarbonate and extract of hydrastia, which the medical profession knew had no effect whatever on diabetes. Cures for cancer were either taken internally and consisted of alcohol or even dye, or were caustic in nature and applied externally. The latter were entirely ineffective in addressing the disease and produced excruciating pain in the patient.

As late as 1909 'Cure-Alls' – remedies for a wide and unconnected range of diseases – were still popular proprietary medicines.[51] The famous *Pink Pills for Pale People* were sold for the cure of rheumatism, skin diseases, sciatica and dyspepsia, and were found to contain primarily ferrous sulphate.[52] They retailed at just under three shillings for a box of thirty pills, but the cost of the ingredients was estimated at one-tenth of a penny. *Beecham's Pills*, advertised for the cure of dozens of diseases of the skin, stomach and nerves, consisted of aloes, ginger and soap, ingredients that cost half a farthing and yet the pills were sold at more than one shilling a box.

The dangers of proprietary medicines were compounded by their widespread sale by unqualified vendors. The practice of pharmacy was a highly skilled and responsible occupation and a measure of control over the quality

[46] *Ibid.*, pp. 114–5.
[47] *Ibid.*, pp. 105–13.
[48] *Ibid.*, pp. 134–41.
[49] *Ibid.*, p. 143.
[50] *Ibid.*, pp. 20–36, 76–82, 117–23.
[51] *Ibid.*, pp. 170–81.
[52] See Peter G. Homan, Briony Hudson, Raymond C. Rowe, *Popular Medicines*, (London: Pharmaceutical Press, 2008), p. 137.

of medicines was inherent in the concept of a professional pharmaceutical practice, with chemists and druggists responsible for compounding and dispensing medicines and acutely aware of the dangers of inferior or debased medicines. In England, as in the United States,[53] a measure of quality control was inherent in the founding of professional pharmaceutical associations, but this was essentially voluntary control by chemists and druggists rather than any kind of mandatory regulation. Unqualified individuals practising as chemists and druggists, unable to judge the quality of the medicines and drugs they purchased wholesale, resulted in inferior products in the market. For example, scammony sold as such could contain only a little of the drug, the rest adulterated with chalk, starch or gum, and yet be undetected by many professing to be chemists and druggists.[54] Education was thus a key element in ensuring that medicines provided to the public were wholesome and safe, and the public good was a motive of equal importance to any desire to raise the status of practitioners when the Pharmaceutical Society was formed in 1841. It was a widely held belief. In 1852 a London chemist and druggist believed that the lack of formal education of most chemists and druggists resulted in inferior medicines being dispensed and sold to the public.[55] He believed that compulsory education and examination of all individuals dispensing or selling medicines, the inspection of drugs dispensed and the prohibition of patent medicines would go a long way towards ensuring the wholesomeness of medicines; he appreciated that it was a matter fraught with difficulties. In the same year a wholesale druggist said that compulsory education and the regulation of chemists and druggists would be far more effective in ensuring the quality of medicines dispensed and sold to the public than government intervention,[56] a view still maintained some thirty years later by the president of the British Pharmaceutical Conference, John Attfield.[57]

---

53 Glenn Sonnedecker, 'Contribution of the Pharmaceutical Profession Toward Controlling the Quality of Drugs in the Nineteenth Century', in John B. Blake (ed), *Safeguarding the Public, Historical Aspects of Medicinal Drug Control* (Baltimore, Md: John Hopkins Press, 1970), pp. 97–100.

54 Report and Minutes of Evidence from the Select Committee on the Pharmacy Bill, *House of Commons Parliamentary Papers* (1852) (387) xiii 275 at qq. 829–41 *per* Thomas Herring, wholesale druggist.

55 *Ibid.*, qq. 589–90 *per* John Savory.

56 *Ibid.*, q. 919 *per* Thomas Herring.

57 John Attfield, *Introductory Address: The Relation of Pharmacy to the State, Delivered to the British Pharmaceutical Conference 19th Annual Meeting, Southampton, 1882* (LSE Selected Pamphlets, 1882).

REGULATORY OBJECTIVES

Despite the known problems with proprietary medicines in Britain at the turn of the eighteenth century, the trade operated outside any formal regulatory regime. Proprietary medicines could contain noxious, addictive, potent or useless ingredients, could be sold by anyone anywhere and members of the public were no nearer being informed as to the nature of the substances they were taking. Even thereafter, statutory regulation of poisons was only partially effective. The absence in England of official control of the manufacture, advertisement and sale of proprietary medicines, even with the most outrageous and unlikely claims, was in striking contrast to other European states, which adopted a far more serious and systematic regulatory approach to such medicines. In France, for example, where, it was said, 'quackery prevails more, if possible, than in [Britain]',[58] the necessity for the legal control of the quality of proprietary medicines to protect the health of the public was fully appreciated throughout the eighteenth and nineteenth centuries.[59] Although the French faced the same difficulty as their British counterparts in attempting to suppress a trade that was so strongly supported by public credulity,[60] successive governments were committed to imposing some legal control on it. Showing a sustained desire to arrive at an effective solution, they constructed a framework of legal regulation.[61] In the eighteenth century they introduced a system of retail control along similar lines to the licence element of the British medicine stamp duty, providing that only apothecaries or licensed individuals could sell proprietary medicines, and enforced this by financial penalties. There was also an attempt at a complete ban on the sale of proprietary medicines by any person in 1790, and in 1803 the Law of Germinal banned their sale by pharmacists or by any person from public stages, and on their advertisement in print. Quality control was attempted by the establishment of an expert commission composed of physicians, surgeons

---

[58] *London Chronicle*, 27–30 September 1783.
[59] Makittrick Adair, 'Essay', pp. 139–40.
[60] Dr Faligot, *La question des Remèdes Secrets sous la Révolution et l'Empire* (Paris: Occitania, 1924) p. 155. For a comprehensive account of unqualified medical practitioners in France in the eighteenth and early nineteenth centuries, see Matthew Ramsey, *Professional and Popular Medicine in France 1770–1830* (Cambridge: Cambridge University Press, 1988).
[61] See generally Matthew Ramsey, 'Traditional Medicine and Medical Enlightenment: The Regulation of Secret Remedies in the Ancien Régime', in Jean-Pierre Goubert (ed.), *La Médicalisation de La Société Francaise 1770–1830* (Waterloo, Ontario: Historical Reflections Press, 1982), p.215–32; Matthew Ramsey, 'Property Rights and the Right to Health: The Regulation of Secret Remedies in France, 1789–1815' in W. F. Bynum and Roy Porter (eds.) *Medical Fringe and Medical Orthodoxy 1750–1850* (London: Croom Helm, 1987), pp. 87–9.

and apothecaries impartially to analyse licensed proprietary medicines and recommend their authorisation or prohibition according to their quality, safety and effectiveness.[62] Beneficial remedies were approved and authorisation given, although very sparingly, dangerous ones were prohibited and medicines of uncertain value were subjected to closer analysis and, if nontoxic, clinical trial. Such a body existed in some form throughout the eighteenth century and into the nineteenth. In 1810 all remedies found on analysis to be useful and beneficial were published to spread knowledge of their efficacy, and all others banned.[63]

This combination of retail and quality control formed the basis of the regulation of proprietary medicines in France until well into the twentieth century.[64] Its effect was to permit the sale of a number of classes of medicines including those prepared according to a physician's prescription, those found in the formularies of the faculties of medicine, those purchased by the government and those approved by various official medical commissions.[65] But although in the 1830s quacks selling their nostrums could be, and were, fined by the police,[66] and the regulations had a material effect on the British export trade in proprietary medicines,[67] it was clear that the French regulatory framework was of limited effectiveness and that the trade remained as robust as it was in Britain. It has been argued that the reason for the failure of the system lay in the potency of private property rights that ultimately dominated over concerns of professional regulation or public health,[68] in multiple possible avenues of authorisation, a want of strict enforcement and a widespread evasion of the law or claims to exemption. 'In the end', observed Professor Ramsey, 'the French continued to draw a chaste veil over trade secrets in medicine'.[69] Nevertheless the French system demonstrated a serious commitment of the state to regulate proprietary medicines in the public interest, and the French never abandoned the principle enshrined in legislation that proprietary remedies were to be submitted to an expert medical body for analysis and evaluation, and

---

[62] For specific examples of the process, see Ramsey, 'Traditional Medicine', pp. 220–31.

[63] For the work of the 1810 commission, see Ramsey, 'Property Rights' pp. 92–100; Matthew Ramsey, 'Academic Medicine and Medical Industrialism: The Regulation of Secret Remedies in Nineteenth-Century France', in Ann La Berge and Mordechai Feingold (eds.), *French Medical Culture in the Nineteenth Century* (Amsterdam; Atlanta: Rodolpi, 1994), pp. 32–3.

[64] Faligot, *Remèdes Secrets*, pp. 154–5.

[65] Ramsey, 'Academic Medicine', pp. 31–2.

[66] (1833) 20 *The Lancet* 87.

[67] *Ibid.*

[68] Ramsey, 'Property Rights' pp. 79–105.

[69] *Ibid.*, p. 100. See too Alex Berman 'Drug Control in Nineteenth-Century France: Antecedents and Directions', in Blake (ed), *Safeguarding the Public*, p. 3.

that those bodies applied the highest medical and pharmaceutical standards before they would officially approve them.[70]

In Britain, when the danger to the public health of the unregulated consumption of proprietary medicines was appreciated to some degree from the end of the eighteenth century,[71] critics were aware that most foreign legislatures had enacted penal laws for their suppression. A genuine desire to protect the public from unscrupulous vendors of harmful medicines combined with the power of vested interests to create a denigration of these medicines and a demand for some form of official regulation along the lines of that found in the rest of Europe. In 1783 the British press praised the French king's action in giving authority to the Royal Society of Medicine in Paris to examine all proprietary medicines and to authorise or ban them, as 'a very salutary measure'.[72] Regulation along French lines, it was said, would 'prevent the unhappy effects of the credulity of the people'.[73] And writing in the late 1790s, James Makittrick Adair, a regular practitioner, compared the English legislature unfavourably with that in France and condemned the absence of state regulation of quackery.[74]

The most insistent voice calling for formal regulation of proprietary medicines was that of the regular medical profession, namely physicians, surgeons and apothecaries. A movement addressing the whole question of unqualified medical practice, professional training, recognition, status and regulation began in the early nineteenth century, and was ultimately successful in securing a reformed, exclusive, regulated and ethically based medical profession.[75] Proprietary medicines formed a central issue because regular practitioners saw the growing culture of self-medication as a threat to their professional status and interests. The public predilection for taking pills for any and every ailment remained as strong in the mid-nineteenth century as it was at the end of the eighteenth. 'Englishmen', a surgeon wrote in 1847, 'are a pill-taking people' who, 'with a courage peculiar to themselves, bolt more drugs, mineral and vegetable, than the rest of the world beside'.[76] Because the regular medical profession regarded many of these preparations as harmful or even lethal,

---

[70] Ramsey, 'Academic Medicine', pp. 25–78.
[71] *St James's Chronicle* or *British Evening-Post*, 25–27 November 1784. See generally Porter, *Quacks*, pp. 193–206.
[72] *London Chronicle*, 27–30 September 1783.
[73] *Ibid.*
[74] Adair, 'Essay', p. 142.
[75] 'Editorial', (1836) 25 *The Lancet* 976, 978.
[76] Frederick Smith Garlick, 'Letters to the Editor: On the Mischief of the Self-Administration of Medicines,' (1847) 49 *The Lancet* 291.

they perceived the purchasing public as lacking common sense and discernment. The commercial nature of the trade, coupled with a complete absence of any requirement for scientific education or training in their manufacture or sale, was anathema to them. The regular practitioners attacked the quacks for their ignorance, their deceit and the harm they caused. The campaign against proprietary medicines was expressed through articles and letters in the professional journals, notably in *The Lancet*, and in the 1830s an Anti-Medical Quackery Society was established with the aim of the 'total suppression of the sale of stamped, patent, and secret medicines'.[77] The quacks defended their medicines as being based on practical experience, proven efficacy and an invaluable source of innovative treatment[78] and, furthermore, one that was easily accessible to the public and provided in a useable form. It was, in short, a public service.

The reactions of members of the regular medical professions to the medicine stamp duty as an instrument of regulation are revealing. By its very existence the demand for formal regulation of proprietary medicines suggested that the regular medical profession did not regard the medicine stamp duty as an instrument of social control, or certainly not a credible one. James Makittrick Adair doubted the wisdom and efficacy of Britain's decision merely to tax, reflecting the contemporary understanding of tax in its traditional sense of an instrument of government finance and suggesting a perception of tax as, at best, a poor alternative to legal sanction.[79] Another physician writing in 1852 condemned the evil of the sale of proprietary medicines saying that he would prevent it 'by every means in the power of the Legislature'[80] – a comment clearly envisaging a complete ban on such articles. Despite a significant demand for formal regulation of proprietary medicines in the late eighteenth and early nineteenth centuries, and a pervasive culture of intense quackery equal to that seen in the rest of Europe, Britain did not follow the lead of her continental counterparts and did not attempt to regulate medicines in an overtly legalistic way. There were two principal and powerful reasons for this.

---

[77] 'Editorial', (1836) 25 *The Lancet* 949; *ibid.*, 976. See Michael Brown, 'Medicine, Quackery and the Free Market:The 'War' against Morison's Pills and the Construction of the Medical Profession, c. 1830- c.1850', in Mark S. R. Jenner and Patrick Wallis (eds.), *Medicine and the Market in England and Its Colonies, c.1450-c.1850* (Basingstoke: Palgrave Macmillan, 2007), p. 238.

[78] Which it was: quacks discovered inoculation and the benefits of using mercury, antimony, opium and the bark: Porter, *Quacks*, p. 21.

[79] Adair, 'Essay', p. 142.

[80] Report and Minutes of Evidence from the Select Committee on the Pharmacy Bill, *House of Commons Parliamentary Papers* (1852) (387) xiii 275 at q. 2206 *per* G. Webster.

The first was professional. Orthodox regulation through penal laws administered by the regular medical professional bodies had already been tried but had failed.[81] The British professional structure was weak, divided, complex, uncoordinated and confused prior to the mid-nineteenth century. There existed a number of bodies that could licence various branches of medical practice in certain areas, namely the professional medical bodies of physicians, surgeons and apothecaries, the universities, the Archbishop of Canterbury and the Crown,[82] but all attempts had been rendered essentially ineffective.[83] The reasons lay in exemptions and a rigid demarcation between the three traditional branches of medical practice which they were determined to maintain. Vested interests, bribery, apathy, inconsistency and practical problems of enforcement against the unqualified practitioners left them free to exercise their trade, unhampered by the professional medical bodies. France too suffered from a multiplicity of authorising bodies in its professional control of the quality of proprietary medicines, but its system was sufficiently robust to transcend these divided powers. In Britain, the lack of any powerful and effective corporate control of the medical profession that could implement state regulation of proprietary medicines allowed the proliferation of proprietary medicines, and was largely responsible for the extent of the trade that made it so attractive as an object of taxation to successive governments.

The second reason for the lack of legal control of proprietary medicines was political. The theory of mercantilism, which had dominated economic thinking for the past 200 years and promoted the increase in national wealth by means of the governmental regulation of its trade, was giving way to laissez-faire in the late eighteenth century. And when in the early nineteenth century laissez-faire came to dominate economic and political thought, as epitomised by Adam Smith, regulation became politically unacceptable. The importance of trade and commerce was recognised, but prevailing theories believed that they were best promoted through the operation of market forces rather than proactive state regulation. Free trade principles were thus applied in their full vigour to all aspects of medical practice.[84] A suggestion in 1876

[81]   For the limitations of regulation of medical practice in England in the seventeenth and eighteenth centuries, see Porter, *Quacks*, pp. 34–9.
[82]   Matthew Ramsey, 'The Politics of Professional Monopoly in Nineteenth-Century Medicine: The French Model and Its Rivals', in Gerald L. Geison (ed.), *Professions and the French State, 1700–1900* (Philadelphia: University of Pennsylvania Press, 1984), pp. 245–6.
[83]   See generally, Sir George Clark, *A History of the Royal College of Physicians*, 2 vols. (Oxford: Clarendon Press, 1964); Leslie G. Matthews, 'Licensed Mountebanks in Britain', (1964) 19 *Journal of the History of Medicine* 34–6; 40–1.
[84]   David L. Cowen, 'Liberty, Laissez-faire and Licensure in Nineteenth Century Britain', (1969) 43 *Bulletin of the History of Medicine* 30.

that the safety of proprietary medicines be decided by a board of chemists and analysts, paid for by the revenue authorities, with potentially dangerous medicines to be registered at the point of sale and sold only by qualified chemists and druggists, was understood to be impossible in view of Britain's free trade policies.[85] Also, although proprietary medicines caused concern to the government in terms of the public health, medical science was not sufficiently advanced to prove that they were a threat to the public. Moreover, until the evil of proprietary medicines was sufficiently widely appreciated to counterbalance their undoubted attractiveness in terms of effectiveness, accessibility and anonymity, the quacks themselves would not be perceived as a sufficiently severe social or political threat.

The combination of professional and political conditions prevailing in eighteenth-century Britain made overt regulation of proprietary medicines difficult if not impossible. In terms of regulatory policy, these conditions left a vacuum that the government, grasping a market opportunity to address a serious financial problem, filled with tax.[86] Although the forces that determine the introduction and retention of any tax are complex, it appears at first sight that any regulatory purpose within the medicine stamp duty was unlikely. There were a number of reasons for this. First, not only has it been seen that the political and fiscal context of the tax strongly suggested an entirely financial motive behind the legislation, but the orthodox view of taxes as exclusively revenue-raising instruments of government left little room for the remedying of social ills. Indeed, throughout the eighteenth and nineteenth centuries governments were notoriously indifferent to any harmful social effects of taxation. For example, the proven detrimental effect of the window tax on the public health was ignored by government for more than twenty years.[87] Second, when Lord John Cavendish first introduced the tax to Parliament in 1783, he did not expressly mention the evils of proprietary medicines, voiced no concerns for the health of the public in this respect and made no regulatory claims for the tax. Third, the new medicine stamp duty was one of a number of new taxes, most of which had no discernible wider policy perspective at all. Only

---

[85] See the papers presented at the Birmingham trade conference held to discuss the formation of a chemists' defence association, reported at 18 *Chemist and Druggist* 237–53 (15 July 1876).

[86] The decision to tax, however, was not just a second best to regulation. In its own right it was overwhelmingly the choice of the government. Taxing quack medicines was simply more attractive from almost every perspective.

[87] Chantal Stebbings, 'Public Health Imperatives and Taxation Policy: The Window Tax as an Early Paradigm in English Law', in John Tiley (ed.), *Studies in the History of Tax Law*, vol. 5 (Oxford: Hart Publishing, 2011), 43.

in relation to the new tax on the registration of births, marriages and deaths did Cavendish mention a policy imperative in addition to the financial one.[88]

Finally, as a regulatory instrument to curb the trade in proprietary medicines, the medicine stamp duty of 1783 was wholly unconvincing. Any proprietary medicine could be sold free of duty as long as the vendor was qualified within the meaning of the Act, and any unqualified vendor could do so as long as the duty was paid and a licence obtained. The legislation did not include any provision to ensure the regulation or scrutiny of applicants for licences. At best, the only control introduced by the Act was the premise that only unqualified individuals would sell dangerous or inappropriate medicines, and qualified persons would not. And so by targeting unqualified vendors and requiring them to go to the expense of purchasing a licence, the Act would control the sale of undesirable medicines. This vestigial quality control was not, as might be thought, entirely undermined by the exemption for established shopkeepers. It suggested that the legislature was particularly concerned with taxing travelling quacks or pedlars. These were generally at the more undesirable end of the proprietary medicine trade, itinerants who sold their wares from village to village and had moved on before the products could reveal their ill effects or be shown to be ineffective. Established medicine vendors could argue they had acquired specialist knowledge and skill through the practice of the sale of medical preparations, with the stability and respectability that expertise brought, an argument that was even stronger if the exempting provision was interpreted as requiring the shop to be for the sale of medicines only.

With the shift in focus in 1785 from the seller to the proprietary medicine itself, however, the qualification of the vendor became irrelevant. Anyone could sell proprietary medicines as long as the medicines were stamped and a licence was purchased. There was still no vetting of any kind by the revenue authorities, who simply sold a licence to anyone who wanted one and could pay for it, and accordingly it imported no suggestion of professional qualification to judge the quality of the product, nor even the probity of the individual vendor. From the point of view of the revenue authorities it was nothing more than an administrative provision to assist in implementing the tax by identifying the vendors of taxable medicines and recording the address of their trading premises, and one that also raised some revenue in its own right. The most a licence requirement could achieve was to exert a market control in that it may have deterred some individuals from entering the trade. For the vendors it was a commercial judgement as to whether it was worth buying the licence, in view of likely profits on the sale of the commodity. So

[88] *Parliamentary Register 1780–1796*, vol. 10, 26 May 1783, p. 72.

when the rates were perceived as unfair, as when the cost of the licence was significantly higher in London and Edinburgh and yet the sales of proprietary medicines were much greater in the provinces, complaints were made to the Chancellor of the Exchequer. Equally, however, some traders paying the higher rate were happy to do so just to achieve a measure of exclusivity in their trade.[89]

Despite these four clear indications that the tax had no social policy objectives, there is evidence to suggest that the British government was well aware that the medicine stamp duty could be exploited politically as at least in part a regulatory measure. When Cavendish introduced the tax in 1783 he famously described proprietary remedies as 'very proper objects of taxation'.[90] This was, of course, equivocal. On the one hand he could have been referring to the extensive nature of the trade that made proprietary medicines an obvious and potentially lucrative source of revenue. On the other hand, he could have had in mind the social evils of proprietary medicines in terms of the physical and moral danger they posed to the public and the consequent appropriateness of imposing a tax on them. It was clear that most contemporary parliamentarians understood him as inclining to the latter and presumed a policy objective. The following day, when discussing a resolution on bills of exchange, Sir John Mawbey was reported as saying that proprietary medicines were proper objects of taxation 'because they were very pernicious to mankind'[91] and another newspaper reported him as calling for a higher tax on proprietary medicines 'for the sake of humanity'.[92] Francis Spilsbury, one of the most outspoken critics of the new tax, certainly believed that it had been imposed to some extent because the government believed proprietary medicines were 'hurtful to the community'.[93] The fact that Pitt, who was well known to be prepared to abolish taxes if they were either unproductive or excessively unpopular, notably the taxes on female servants, carts, tallow candles and gloves, maintained the medicine stamp duty two years later even though it had failed dismally, could suggest that he saw a purpose in it – to repress a social evil – a characteristic not shared by the duties that he did abolish. A century later, Stephen Dowell, Inland Revenue officer and pioneer historian of English taxation, believed that the tax was imposed not just in the interests of the revenue and regular

---

[89] Stephen Dowell, A *History of Taxation and Taxes in England*, 4 vols. (London: Longmans, Green and Co., 1884), vol. 4, pp. 371–2.

[90] *Parliamentary Register 1780–1796*, vol. 10, 26 May 1783, p. 71.

[91] *Gazetteer and New Daily Advertiser*, May 28, 1783.

[92] *Parker's General Advertiser and Morning Intelligencer*, May 28, 1783.

[93] Spilsbury, *Discursory Thoughts*, p. 41.

medical practitioners, but also in the interests of the public,[94] a perception widely shared in the nineteenth century.[95]

It was also the case that a tax objective beyond mere revenue-raising was rare but not unknown to English law. Customs duties, for example had long been used to achieve strategic economic objectives, and, more significantly, there were some instances of specific taxes being used explicitly to address social ills. A precedent was the eighteenth-century gin tax, when after a number of attempts at prohibitive taxation had failed due to their severity, a moderate and effective tax was imposed in 1751 on the manufacture of spirits that raised the price above that affordable by most people as a daily commodity.[96] Similar social purposes can be found within a range of stamp duties. When stamp duties on dice and playing cards were introduced in 1711, they were arguably instruments not only of revenue-raising but of social control. A similar regulatory motive, although ancillary to its financial purpose and only subsequently articulated, lay behind the stamp duty on almanacs and newspapers, introduced in 1711–12. Again the objective was a dual one: to raise money to finance the war of the Spanish succession and to curb the increasingly vitriolic political wars conducted in a now unregulated press. It has been argued that Parliament preferred to regulate press freedom through taxation, and that contemporary albeit circumstantial evidence reveals Pitt as increasing the newspaper duty in 1789 as an instrument of censorship to curb the radical press in Britain, which was reporting about the progress of the French Revolution.[97] Finally, there were clear non-fiscal reasons for maintaining the gambling stamp duty in the first half of the nineteenth century, despite widespread evasion.

The experience of the gin tax, the newspaper stamp duty, taxes on dice and playing cards all confirmed that it was not unknown to English law to impose a tax with social as well as financial objectives. However, only rarely was a tax's social objective more important than the financial one, as in the gin tax

---

[94] Dowell, *History of Taxation*, vol. 4, p.366.

[95] See counsel in the litigation reported in 'Action to Recover a Charge for Patent Medicines', (1846) 48 *The Lancet* 600.

[96] Sale of Spirits Act 1750, 24 Geo. II c. 40. See generally Dowell, *History of Taxation*, vol. 4, pp. 103–9.

[97] Pauline Sadler and Lynne Oats, '"This Great Crisis in the Republick of Letters" – The Introduction in 1712 of Stamp Duties on Newspapers and Pamphlets' (2002) *British Tax Review* 353, 363–4; Lynne Oats and Pauline Sadler, 'Stamp Duty, Propaganda and the French Revolutionary and Napoleonic Wars', in John Tiley (ed.), *Studies in the History of Tax Law Volume 1* (Oxford: Hart Publishing, 2004), p. 243 at pp. 252–3; Lynne Oats and Pauline Sadler, 'Political Suppression or Revenue Raising? Taxing Newspapers during the French Revolutionary War', (2004) 31 *Accounting Historians Journal* 93.

and, to some extent, the newspaper stamp duty. What was more common was the introduction of a tax with the primary purpose of raising finance, but having a regulatory by-product that was welcomed by legislators. The medicine stamp duty was one such tax. Although the central government promoted the view that it was introduced entirely for financial reasons, contemporary evidence demonstrates a social policy dimension to the tax, albeit one carefully expressed in official neutrality. The Commissioners of Stamps said that all proprietary medicines by whomsoever sold should be subject to the charge if it were indeed the case that they were 'in themselves pernicious, and, therefore, that the use of them ought to be discouraged'[98] or that they constituted a fruitful source of public revenue. Nevertheless, correspondence between the commissioners and the Treasury in 1785 shows conclusively the intention of the drafters of the medicine stamp duty legislation. Raising public revenue was not the sole rationale of the medicine stamp duty, because it was also intended to affect behaviour and suppress a perceived evil. The correspondence asserts that the object of the tax was to act as 'a Regulation of Police, or as a Law of Revenue, by restraining the immoderate use of certain Medicines, commonly called Quack Medicines'.[99] Furthermore, when observing that since the 1783 Act resulted in qualified individuals selling proprietary medicines free of the duty and therefore at a cheaper rate than the non-exempt quack, the tax did nothing to lessen the trade, the writer stressed that 'the proposed advantage to the public [was in] every way defeated'.[100] In other words the intention was both to control and limit the use of proprietary medicines and to raise public revenue.

With the precedent of the dual purpose inherent in the gin tax and the newspaper stamp duty, the introduction of the medicine stamp duty with the ancillary purpose of controlling proprietary medicines in the interests of the public health was neither new nor surprising. The imposition of a measure of control over the trade was a subsidiary and scarcely articulated intention behind the new tax. Indeed, intention is too strong: it was at most an official understanding that the new tax could have a regulatory effect on the trade, that it could send out a signal that proprietary medicines were perceived by the government as commodities that were not to be encouraged and that the new tax could be publicly justified on social as well as financial grounds. This was an enduring awareness on the part of the revenue authorities, who even

---

[98] *Stamp Office: Observations upon the present Medicine Act and Proposals for an Improvement of that Duty*, 21 May 1785: TNA: T1/624/514.

[99] *Ibid.*

[100] *Ibid.* The words 'to the public' are underlined in the original document.

in the twentieth century would say that the burden on the community by the taxation of proprietary medicines was 'more readily justified' than the burden imposed by other duties such as those on sugar, tea and coffee.[101]

REGULATORY EFFECTS

The Select Committee on Patent Medicines concluded in 1914 that the law relating to proprietary medicines in general was totally unsatisfactory. Other than legislative control of certain poisons introduced in 1868, the law was powerless to prevent any person from making a medicine, however useless or harmful, advertising it in fulsome terms as an effective cure for almost any ailment and selling it for any price the market could bear. The only constraint was the payment of a small tax on those medicines coming within the terms of the medicine stamp duty legislation.[102] Until well into the nineteenth century, therefore, the medicine stamp duty constituted the only official state involvement in the proprietary medicines trade. Because the primary intention of the tax was financial, and was never to ensure the wholesome quality of the proprietary medicines it attached to, let alone their effectiveness, this lack of consideration given to the integrity of the medicines themselves was unsurprising. Moreover, given that the tax was conceived, implemented and maintained around a commercial model, with the object of charge being defined entirely by its characteristics as a commodity, the regulatory function of the medicine stamp duty could only be in the market sense. The imposition of the stamp duty undoubtedly made proprietary medicines more expensive for the customer. Chemists and druggists, and other vendors of proprietary medicines, would have to purchase a licence, raise their prices to cover the cost of the stamp, take the time and trouble within their working lives to correspond with the revenue authorities to check whether any new products, or uncertain products, were dutiable and, if they breached the Act, would be liable to the heaviest financial penalties. It could be anticipated that such products would become less attractive to the consumer and less profitable to vendors, thereby reducing the volume of the trade in proprietary medicines.

Sellers of medicines, above all the chemists and druggists, certainly predicted a commercial impact as soon as the tax was first enacted in 1783. Francis Spilsbury said the stamp was bound to act 'as a scare-crow to drive ...

---

[101] *Board of Customs and Excise and Predecessor: Private Office Papers, The Medicine Stamp Duties 1783–1936*, TNA CUST 118/366 at p. 125.
[102] Report and Minutes of Evidence from the Select Committee on Patent Medicines, *House of Commons Parliamentary Papers* (1914) (Cd. 414) ix 1 at p. ix.

customers to another shop' where the legislation permitted an exemption.[103] Certainly qualified individuals under the 1783 Act were quick to stress their exempt status in the advertisements for their remedies. So, for example, the advertisement for *Bennett's Dentilave Tincture* and his *Dentifrice Powder* stated that they were sold exempt from the duty on quack medicines because the medicines were the property of a regular practitioner.[104] Francis Newbery, the proprietor of the celebrated remedy *Dr James's Powder* and well-known vendor of proprietary medicines in general, advertised the rise in his prices and included various marketing ploys to retain his customers, including the offer of discounts on bulk buying.[105]

As an economic regulator, however, the medicine stamp duty was demonstrably and consistently unsuccessful. The Stamp Commissioners observed that the Act of 1783, an acknowledged financial failure, 'had done nothing to moderate the public demand for and consumption of quack medicines' and that there remained 'as great a demand as ever for such Medicines'.[106] The reformed tax from 1785 did no better in that respect: it is known that by 1900 there had been a fivefold increase in the use of proprietary medicines in the previous fifty years. Nevertheless, in the absence of any formal regulation, market control of the medicine stamp duty, however slight, was regarded by many as the only viable control of proprietary medicines. James Drew, a wholesale druggist giving evidence to the Select Committee on the Adulteration of Food in 1856, agreed that their legal prohibition was desirable but entirely impractical, in view of the vested interests concerned, not least the newspapers' income from advertisements.[107] He believed that the only solution to control proprietary medicines was to double the rate of the tax because it would 'tend to check the sale'.[108] Certainly *The Lancet* believed that if the control of the medicine stamp duty were removed by abolishing the tax, a new control would have to be introduced to prevent the unchecked sale of cheap proprietary medicines,[109] and the underlying view that the medicine stamp duty did to some degree at least restrict the sale of proprietary remedies persisted to the end of the nineteenth century. But its regulatory effects were

---

[103] Spilsbury, *Discursory Thoughts*, p. 9.

[104] *General Advertiser*, 13 December 1784.

[105] *Morning Post and Daily Advertiser*, 6 January 1786. See too *E. Johnson's British Gazette and Sunday Monitor*, 24 January 1802.

[106] *Stamp Office: Observations upon the present Medicine Act and Proposals for an Improvement of that Duty*, 21 May 1785: TNA: T1/624/514.

[107] Report and Minutes of Evidence, Select Committee to inquire into Adulteration of Food, Drinks and Drugs, *House of Commons Parliamentary Papers* (1856) (379) viii 1 at qq. 3191–4.

[108] *Ibid.*, q. 3169.

[109] 'Patent Medicines', (1870) 95 *The Lancet* 358.

not limited to this minor and ephemeral commercial control. The law and practice of the tax had a material effect on the quality of medicines in three entirely different ways. The first related to public perceptions of quality and safety, the second to promoting the development of scientific analysis and the third to creating a practice of disclosure.

PERCEPTIONS OF QUALITY AND SAFETY

Any official recognition of a product affected public perceptions of quality and safety. It was well known that letters patent granted for proprietary medicines 'bestowed virtues and efficacy on any quack medicine',[110] masked their true often dangerous qualities and encouraged their sale. Proprietary medicines enjoyed similar de facto privileges as a result of the medicine stamp duty regime because even the mere recognition of proprietary medicines as objects of a charge to tax endowed them with an aura of respectability. This was so despite the tax being widely regarded as a punitive measure imposed by an impoverished government on a commodity deserving of the impost due to its unwholesome characteristics. Francis Spilsbury maintained that Lord John Cavendish had said that 'as quack medicines had done much harm to the public, it was fair game to tax them'.[111] This imported notions of fault, justification and blameworthiness, but it was felt that by directly taxing quacks in 1783 the legislature was somehow legitimising them, giving them credibility and a measure of respectability and thereby constituted an active stimulus to the trade. Spilsbury said that to tax quacks was akin and equally objectionable to taxing highway robbers and footpads.[112] It would 'screen them from justice', allow dangerous medicines to proliferate and thereby cause great harm to society.[113] It was nothing short, he said, of raising 'specie from filth'.[114] One newspaper in the early days of the tax said in relation to the sale of medicines containing antimony and mercury that '[t]o licence such practices is to render poisoning legal'.[115] This perspective persisted. In 1834 a leading surgeon, Sir Astley Cooper, observed: 'I am sorry to say that quacks are extremely promoted in this country. The Government support them, and that, merely because

---

[110] *Parliamentary Register 1780–1796*, vol. 20, 28 April 1786, p. 142 *per* Mr Courtenay.
[111] Spilsbury, *Discursory Thoughts*, p. 1. This was not reprinted in the *Parliamentary History* but the accurate reporting of parliamentary debates in 1783 was in its infancy and was neither comprehensive nor regulated.
[112] *Ibid.*, p. 2.
[113] *Ibid.*
[114] *Ibid.*, p. 40.
[115] *St. James's Chronicle or the British Evening-Post*, 25–27 November, 1784.

there is a certain sum accruing to Government for the sale of their medicines. Government is therefore in fault, in that respect'.[116] Chemists and druggists shared this view.[117] The fact that the sum raised was small merely fuelled this opposition. *The Lancet* argued that 'official obstinacy perpetuates an impost which is productive of infinite harm, and in favour of which not a single plea exists'.[118] The journal castigated the Chancellor of the Exchequer as 'the patron of all the stinking liniments, filthy unguents, and visceral persuaders, vended under the Government stamp' and as such he was 'the greatest quack doctor in Great Britain'.[119]

   This official recognition of proprietary medicines in the fiscal system had its physical expression in the form of the red medicine stamp affixed to all chargeable medicines, 'a standing witness' as to whether the duty had been paid.[120] Aware that the ubiquitous government stamp was taken as a mark of official recognition and, by implication, approval and indeed efficacy, it was exploited to the full in the advertisement of the products, that key characteristic of proprietary medicines.[121] The words 'with the Government Stamp' generally took a prominent place in the advertisements and they were phrased in such a way as to reinforce the suggestion of purity and usefulness and thereby increase the volume of sales. A common practice was to advertise medicines with the words 'None Genuine unless guaranteed by the Government stamp'. At the point of sale too it was said that that vendors made commercial use of the stamp, telling gullible customers that they had to pay the government for permission to sell the medicine, and that the government would not allow them to do so if the medicine was harmful. So commercially powerful was the stamp that even where a product was exempt from the tax, manufacturers would imitate the government stamp as closely as they could short of being guilty of forgery. This practice continued for the entire life of the tax. In the 1930s *Yeast-Vite* was not liable to the duty, yet the packet bore an imitation government stamp with the word 'guarantee' written on it. And at the time of writing, some seventy-five years after the tax was abolished, the packet containing *J. Collis Browne's*

[116] Report from the Select Committee on Medical Education with Minutes of Evidence, *House of Commons Parliamentary Papers* (1834) (602) xiii 1 at q. 5575.
[117] 'On the Professional Character of the Pharmaceutical Chemist', (1842) 2 *Pharmaceutical Journal* (series 1) 1, 2.
[118] 'Editorial', (1857) 69 *The Lancet* 172.
[119] *Ibid.*
[120] *Board of Customs and Excise and Predecessor: Private Office Papers, The Medicine Stamp Duties 1783–1936*, TNA CUST 118/366 at p. 123.
[121] The schedules themselves, namely the lists of named remedies subject to the medicine stamp duty, also constituted powerful publicity for the owners of the medicines concerned.

Mixture bears an image of the government stamp, although very few people would understand its meaning today.

Certainly the presence of the instantly recognisable red government stamp served the trade well. The sale of proprietary medicines was flourishing in the nineteenth century as the population grew, and was not hindered by increasing population mobility because as people moved from the countryside to the city, and from city to city, recognised brands, and the presence of the familiar stamps, gave them an element of security that they were purchasing the same proprietary medicine they were accustomed to using.[122] This was equally true when consumers travelled abroad, whether on holiday or permanently. For example, there developed a thriving trade on the French Riviera in British proprietary medicines, with British chemists specializing in such preparations specifically for the expatriate market.[123]

It was, however, through the use of 'appropriated' stamps that the commercial power of the government stamp was exploited to its fullest extent. Under the original medicine stamp duty legislation in 1783, vendors were required to send their own medicine wrappers and labels to the revenue authorities for stamping.[124] This regulation was presumably to ensure a measure of standardisation, and certainly labels had to state the vendor's name and the value at which the medicine was to be sold. From 1802 the Stamp Office provided the stamps[125] and, probably to reduce the impact on the trade of the change of system, it allowed vendors to include their names and that of the product on the stamp. One of the earliest examples of such medicine stamps were those of Francis Newbury, the proprietor of *Dr James's Fever Powder*. Requests would be made directly to the board to have an individual vendor's name and address engraved on the medicine stamp label, along with, where appropriate, an indication that the vendor was the proprietor of a particular remedy.[126] All costs were met by the individual requesting the appropriated stamps: vendors paid a sum to have a personal die engraved and their exclusive stamps printed and held by the revenue authorities for them to call for as necessary. In 1936 an appropriated stamp cost £12.[127] The management of appropriated

---

[122] Dowell, *History of Taxation*, vol. 4, p. 371.

[123] For example, Reilly & Co., Nice, France, chemists and druggists, importers of English and American proprietary medicines. See Figure 7.

[124] Medicine Stamp Duty Act 1783 (23 Geo. III c. 62) s. 6.

[125] 42 Geo. III c. 56 s. 10 (1802).

[126] *Minutes on Medicine, Card and Dice Duties*, 1811–36: TNA IR 83/203, 3 September 1835.

[127] Report and Minutes of Evidence from the Select Committee on Medicine Stamp Duties, *House of Commons Parliamentary Papers* (1937) (Cmd. 54) viii 129, Memorandum of C. J. Flynn of the Board of Customs and Excise, p. 166. Minimum £8 in 1904: *Taxes, Precedent Book, 1892–1910*: TNA IR 83/61.

stamps was a consideration in any sale of the business, so when Charles Butler sold the goodwill of his business as a 'patent medicine vendor' to his brother, Thomas, in 1833 there followed a correspondence of some months with the tax authorities to ensure that the medicine stamp plates were altered from 'Charles Butler' to simply 'Butler'. It was ultimately agreed to by the board, with Thomas Butler agreeing to meet the expense.[128]

These customised medicine stamps were immensely popular with vendors of proprietary medicines as marketing tools. They constituted advertisements in their own right, and hundreds made use of the privilege.[129] James Dalby purchased appropriated labels for his *Carminative* from the Stamp Office in the early nineteenth century[130] and in 1861 Johnson Da Silva of London paid £16 for medicine labels bearing the name of his medicine, *Dr Hugo's Medical Atoms*.[131] The proprietors of *Aspro*, *Beecham's Pills* and *Dr J. Collis Browne's Chlorodyne* all paid for appropriated stamps.[132] Over four years at the beginning of the twentieth century, of the 1½d stamps issued, ten million were unappropriated and nineteen million were appropriated; of the 3d stamps three million were unappropriated and five million were appropriated.[133] The use of appropriated stamps for *Aspro* alone brought in more than £100,000 pa in 1935–6.[134] By 1936 some two thirds of the revenue from medicine stamp duty came from appropriated stamps.[135]

Appropriated stamps intensified the connection in the public mind between the medicine stamp and the quality of the product. It was the usual practice for the vendors of proprietary medicines to exploit every nuance of

[128] Board of Stamps, Miscellaneous Letter Books: TNA IR 45/18. See too *Minutes on Medicine, Card and Dice Duties, 1811–36*: TNA IR 83/203, 14, 19 August 1833.

[129] For a list of firms and products advertising on medicine stamps, see George Griffenhagen, *Medicine Tax Stamps Worldwide* (Milwaukee, Wisc: American Topical Association, 1971), pp. 15–26. So popular were these stamps that the revenue authorities became anxious that appropriated stamps should not become an administrative burden and requested in 1833 that orders of appropriated stamps should not be less than £30 in value at one time, should be sold in quires or sheets but 'no odd stamps' and that due notice of orders should be given: TNA IR 45/18.

[130] *Stamp Commissioners' Orders, 1810–20*: TNA IR/72/2.

[131] TNA IR 40/2003A.

[132] For a full list of appropriated stamps in force in 1936 see *Board of Customs and Excise and Predecessor: Private Office Papers, The Medicine Stamp Duties 1783–1936*: TNA CUST 118/366 at pp. 182–8.

[133] Report and Minutes of Evidence from the Select Committee on Patent Medicines, *House of Commons Parliamentary Papers* (1914) (Cd. 414) ix 1 at q. 61, *per* Sir Nathaniel Highmore, solicitor to the Customs and Excise.

[134] *Board of Customs and Excise and Predecessor: Private Office Papers, The Medicine Stamp Duties 1783–1936*: TNA CUST 118/366 at p. 182.

[135] *Ibid.*, at pp. 93, 188.

the requirement to bear a medicine stamp. Because the penalties for forging a stamp were severe, and proceedings would invariably be taken by the revenue board against a counterfeiter, the appropriated stamp was regarded as a particularly powerful indicator that the medicine in question was the genuine product of the named maker. It was therefore common for advertisements to direct the purchaser to check that the maker's name was on the stamp, for without it the product was not genuine. As early as 1790 newcomers to a medicine were being thus cautioned.[136] B. H. Inglish, the proprietor of *Dr Anderson's Scots Pills*, was quick to see the commercial potential in the medicine stamp duty. An advertisement notice in the *London Gazette* in 1802 proclaimed that in order to ensure that the public purchased only the true pills, not a counterfeit product, the proprietor was availing himself of the new Medicine Stamp Act to ask the public to look for the stamp in his name. Stating the penalty for forgery of the stamp was death, the implication was that a medicine bearing that stamp was indeed the genuine product.[137] An advertisement for *Hogarth's Genuine Compound Oxymel of Horehound*, 'an infallible remedy for coughs, colds, asthmas and consumption', instructs the reader to 'OBSERVE THIS CAUTION. None are genuine, unless the name G.S. Hogarth is written on the Stamp ...' In a commercial catalogue of proprietary medicines sold by Mr W. Bacon at the end of the nineteenth century, he repeatedly stressed that his name was signed on every stamp, 'as a proof of authenticity',[138] 'a guard against fraud'.[139] If anything, this practice intensified over time. The Select Committee inquiring into the sale and advertisement of proprietary medicines in 1914 found some extreme examples. An advertisement for *Therapion* read '*Therapion* appears on the Government Stamp, affixed to every package by his Majesty's Hon. Commissioners, and without which it is a forgery'. On another publication the owners of *Therapion* wrote the words 'Protected by His Majesty's Hon. Commissioners'.[140] Another example read: 'On the 24th May 1839, Her Majesty's Honourable Commissioners of Stamps ordered the name of "John Steedman, Chemist" to be engraved on the Government Stamp affixed to each packet, without which none after that date can be genuine'.[141]

[136] Revd Dr Trusler, *The London Adviser and Guide*, 2nd edn, (London: Literary Press, 1790), p.160.
[137] *London Gazette*, 7 December 1802, p. 1303.
[138] W. Bacon, *An Account of several Valuable and Excellent Genuine Patent and Public Medicines* (London: ca. 1790), p. 10.
[139] *Ibid.*, p. 17.
[140] Report and Minutes of Evidence from the Select Committee on Patent Medicines, *House of Commons Parliamentary Papers* (1914) (Cd. 414) ix 1 at q. 3641 *per* Edward Harrison, analytical chemist.
[141] *Ibid.*, q. 3642.

A more detailed barefaced use of the legal requirement to stamp a medicine to imply a guarantee of quality was seen in relation to *Clarke's Blood Mixture*, which announced that 'To prevent fraud, His Majesty's Commissioners of Inland Revenue have ordered the words "Lincoln and Midland Counties Drug Company, Lincoln, England," to be printed in white letters on a red ground on the Government Stamp which is affixed over the cork of each bottle, and to imitate which is a felony'.[142] Such statements constituted a clever manipulation of the statutory obligation on proprietary medicines to bear a stamp to achieve a commercial advantage.

That the medicine duty stamp constituted an implicit approval of the product by the government, and thereby a guarantee of its quality, purity, safety and effectiveness,[143] was an entirely unfounded but widely held public perception. The scepticism of a wholesale druggist in 1856 who maintained that if the public was deceived into thinking the stamp implied a government sanction of the product, 'it must be amongst a very ignorant class of people indeed',[144] was shared by very few. The danger that this increased the trade in unproven and sometimes dangerous proprietary medicines, encouraged self-medication and preyed on the gullibility of the sick was fully appreciated in the nineteenth century by the regular medical profession and the government itself.[145]

Although Charles Warton failed in the early 1880s to procure any amendment to the poisons legislation to ensure it covered proprietary medicines, it did allow him to address directly the problem as he saw it that 'a good deal of quackery was promoted by the Government stamp', and that the stamp was 'an apparent sanction'.[146] He argued that many people 'believed that both Houses of Parliament had in some way sanctioned and almost sanctified those medicines', and believed that it was utterly wrong for the government to derive any revenue from such an 'unworthy' and 'shameful' source.[147] He

---

[142] *Ibid.*

[143] *Board of Customs and Excise and Predecessor: Private Office Papers, The Medicine Stamp Duties 1783–1936*: TNA CUST 118/366 at p.43.

[144] Report and Minutes of Evidence from the Select Committee to inquire into the Adulteration of Food, Drinks and Drugs, *House of Commons Parliamentary Papers* (1856) (379) viii 1 at q. 3170 *per* James Drew.

[145] 'On the Mischief of the Self-Administration of Medicines', (1847) 49 *The Lancet* 291; 'On the Injury Inflicted on the Public by the Legalized Sale of Quack Medicines', (1848) 51 *The Lancet* 699, 700; Report and Minutes of Evidence from the Select Committee on Medicine Stamp Duties, *House of Commons Parliamentary Papers* (1937) (Cmd. 54) viii 129, Memorandum of the British Medical Association at p. 27 and qq. 1118–19, 1132–3 *per* Dr J. W. Bone, British Medical Association.

[146] *Parl. Deb.*, vol. 269, ser 3, col. 595, 12 May 1882 (HC); *per* Charles Warton; *ibid.*, vol. 286, cols. 801–4, 26 March 1884 (HC).

[147] *Ibid.*, vol. 286, ser 3, col. 802, 26 March 1884 (HC)

suggested that if the Chancellor of the Exchequer insisted on retaining the tax, he should at least restrict the use of the words on the stamped label. He proposed the following phrase: 'This duty is levied for fiscal purposes, and there is no Government guarantee of the goodness of the medicine'.[148] The bill was rejected, but the Chancellor of the Exchequer did discuss the matter with the Board of Inland Revenue and announced in 1885 that 'the stamp will be altered, so as to show clearly and make it plain that there is no Government guarantee of the medicine'.[149] New plates were engraved, old stock used up, and two months later new stamps were introduced, bearing the words 'This Stamp implies no Government guarantee of the medicine',[150] later shortened to 'No Government guarantee'.[151] This was a result of a communication from the Privy Council Office to the Treasury rather than any initiative by the revenue authorities.[152] At that point, the appropriated stamps should have become nothing more than a 'commercial convenience',[153] but in practice such was the potency of the government stamp that the disclaimer had little effect. The revenue authorities still felt it necessary to stress that appropriated stamps did not 'have the effect of Letters Patent, the only security afforded being that they are supplied solely to the person for whom the special Plate was engraved, or to his authorised Agent',[154] and that officers were bound to issue the stamp to any proprietor of a medicine liable to duty who paid for it.[155]

THE GOVERNMENT LABORATORY

The effect of the medicine stamp in persuading the public that proprietary medicines were safe and effective had no scientific, medical or pharmaceutical foundation and did nothing to promote any improvement in the integrity of proprietary medicines. Indeed, arguably, it hindered it by engendering a false confidence in a large section of the public. The medicine stamp duty, however, did have a second material, if indirect, effect that contributed to the

---

[148] *Ibid.*, vol. 269, ser. 3, col. 595, 12 May 1882 (HC).

[149] *Ibid.*, vol.297, ser. 3, col. 1158, 30 April 1885 (HC) *per* Hugh Childers.

[150] *Ibid.*, vol.299, ser. 3, col.428, 13 July 1885 (HC) *per* Sir Henry Holland, secretary to the Treasury.

[151] See Figure 8.

[152] Report and Minutes of Evidence from the Select Committee on Patent Medicines, *House of Commons Parliamentary Papers* (1914) (Cd. 414) ix 1 at q. 257 *per* Sir Nathaniel Highmore, solicitor to the Customs and Excise.

[153] Alpe, *Handy Book*, p. 22.

[154] *Taxes, Precedent Book, 1892–1910*: TNA IR 83/61.

[155] Twenty-eighth Report of the Commissioners of Inland Revenue, *House of Commons Parliamentary Papers* (1884–85) (4474) xxii 43 at p. 96.

long-term greater safety of medicines, and that was the contribution of the tax authorities to the development of their scientific analysis.

Facilities for such analysis were first introduced in 1842, when the Inland Revenue laboratory was established in Old Broad Street, London, at the headquarters of the Board of Excise.[156] When an Act was passed prohibiting the adulteration of tobacco,[157] it was clear that the law would be inoperative unless scientific methods were developed to identify this increasingly sophisticated fraud. Tobacco could be adulterated with alum, sugar, liquorice, chicory leaves coated with tar and molasses or dried rhubarb leaves. Snuff could be adulterated with various substances including lime, wood, earth, salt and roasted oatmeal.[158] The laboratory regarded the prevention of the adulteration of tobacco as its most important duty[159] and concentrated entirely on it. It provided a service of the highest quality and soon proved its usefulness. Entry was competitive, the scientific training rigorous [160] and the processes meticulous.[161] Its remit was extended to all exciseable articles capable of adulteration, notably soap, pepper, coffee, tea and beer,[162] it undertook analyses for the boards administering all the taxes and by the 1850s it had become 'an essential and prominent part' of the British tax system.[163]

[156] First known as the Laboratory of the Board of Excise (1842–49) and then successively as the Inland Revenue Laboratory (1849–94), the Government Laboratory (1894–1911), the Department of the Government Chemist (1911–59), then part of a succession of different departments until it finally became an executive agency. It was located in Somerset House from 1859 to 1897 when it moved to better premises in Clement's Inn Passage off the Strand. For a comprehensive and insightful history of the laboratory, see P. W. Hammond and Harold Egan, *Weighed in the Balance, A History of the Laboratory of the Government Chemist* (London: HMSO, 1992). See too John St Clair Cholmondeley, *The Government Laboratory* (London: C. Fry, 1902).

[157] Tobacco Act 1842 (5 & 6 Vict c. 93).

[158] Second Report of the Commissioners of Inland Revenue, *House of Commons Parliamentary Papers* (1857–8) (2387) xxv 477 at pp. 493–5.

[159] First Report of the Commissioners of Inland Revenue, *House of Commons Parliamentary Papers* (1857) (2199 sess. 1) iv 65 at p. 120.

[160] For the education and training of the laboratory personnel, see Hammond and Egan, *Weighed in the Balance*, pp. 68–85.

[161] *Ibid.*, p. 39.

[162] First Report of the Commissioners of Inland Revenue, *House of Commons Parliamentary Papers* (1857) (2199 sess. 1) iv 65 at pp. 121–7; Hammond and Egan, *Weighed in the Balance*, pp. 33–6.

[163] Second Report of the Commissioners of Inland Revenue, *House of Commons Parliamentary Papers* (1857–8) (2387) xxv 477 at p. 510. Ultimately its non-revenue work increased, and it was used by other government departments, including the Board of Trade, the Admiralty, the India Office and the Local Government Board, and, from 1875, in connection with the administration of the Food and Drugs legislation: Report of the Principal Chemist of the Government Laboratory, *House of Commons Parliamentary Papers* (1910) (Cd. 5283) xxxi 635. See too Derek J. Oddy, 'Food Quality in London and the Rise of the Public Analyst, 1870–1939', in Peter J.

The laboratory undertook analyses in relation to the medicine stamp duty, providing scientific advice as to the nature of a medicine to the revenue boards. The reference normally arose when a revenue official had purchased unstamped a medicine that he thought should be stamped, but many originated from applications by individual chemists and druggists directly to the revenue authorities for a ruling as to the liability of a particular medicine to the medicine stamp duty. It was standard procedure for the board to ask for a sample and the formula, to forward it to the laboratory and to give a definitive answer on the basis of the analysis and the advice of the laboratory, a service that was impressively prompt.[164] The board almost invariably adopted the view of the laboratory.[165] The board informed taxpayers of their decision in the most general terms.

The analyses related almost exclusively to the exemptions to the tax. For example, in the case of the *known, admitted and approved* remedy exemption, the reference usually concerned the adequacy of the formula disclosed. In this respect the laboratory advised the board not to accept disclosures in foreign languages, nor contracted names, nor names other than those generally known in the trade. Foreign medicines were analysed to establish their liability to stamp duty. The Medicine Stamp Act 1812 imposed the duty on 'foreign medicines of all kinds, except drugs'.[166] This was interpreted to mean that an imported foreign medicine was not liable to the duty if it consisted of only one drug and so samples were sent to the laboratory to ascertain whether they contained one or more drugs, a process of considerable difficulty.[167] Similarly, the laboratory tested to ascertain whether a preparation could claim the pure drug exemption, as with its analysis in 1892 of *Lady Rachel's Secret Ointment*, where it found that it was composed of cocoa nut oil scented with geranium, and was not a pure drug and so had to be stamped.[168] Other preparations denied

---

Atkins (ed.), *Food and the City in Europe Since 1800* (Farnham: Ashgate, 2008), p. 91. For the breadth of the laboratory's work, see Tom Pocock, 'Chemists Behind the Law', *Leader Magazine*, 5 October 1946.

[164] See the cases in TNA IR 40/2276, which are all acknowledged within a week, and the query answered definitively usually within a month.

[165] A rare example when the board did not follow the laboratory's advice was in the case of *Savory & Moore's Digestive Candy*, deciding that although the laboratory said the presence of rhubarb and magnesia made it a medicine, it was not held out as a medicine nor recommended, and so was not liable to the duty: *Board of Inland Revenue decisions on medicine stamp duty*, 1892: TNA DSIR 26/138.

[166] 52 Geo. III c. 150, schedule (1812).

[167] Twenty-second Report of the Commissioners of Inland Revenue, *House of Commons Parliamentary Papers* (1878–79) (2406) xx 635 at p. 722. See too Report and Minutes of Evidence from the Select Committee on Medicine Stamp Duties, *House of Commons Parliamentary Papers* (1937) (Cmd. 54) viii 129 at qq. 291–308 per Dr J. J. Fox, Government Chemist.

[168] *Board of Inland Revenue decisions on medicine stamp duty*, 1892: TNA DSIR 26/138.

the pure drug exemption after analysis included *Harmer's Concentrated Syrup or Fluid Extract of Senna, Soden Mineral Pastilles* and *Elixir of Cascara*.[169] *Witch Hazel*, on the other hand, was emphatically found to be a pure drug and not liable.[170] Another common analysis was to establish whether a wine was sufficiently medicated so as to bring it within the tax as a medicine and allow it to be sold by chemists and druggists without an excise licence.[171] The general test was whether to drink it as an ordinary beverage would be 'nasty'[172] so if a person could drink half a pint of it, it would be wine and not medicine.[173] But where medicinal wines were listed in the *British Pharmacopoeia*, as for example orange quinine wine, the laboratory used the standards there laid down. A wide range of samples were analysed, including waters and mud compresses alleged to have radioactive properties and have beneficial medical effects, as well as various pills, powders, plasters, ointments, medicinal snuff, herbal preparations, corn cures, embrocation and various liquid and solid preparations sold as 'remedies'.[174] It also analysed well-known proprietary products such as *Liebig's Extract of Beef and Tonic Wine*[175] and *Friar's Balsam*.[176]

The exemption for mineral waters caused particular problems because the law was imperfectly understood by manufacturers, retail chemists and even by many local revenue officials.[177] In 1900, for example, the firm of Souter Mackenzie, manufacturers of mineral waters in Dover and Folkestone, wished to label bottled citrate of piperazine as follows: *Aerated Citrate of Piperazine. A Specific for Gout. And the best solvent for uric acid.* The firm said it understood the legislation to provide that if a single substance were advertised as a remedy it was not liable to the duty, so if they advertised just *Piperazine* it would not be liable. A board official queried whether this would constitute a

[169] *Ibid.*
[170] *Ibid.*
[171] *Ibid; Precedents and Instructions*, 1904: TNA IR 78/60 at p.157.
[172] Report and Minutes of Evidence from the Select Committee on Medicine Stamp Duties, *House of Commons Parliamentary Papers* (1937) (Cmd. 54) viii 129 at qq. 280–81 *per* Dr J. J. Fox, Government Chemist.
[173] And a wine licence would be needed to sell it. Report and Minutes of Evidence from the Select Committee on Patent Medicines, *House of Commons Parliamentary Papers* (1914) (Cd. 414) ix 1, q. 44, *per* Sir Nathaniel Highmore, solicitor to the Customs and Excise.
[174] Report of the Government Chemist, *House of Commons Parliamentary Papers* (1912–13) (Cd. 6363) xxix 453 at p. 465.
[175] Twenty-first Report of the Commissioners of Inland Revenue, *House of Commons Parliamentary Papers* (1878) (C. 2158) xxvi 717 at p. 814.
[176] Twenty-second Report of the Commissioners of Inland Revenue, *House of Commons Parliamentary Papers* (1878–79) (C. 2406) xx 635 at p. 730.
[177] See Chapter 2.

medicinal drug vended entire, and whether the exemption in favour of mineral waters would apply. The laboratory confirmed that the chemical compound citrate of piperazine would be regarded as a pure drug and so would be exempt from stamp duty. Whether it would still qualify for exemption when dissolved in water aerated with carbonic acid gas was a matter for the board's solicitor, but suggested that it was possible that it could then contain mineral salts that generated carbonic acid when mixed, and that could not constitute a pure drug. Neither, suggested the laboratory, would it seem to come within the mineral waters exemption.[178] Within a week the solicitor, and the board, confirmed that *Aerated Citrate of Piperazine* did not fall within the exemption for drugs vended entire, and that it had accordingly to be sold stamped. The letter gave no explanation for the reasons, legal or scientific, behind the decision.

In a similar case in 1901 a Mrs Brice wrote to the board asking as to the liability of *Lindale's Effervescing Tablets* sold for the relief of rheumatism. She provided a bottle of the preparation and gave the formula as 'urotropine and ordinary effervescing material'. The laboratory confirmed this, and, referring to the precedent of the *Citrate of Piperazine* case, observed that the mixture was neither within the exemption in favour of materials for making artificial mineral waters, nor that for pure drugs. Because it came within neither exemption, its recommendation on the label for rheumatism and other ailments brought it within the charge to medicine stamp duty and so the tablets not only had to bear a stamp but the vendor had to hold a valid licence.[179] So where a firm in Margate queried in 1905 whether a combination of three salts – lithium carbonate (lithia), phenocoll and piperazine in carbonated water and sold as *Gout Water* – was liable to the duty, the board looked to its decision on piperazine water and replied that it was dutiable.[180] In response to a query in 1907 from a drug company asking whether theatres needed a licence to sell *Bromo-Seltzer*, the laboratory found that the preparation was a white powder containing sugar, other substances used in making mineral waters and a medicinal ingredient. If sold in powder form it did not come within the exemption for articles employed for compounding artificial mineral waters, and so the vendor would need to purchase a medicine licence. And if sold in the form of a beverage prepared from the powder, it was dutiable on the same grounds as the *Aerated Citrate of Piperazine*. *Bromo-Seltzer* was, therefore, a proprietary medicine and chargeable as such.

178 TNA IR 40/2276.
179 *Ibid.*
180 *Ibid.*

Analysis of proprietary medicines, however, formed a relatively small proportion of the laboratory's work. At first medicines were not distinguished in the records, which noted the analysis of 'miscellaneous samples', including, although not quantifying, proprietary medicines, wines, confectionary and toiletries, all of which could have been analysed for the purposes of the medicine stamp duty.[181] The numbers ranged from some 175 'miscellaneous samples' in the early 1860s[182] rising to more than 2,000 in 1909,[183] but are of little assistance. Only from 1911 did the official reports distinguish samples of medicines, and the extent of the work of the laboratory in this respect was clear. From a peak of ninety-seven samples analysed in 1912–13,[184] it dwindled to only nine in 1919–20.[185]

The availability of expert government chemists with a sophisticated and well-equipped laboratory devoted, initially at least, to undertake analyses for the revenue departments, potentially constituted an obvious and effective safeguard to the public health. In its revenue work, however, the laboratory was not concerned with the quality of the medicines it was called upon to analyse. From its inception, it existed to protect the public revenue and not the public health. Far from analysing medicines to ascertain whether they were harmful to the public, the purpose was exclusively to establish their liability to the tax. The imperative was, therefore, entirely fiscal. Nevertheless, and despite the relatively small volume of analyses, the work of the laboratory was of twofold importance. First, the laboratory was a leader in the development of rigorous scientific analytical techniques, applying them to the very challenging subject of proprietary medicines.[186] Second, the fact that these medicines were being analysed at all, and their compositions subject to expert scrutiny, with the publication of the results in official and publicly available reports was important in the history of legislative control over the integrity of proprietary medicines. It created a culture of formal and rigorous scientific attention to medicines that had always operated, despite their vendors' protestations, as an

[181] First Report of the Commissioners of Inland Revenue, *House of Commons Parliamentary Papers* (1857) (2199 sess. 1) iv 65 at p. 127. See too Reports of the Principal Chemist, *House of Commons Parliamentary Papers* (1898) (C. 9035) xxxiii 249; 1899 (C.9408) xxix 227; 1900 (Cd.348) xxvi 449; 1901 (Cd.765) xxiii 515; 1902 (Cd.1189) xxxiv 447.

[182] Seventh Report of the Commissioners of Inland Revenue, *House of Commons Parliamentary Papers* (1863) (3236) xxvi 205 at p. 257.

[183] Report of the Principal Chemist of the Government Laboratory, *House of Commons Parliamentary Papers* (1910) (Cd. 5283) xxxi 635 at p. 658.

[184] Report of the Government Chemist, *House of Commons Parliamentary Papers* (1913) (Cd. 7001) xx 557 at p. 569.

[185] Report of the Government Chemist, *House of Commons Parliamentary Papers* (1920) (Cmd. 881) xvii 23 at p. 32.

[186] For the difficulties involved in undertaking a precise analysis of proprietary medicines see British Medical Association, *Secret Remedies* (1909), pp. 10–12.

art rather than a science, and outside the orthodox discipline of science and regular medicine.[187]

DISCLOSURE

The third, and arguably the most important, effect of the medicine stamp duty on the quality of proprietary medicines was as the catalyst for the public disclosure of their ingredients. The medicine stamp duty legislation itself did not require disclosure of the full formula of proprietary medicines. So, with no legal duty to state the ingredients of their medicines, the manufacturers and vendors, including the individual chemists and druggists who sold their own preparations, offered no safeguard to the public as to what their remedies contained. Ignorant of the constituents, blinded by the power of advertising and the perceived protection of the medicine stamp, customers had no safeguard against harmful ingredients or a variable composition.[188] Such an uninformed reliance was, said *The Lancet* in 1836, nothing short of 'monstrous'.[189]

The first step towards disclosure came as a result of the judicial understanding of the *known, admitted and approved* remedy exemption in the case of *Farmer v. Glyn-Jones* in 1903, and its subsequent interpretation by the revenue authorities.[190] One of the two conditions for claiming the exemption was that the ingredients of the medicine in question should be disclosed.[191] That was easily achieved by ensuring that the label either bore an 'adequate indication of the ingredients' of the medicine, or, on payment of a modest (if any) fee, indicated that the medicine's formula was registered in an approved book of pharmaceutical formulae,[192] namely the *British Pharmacopoeia* 'or well-known and recognized books of reference'.[193] Because of the widespread desire among chemists and druggists to claim the *known, admitted and approved* remedy exemption from the medicine stamp duty, within a year of the decision in *Farmer* there began a flood of registrations of formulae in recognised books of reference.

[187] Note that the large manufacturing chemists adopted higher standards of quality of ingredients and products than was usual in the world of proprietary medicines, and came to underpin their businesses with rigorous scientific pharmaceutical research.

[188] C. J. Arblaster, 'Patent Medicines', 18 *Chemist and Druggist* 250 (15 July 1876).

[189] 'Editorial', (1836) 25 *The Lancet* 949.

[190] See Chapter 2.

[191] The other was that the vendor should hold a professional pharmaceutical qualification: *Taxes, Precedent Book, 1892–1910*: TNA IR 83/61.

[192] *Taxes, Precedent Book, 1892–1910*: TNA IR 83/61. See Leslie G. Matthews, *History of Pharmacy in Britain* (Edinburgh: E. & S. Livingstone, 1962), pp. 100–11.

[193] *Precedents & Instructions, 1904*: TNA IR 78/60 at p. 123.

Pharmacopoeias were reference works containing the specification of pharmaceutical drugs to ensure a uniform standard of composition and purity. Under the statutory authority given to the General Medical Council by the Medical Act 1858, the first *British Pharmacopoeia* was published in 1864, replacing the older individual regional publications. It was regularly updated, its fourth edition in 1898 involving the Pharmaceutical Society for the first time in its production to contribute essential pharmaceutical expertise, and a notable revision in 1914. It formed, in practice, the legal standard for the purity of drugs and medicines it contained.[194] By section 15 of the Pharmacy Act 1868, the standards of the *Pharmacopoeia* had to be adhered to for the preparation of the medicines it contained. In its own right, therefore, it promoted a national uniform standard of composition, purity and strength of medicines.

The revenue authorities would only recognise the *Pharmacopoeia* and certain books of reference for the purpose of tax exemption, but these were not comprehensive. Accordingly, chemists and druggists wishing to claim the exemption in this way pressed for the compilation of a special chemists' formulary containing the formulae of a wider range of common remedies. The board was prepared to recognise a formulary published by a body such as the Pharmaceutical Society. This further promoted a recognised standard for many medicines that were in widespread use by the public. The board then began periodically to publish lists of approved books of reference in its instructions to its officers,[195] works that were not named in any Act of Parliament, but entirely the product of the revenue authorities.[196] In 1904, for example, the board informed its officers that the *British Pharmacopoeia, Pharmaceutical Journal Formulary, Chemist and Druggist Diary, Pharmaceutical Formulas, Pharmacopoeias of the London Hospital, Diary of British and Colonial Druggist, Martindale's Extra Pharmacopoeia, British Homoeopathic Pharmacopoeia, Druggist General Receipt Book (Henry Beasley), Book of Prescriptions (Henry Beasley), Pharmaceutical Formulary (Henry Beasley), Cyclopaedia of Receipts (Cooley), Physicians' Vade Mecum (Hooper)* and the *Selecta e Praescriptis (Dr J Pereira)* were all recognized for the purposes of the exemption.[197] Disclosure of formulae was extensive. In 1904, for example, the *Pharmaceutical Formulae* published by the *Chemist and Druggist* contained the formulae of nearly 700 mixtures for coughs, for diarrhoea and for neuralgia alone. The recognition that the medicine stamp duty gave to the authoritative *Pharmacopoeia* and

---

[194] See T. D. Whittet, 'Drug Control in Britain: From World War I to the Medicines Bill of 1968', in Blake (ed), *Safeguarding the Public*, pp. 27–37.

[195] *Taxes, Precedent Book, 1892–1910*: TNA IR 83/61.

[196] 'Liability to Medicine Stamp Duty', (1903) 71 *Pharmaceutical Journal* (series 4) 97, 98.

[197] *Taxes, Precedent Book, 1892–1910*: TNA IR 83/61.

other well-known books of reference constitutes one of its contributions to the regulation of the quality of proprietary medicines.

The requirement for disclosure created by the revenue authorities for claiming exemption from the medicine stamp duty created a culture of openness and undermined the secrecy popularly, actually and legislatively associated with proprietary medicines. As such it gave forcible impetus to the intense discussion within the medical profession in the early years of the twentieth century about protecting the public from dangerous or useless proprietary medicines, primarily by disclosure and ultimately through legislative control. In 1911, for example, the Royal College of Physicians urged the home secretary to require manufacturers and vendors of proprietary medicines fully to disclose the exact composition of their medicines on the label.[198] But it was the publication by the British Medical Association of its two *Secret Remedies* volumes of analyses of the most common proprietary medicines in 1909 and 1912 that most forcibly promoted the idea of requiring disclosure of composition and ingredients, to act as warning to the public, who could compare the extravagant claims of the vendors with the commonplace nature of the ingredients.[199] The titles of these volumes make it clear that the British Medical Association saw the secrecy in proprietary medicines as constituting their chief problem and, indeed, their attraction. The secrecy of the composition left a manufacturer free to use the cheapest ingredients, some of which were dangerous, and to make extravagant claims for the efficacy of a remedy whose origins and composition could not be checked. It was understood, however, that secrecy held a popular fascination, and the vendors of proprietary medicines continued to exploit this 'common foible of human nature' by seeking to impress a gullible public with the mystery of the composition.[200] The solution was publicity, exposing the facts to enable the public to appreciate the disparity between the extravagant claims of the medicine vendors and the commonplace nature of their products' ingredients. In this respect the two *Secret Remedies* volumes had a potent impact, not least because of the 'juxtaposition of analytical facts and advertising fancies ... the fancy is so free and the fact so simple.'[201] Secrecy led to fraud, but the degree of fraud varied considerably between medicines. Some medicines contained the drugs that were commonly prescribed for the condition in question, notably those for the cure

---

[198] *Board of Customs and Excise and Predecessor: Private Office Papers, The Medicine Stamp Duties 1783–1936*: TNA CUST 118/366 at p. 95.
[199] British Medical Association, *Secret Remedies* (1909), p. 184.
[200] *Ibid.*, p.v.
[201] *Ibid.*, p. vi.

of epilepsy containing bromide salts,[202] and some were made up from medical practitioners' prescriptions. The danger to the public in such cases lay primarily in the excessive claims made for the medicines causing delay in seeking skilled medical advice, their high price and their unsuitability in individual cases. Other medicines, however, had no medical origin, however slight, and contained essentially inert preparations. These, observed the British Medical Association, were among the most extravagantly advertised preparations, which 'set out consciously and deliberately to deceive'.[203] The advertisements, including fulsome testimonials, exploited individuals who were ill and frightened them into purchasing the products with images of suffering and death, and enticed nervous individuals into purchasing them by way of prevention. The extravagance of the claims and the banality of the composition revealed to the public for the first time with scientific proof the extent of the quackery involved. It was clear that the cost of producing these medicines was generally a tiny fraction of the sale price.

The *Secret Remedies* publications did not ignore the medicine stamp duty. The first volume in 1909 contained a brief appendix on the tax, and a table enumerating the price of the article without the stamp, the stamp, and the price paid by the public. It estimated that the public spent more than £2 million on proprietary medicines in the year 1907–8.[204]

The practice of public disclosure of the ingredients of proprietary medicines was a positive outcome of the administration of the medicine stamp duty, being the result of the bureaucratic practice of the revenue authorities in relation to the *known, admitted and approved* remedy tax exemption. It was limited, because if the point of the disclosure was to enable ordinary customers to get the information about the medicine themselves, the use of scientific names to describe common medicines restricted its usefulness considerably. Ultimately this was one reason why the Select Committee on Patent Medicines in 1914 rejected the expert medical view that all remedies sold should be required to state their composition on the label.[205] The disclosure of ingredients, however, was a central element in the growth of quality control, and it is in this context that the tax made a material contribution to the regulation of medicines in the history of pharmacy and the longer-term evolution of therapeutic drugs. Some in the medical profession appreciated the beneficial effects of disclosure

---

[202] *Ibid.*, pp. 124–9.
[203] *Ibid.*, p. 21.
[204] *Ibid.*, p. 184.
[205] The committee also considered that it would be commercially ruinous to the proprietors of many secret remedies.

under the medicine stamp duty in regulating the manufacture and sale of proprietary medicines and understood it as a model to be adopted.[206]

Despite the encouragement that exemption from the tax gave to the publication of the contents of proprietary medicines, it still remained the case that if the duty were paid, then the contents of the medicine did not need to be disclosed. This could only end when the tax was abolished by the Pharmacy and Medicines Act 1941, but then equally the incentive to disclose the ingredients would end too. In an implicit recognition of the immense value of the medicine stamp duty in encouraging such disclosure, the Act of 1941 required, for the first time, a full disclosure of the active ingredients of proprietary medicines on the label.[207] It was no coincidence that the Act that abolished the medicine stamp duty in 1941 was the very Act that introduced compulsory disclosure for the first time and, indeed brought with it the first effective regulation of proprietary medicines.

CONCLUSION

The legislators of the late eighteenth century intended the medicine stamp duty to take its place among a series of taxes on commodities in order to make a small but material contribution to the public revenue. The forces that drove it were financial, and therefore political, rather than social. Britain's need for increased revenue was the real imperative. The government chose not to regulate overtly because political conditions and fiscal policy in Britain were not conducive to it and because it understood from the French experience that to legislate against proprietary medicines, however strongly, was unlikely to be effective. The government knew that to tax was not a robust alternative to the formal regulation of dangerous medicines and unqualified medical practice, but appreciated that if neither formal regulation nor taxation were effective as a mechanism of control, at least taxation had a fiscal benefit. It is also possible that Britain perceived that the effective regulation of proprietary medicines could not be achieved by one single regime, and that various techniques were legitimate instruments of control. To impose a tax and eschew formal regulation was an astute and realistic political compromise. In its pragmatism, therefore, Britain was not entirely misguided. Although driven primarily by financial motives, the legislators nevertheless welcomed – and to some extent sought – the tax's potential regulatory effect in acting as an albeit slight market

[206] Eric Pritchard, 'The Regulation of the Sale of Proprietary and Secret Drugs' (1911–12) 9 *Transactions of the Medico-Legal Society* 87, 98.
[207] Pharmacy and Medicines Act 1941 (4 & 5 Geo. VI c. 41) s. 11.

curb on the undesirable trade in proprietary medicines. And as an exception to the policy of laissez-faire, taxation provided a measure of control under a politically acceptable guise, a regulation that could be denied at will and justified as pure taxation for the sole purpose of revenue-raising.

Had regulation been a material ambition, the government would inevitably have been conflicted. On the one hand it would want the trade to remain buoyant to maintain a worthwhile income stream to the Treasury and would be unlikely to look upon its abolition with equanimity. On the other hand it would wish the trade to be curtailed in the interests of the public health. This tension between social and fiscal policy could only increase as the danger to the public health from unregulated proprietary medicines became established from the early nineteenth century. In practice, however, no such tension was apparent for most of the life of the tax. When the evils of the trade were balanced against the benefits of a new taxable object with a material yield, the profit motive dominated, and the government's concern was entirely with the revenue yield of the tax. Any regulatory effect of the tax was purely fortuitous, minor, quantitative rather than qualitative and, being unambiguously ancillary to the revenue-raising objective, was left to take its course with no attention from the legislature or government. At most, the fact that the subsidiary regulatory effect was recognised and welcomed by government, even if only for political reasons, confirms a measure of official appreciation of the dangers of proprietary medicines and the desirability of official action.

This lack of overt legal control of proprietary medicines in the interests of public health – with the exception of the poisons legislation – was compensated for to some extent by the less obvious regulatory effects of the revenue-raising medicine stamp duty. Its market control, a perception, indeed an expectation, albeit misguided, that government recognition of proprietary medicines brought with it a measure of guarantee of purity, the advancement of scientific analytical techniques and a promotion of the disclosure of ingredients all combined to create the foundations of formal control based on quality. Ultimately, however, it was the poisons legislation, the mandatory education of chemists and druggists and, above all, the advent of prescription-only medicines that were responsible for ensuring the integrity of medicines that the public enjoyed from the twentieth century. Only then was an effective regulatory system developed by the state to ensure the quality of medicines.[208]

---

[208] See too Ernst W. Stieb, 'Drug Control in Britain, 1850–1914', in Blake (ed.), *Safeguarding the Public*, pp. 15–26; Stuart Anderson, 'Drug Regulation and the Welfare State', in Virginia Berridge and Kelly Loughlin (eds.), *Medicine, the Market and the Mass Media* (Abingdon: Routledge, 2005), pp. 193–217

FIGURE 8 Medicine duty stamp, 1915.

5

The Demise of the Tax

"There is a troublesome question of long standing to which I propose to give a final quietus."[1]

INTRODUCTION

The medicine stamp duty was introduced as a revenue-raising instrument and was never regarded as anything else. It did not aim to regulate the trade in any meaningful way; on the contrary, the aim was to exploit it. The yield was small, but it was certain, and as long as it remained politically, financially and legally tenable, there was no question of its repeal. Politically, in the sense of public toleration of it, the medicine stamp duty was widely accepted. The consumers of proprietary medicines were used to it, they liked the security they felt the stamp gave them, and, crucially, the chemists and druggists liked it because they saw its considerable commercial advantages. Financially, the yield, never large, did begin to decline in the 1930s and would shortly have been out-weighed by the costs of administration and thus become financially unten-able. This was not, however, the cause of the tax's ultimate downfall, although it did lead to its close examination. The demise of the medicine stamp duty was caused by the revenue authorities losing control of it. It has been seen that the defining characteristic of the tax was the exceptionally high degree of bureaucratic practice that was central to its administration and pervaded its very substance.[2] This was the result of a fundamentally flawed tax, lacking robust definition and left unreformed and outdated, and so, inevitably, having to be implemented by the revenue authorities through the development of

---

[1] *Parliamentary Debates* [hereafter *Parl. Deb.*], vol. 346, ser. 5, col. 990, 25 April 1939 *per* Sir John Simon, Chancellor of the Exchequer.

[2] See Chapter 2.

their own practices. So encrusted did the tax become with revenue practice of doubtful legality that its original provisions were almost obscured. Ultimately, the revenue authorities went too far and overreached themselves. They paid the price of bureaucratic administration of a tax.

THE ABUSE OF REVENUE PRACTICE

The first indication of the downfall of the tax was a collapse of the yield in the 1930s, caused by the exploitation, if not abuse, of revenue practice.[3] Having peaked in 1928–29 at more than £1 million, by the middle of the next decade, even though there had been a rise in the number of licences granted, the yield had halved.[4] Consistent with its prime and enduring character as a revenue-raising instrument, the revenue board looked to the collapse of the yield with considerable concern.[5] The principal cause was the legitimate exploitation by large manufacturing chemists of the *known, admitted and approved* remedy exemption, and its interpretation by the revenue authorities after the decision in *Farmer* v. *Glyn-Jones* in 1903.[6] Because the judicial decision was impossible in practical terms to implement, the board had drawn the exemption so widely that it was virtually unrestricted and required only professional qualification and adequate disclosure of the medicine's ingredients. Its original purpose, which was to exempt qualified retail chemists in small shops from the burden of the tax in selling common remedies without any quackery, prevailed for some years after the *Farmer* decision with the exemption being claimed almost exclusively by individual chemists for their own medicines sold in their name. Large manufacturers of advertised proprietary medicines rarely claimed it, probably because some, such as the manufacturers of *Beecham's Pills*, were reluctant to disclose the ingredients of their products,[7] possibly because they

---

[3]   For the annual yield of the medicine stamp duty from 1800 to 1936 see *Board of Customs and Excise and Predecessor: Private Office Papers, The Medicine Stamp Duties 1783–1936*: TNA CUST 118/366 at pp. 189–93.

[4]   Report and Minutes of Evidence from the Select Committee on Medicine Stamp Duties, *House of Commons Parliamentary Papers* (1937) (Cmd. 54) viii 129 at p. 138. In 1926–7 the yield from sale of licences was £14,928 from sale of 59,732 licences. By 1935–36 the yield was £38,647 from sale of 154,578 licences: *ibid.*, Memorandum of C. J. Flynn of the Board of Customs and Excise at p.166.

[5]   *Board of Customs and Excise and Predecessor: Private Office Papers, The Medicine Stamp Duties 1783–1936*: TNA CUST 118/366 at pp. 107–8.

[6]   See Chapter 2.

[7]   *Board of Customs and Excise and Predecessor: Private Office Papers, The Medicine Stamp Duties 1930–36*: TNA CUST 118/367 at p.6.

were unaware of the breadth of the exemption under the revenue practice,[8] or again because of the revenue authorities' insistence from 1909 that the exemption be limited to remedies in which no proprietary rights were claimed.[9] At first, therefore, the use of the exemption for such branded remedies was exceptional.

The first signs of a change in the nature of claimants came in the mid-1920s, when large manufacturing chemists began to bring themselves within the conditions to claim the exemption, partly because, as a war measure, the rates of the tax had doubled. Popular and hitherto stamped medicines began to be sold unstamped through the practice of 'branding and de-stamping'. By publishing the formula of their medicine in well-known trade formularies, and printing the name of the formulary and the number of the formula on the medicine's label, manufacturers could satisfy the disclosure requirement for the *known, admitted and approved* remedy exemption. They would also expressly disclaim any proprietary rights in the formula, but would retain their commercial property by including a brand name for the article. This was on the basis that because the legislation said that liability rested on 'a proprietary claim in the making or preparing of the drug', if a medicine was well known, then the manufacturer calling it by his or her own name would not necessarily signify a proprietary claim to an exclusive right to make the medicine. The dividing line was difficult to draw, and although the revenue authorities did not have a clearly understood policy, even within the department,[10] they were advised by their solicitor that in such circumstances there was no proprietary claim within the meaning of the medicine stamp duty legislation, and so the medicine was not dutiable on those grounds.[11] Manufacturers could, therefore, rely on their trade mark for protection from competition rather than the secrecy of their product.

The *known, admitted and approved* remedy exemption was requested for *Vick Brand Vapour Rub* and *Aspro*.[12] So whereas *Vick Vapour Rub* used to be dutiable, it ceased to be so once it was renamed in the late 1920s as *Vick Brand Vapour Rub*. Similarly *Phosferine Tonic* became *Phosferine Brand*

---

[8] *Board of Customs and Excise and Predecessor: Private Office Papers, The Medicine Stamp Duties 1783–1936*: TNA CUST 118/366 at p.105.

[9] *Ibid.*, p. 86.

[10] *Ibid.*, pp. 105–6.

[11] Report and Minutes of Evidence from the Select Committee on Medicine Stamp Duties, *House of Commons Parliamentary Papers* (1937) (Cmd. 54) viii 129 at q. 127 *per* C. J. Flynn of the Board of Customs and Excise.

[12] *Board of Customs and Excise and Predecessor: Private Office Papers, The Medicine Stamp Duties 1783–1936*: TNA CUST 118/366 at p. 105.

Tonic, a development of particular concern to the revenue authorities. Until 1929 this very popular remedy had always been sold with a stamp, but in 1930 it began to be sold unstamped under the *known, admitted and approved* remedy exemption, with a reference to its formula on the label and a statement that no proprietary right was claimed in the preparation of the medicine, only in the registered trade mark, *Phosferine*. The revenue authorities wrote to the Chancellor of the Exchequer observing that the claim was legitimate[13] because the formula was disclosed and any proprietary right, other than in the trade mark name, disclaimed, but that it could result in some £30,000 in lost revenue a year.[14] Indeed the revenue authorities feared that if the general movement continued, the very viability of the tax would be compromised, because the board believed that the practice of 'branding and de-stamping' was responsible for the decline in the overall yield of the tax in the early 1930s.[15]

All the revenue authorities could do was to make the requirements for claiming the exemption more stringent. They adopted a more rigorous practice in 1930, insisting on full disclosure of the actual ingredients rather than mere reference to a formula and a robust express disclaimer of proprietary rights in the preparation of the medicine on every label before they allowed the exemption.[16] Many chemists refused to comply and the revenue authorities were forced to take legal proceedings. The test case concerned the sale unstamped of a preparation called *Vapour Rub*, recommended for chest and throat complaints, with its label referring to a formula for a product called *Chest Vapour Rub* in a recognised book of reference. In *Attorney General v. Lewis and Burrows Ltd* in 1932 Rowlatt J said that had the preparation been called *Chest Vapour Rub* he would have held that it came within the exemption because its formula was found under that name in the book of reference.[17] Because it was called merely *Vapour Rub*, it could not claim the exemption because although the properties of an ointment *Chest Vapour Rub* might be regarded as *known, admitted and approved* by reason of the formula appearing in a book of well-known pharmaceutical formulae

---

[13] See too the advice of the Assistant Solicitor in 1930: *ibid.*, p. 112.

[14] *Ibid.*, at p. 107.

[15] *Ibid.*, at p. 109.

[16] *Ibid.*, at p.110. *Board of Customs and Excise and Predecessor: Private Office Papers, The Medicine Stamp Duties 1930–36*: TNA CUST 118/367 at p.6; Report and Minutes of Evidence from the Select Committee on Medicine Stamp Duties, *House of Commons Parliamentary Papers* (1937) (Cmd. 54) viii 129, Memorandum of C. J. Flynn of the Board of Customs and Excise at pp. 164–5.

[17] *Attorney General v. Lewis and Burrows Ltd* [1932] 1 KB 538.

under that name, this was no ground for taking the view that an ointment manufactured in accordance with the same formula but sold as *Vapour Rub* was the same article. The revenue authorities took the decision to mean that if the name or specific description under which a medicine was sold was identical to that found in a recognised book of reference, it became a *known, admitted and approved* remedy and was thus exempt.[18] The decision was 'troublesome'[19] to the revenue authorities, and they consulted counsel to determine whether there was any chance of overturning the decision on appeal. They were advised against it because the ambiguity of the law would make the outcome too uncertain.[20] As a result they were forced to abandon their revised practice and to allow exemption where there was a definite statement disclaiming any proprietary right, the formula or an indication that the medicine was made in accordance with the formula in a recognised book of reference.

Even though the stringent conditions that the revenue authorities desired had been held by the courts to be legally unenforceable, and some manufacturers abided by them,[21] they had little effect. The reach of the exemption had become widely known and was frequently claimed. The revenue authorities believed there was a deliberate movement by the large manufacturing chemists to bring their medicines within the exemption. The pharmaceutical press portrayed this use of the exemption by the large manufacturers as an undermining of the 'age-long privilege' of the chemist.[22] The fact that the manufacturers continued to charge the same price for their products, and that their profits were seen to increase considerably, simply exacerbated the tension.[23] By 1935 most widely advertised proprietary medicines were sold under a trade mark and, when sold by a qualified chemist, did not have to bear a stamp. *Beecham's Brand Powders, Carter's Brand Little Liver Pills, Listerine Brand Antiseptic, Veno's Brand Lightning Cough Cure, Vick Brand*

[18] Letter from Sir C. E. FitzRoy to Parliamentary Counsel in 1932, *Board of Customs and Excise and Predecessor: Private Office Papers, The Medicine Stamp Duties 1930–36*: TNA CUST 118/367 at p. 16.
[19] Letter from E. R. Forber, the chairman of the board of Customs and Excise, to Sir Arthur Robinson of the Ministry of Health: *Board of Customs and Excise and Predecessor: Private Office Papers, The Medicine Stamp Duties 1930–36*: TNA CUST 118/367 at p. 32.
[20] *Ibid.*, p. 60.
[21] *Board of Customs and Excise and Predecessor: Private Office Papers, The Medicine Stamp Duties 1783–1936*: TNA CUST 118/366 at pp. 114–16 (the Vapour Rub case).
[22] *Ibid.*, p. 109.
[23] For the increase in the profits of the manufacturers of *Beecham's Pills*, see *Board of Customs and Excise and Predecessor: Private Office Papers, The Medicine Stamp Duties 1783–1936*: TNA CUST 118/366 at p. 113–14.

Vapour Rub and *Yeast-Vite Brand Tablets* were just a few. The tax yield was bound to suffer. 'The effect is', stated a departmental report in 1936, 'that under the authority of extra-statutory concessions, the medicine stamp revenue has been roughly halved during the last seven years' and in real terms the loss to the revenue far exceeded the annual yield of the tax.[24] 'Revenue', observed C. J. Flynn of the Board of Customs and Excise, 'is the crux of the whole situation'.[25]

The *known, admitted and approved* remedy exemption was not the only aspect of revenue practice that was exploited and caused a decline in the yield. Breaking bulk was abused to some extent,[26] as was the exemption for entire drugs sold unmixed, commonly known as the pure drugs exemption. The original purpose of the pure drugs exemption had been to safeguard the qualified medical practitioner and chemist practising their profession by enabling them to buy their raw materials free of duty, but it came to be used to sell free of duty single drugs not under their chemical names but under 'fancy and proprietary names and recommended for various human ailments',[27] a practice that increased with advances in chemistry and pharmacy. Headache and influenza powders escaped duty under this exemption because they were made of a single drug, even though they were sold as proprietary remedies and with recommendations for treatment of ailments. Notable examples were *Daisy Powders* and *Grace's Fever Powder*,[28] but cod liver oil, castor oil and *Vaseline* were also sold free of duty under this exemption.[29] Both the revenue authorities and the Royal Pharmaceutical Society thought this was inappropriate.[30] The duty remitted under all these concessions came to far exceed the total collected.

---

[24] *Board of Customs and Excise and Predecessor: Private Office Papers, The Medicine Stamp Duties 1783–1936*: TNA CUST 118/366 at p. 113.

[25] *Board of Customs and Excise and Predecessor: Private Office Papers, The Medicine Stamp Duties 1930–36*: TNA CUST 118/367 at p. 52.

[26] Report and Minutes of Evidence from the Select Committee on Medicine Stamp Duties, *House of Commons Parliamentary Papers* (1937) (Cmd. 54) viii 129 at qq. 1522–9 *per* John Weir, Scottish Pharmaceutical Federation.

[27] *Ibid.*, Memorandum of C. J. Flynn of the Board of Customs and Excise, p. 164.

[28] *Ibid.*, qq. 81–2.

[29] *Board of Customs and Excise and Predecessor: Private Office Papers, The Medicine Stamp Duties 1783–1936*: TNA CUST 118/366 at pp. 53–5.

[30] Report and Minutes of Evidence from the Select Committee on Patent Medicines, *House of Commons Parliamentary Papers* (1914) (Cd. 414) ix 1, q. 194, *per* Sir Nathaniel Highmore, solicitor to the Customs and Excise; Report and Minutes of Evidence from the Select Committee on Medicine Stamp Duties, *House of Commons Parliamentary Papers* (1937) (Cmd. 54) viii 129, Memorandum of H. N. Linstead, Secretary of the Royal Pharmaceutical Society of Great Britain, at pp. 197–8.

THE QUESTION OF LEGALITY

The *known, admitted and approved* remedy exemption became widely used
for the most popular proprietary medicines, providing they were sold by a
qualified chemist and druggist. In the early 1930s, Messrs F. W. Woolworth
wanted to extend their business into proprietary medicines, but, not being
chemists, could not compete with qualified chemists, including Boots and
Timothy Whites, who could sell such medicines duty-free under the exemption whereas Woolworth's had to sell them stamped. In a spirit of reprisal
for an earlier action taken by the revenue authorities against Woolworth's for
selling *Milton* disinfectant and antiseptic unstamped,[31] the company decided
to challenge the board's interpretation of the *known, admitted and approved*
remedy exemption in 1935.[32] This challenge began a chain of events that
would ultimately lead, six years later, to the total repeal of the tax.

Woolworth's began by taking expert advice on the legality of the exemption
as implemented by the revenue authorities. The three barristers who joined
to give an opinion, Wilfrid (later Lord Justice) Greene, J. Millard Tucker and
H. Lloyd Williams,[33] took the view that both requirements laid down in the
statutory provision – professional qualification and an absence of recommendation – had to be satisfied and if they were not, the medicine in question was
dutiable. On the issue of qualification for the exemption, the courts had construed the statutory provision strictly, holding that the seller had to be qualified by a regular apprenticeship in writing and enforceable at law under the
provisions of the Apprentices Act 1814.[34] Although it was clear that this kind of
apprenticeship was no longer in general use in the medical and pharmaceutical professions, and that legislative provision had been made for alternative
modes of qualification, it followed that no corporate body could legally claim
the exemption.[35] That meant that the revenue authorities' practice of allowing corporate bodies entitled to carry on the business of chemist and druggist
through having complied with the poisons legislation[36] to take advantage of
the *known, admitted and approved* remedy exemption to the medicine stamp

---

[31] *Board of Customs and Excise and Predecessor: Private Office Papers, The Medicine Stamp Duties 1930–36*: TNA CUST 118/367 at p. 137. Woolworth's argued it was exempt as a 'water', but the Crown said it was primarily a medicine.

[32] *Board of Customs and Excise and Predecessor: Private Office Papers, The Medicine Stamp Duties 1783–1936*: TNA CUST 118/366 at pp. 117–22.

[33] *Ibid.*, pp. 178–81.

[34] *Kirkby v. Taylor* [1910] 1 KB 529; Apprentices Act 1814 (54 Geo. III c.96).

[35] *Board of Customs and Excise and Predecessor: Private Office Papers, The Medicine Stamp Duties 1783–1936*: TNA CUST 118/366 at p. 179.

[36] Pharmacy Act 1868 (31 & 32 Vict. c. 121) s. 3.

duty was illegal. As to the requirement that the medicine should never have been recommended to the public as beneficial for a human ailment by the owners, proprietors, makers, compounders or original or first vendors, counsel confirmed this had to be satisfied.[37] The practice of the revenue authorities in permitting this requirement to be disregarded was therefore also illegal. Furthermore, because only the Commissioners of Inland Revenue or the Attorney General had the power to institute proceedings for selling dutiable medicines unstamped, then by simply choosing not to take any action, the revenue authorities had been able to implement the exemption as they chose.[38] Counsel's opinion was uncompromising. Adopting a strict and literal interpretation of the statutory words, they found that the practice of the revenue authorities in relation to the *known, admitted and approved* remedy exemption amounted, they said, 'to taxation at their discretion, and also to an assumption by them of a power to grant general exemptions from taxes which Parliament has expressly decreed shall be imposed. In our opinion this procedure is illegal, and unconstitutional'.[39]

As a result, and on that basis, Woolworth's began their action against the revenue authorities to determine the true construction of the medicine stamp duty Acts, claiming that the revenue authorities had ignored the statutory requirements governing the *known, admitted and approved* remedy exemption. In short, Woolworth's maintained that chemists were unlawfully given special and beneficial treatment, with the same article being sold at different prices by different traders when the same article should be sold for the same price, whatever the status of the vendor, and that the revenue authorities were 'wholly wrong in principle' in administering the Act in this way.[40] Represented by Messrs Lovell, White and King, Woolworth's sought a declaration requiring the board to administer the duty in accordance with the law.

Coeval with the growth of revenue practice to make the medicine stamp duty workable was a long-standing appreciation by the executive and the chemists and druggists that it was fundamentally illegal. Although that

[37] *Board of Customs and Excise and Predecessor: Private Office Papers, The Medicine Stamp Duties 1783–1936:* TNA CUST 118/366 at pp. 179–80.
[38] *Ibid.*, p. 181.
[39] *Ibid.*.
[40] Minutes of Evidence before the Select Committee on Medicine Stamp Duties, *House of Commons Parliamentary Papers* (1937) (Cmd. 54) viii 129, Memorandum of F. W. Woolworth & Co Ltd at p. 313.

illegality had been recognised privately by the revenue authorities, they had never admitted it in public, and even justified their practices when the chemists and druggists challenged them. The threat of exposing an unsustainable illegal practice to the public scrutiny was taken very seriously by the government. The Solicitor General wrote to Sir Charles FitzRoy, the board's solicitor, in 1937 that he took 'a rather serious view of the present position'.[41] 'The point', he said, 'is so frequently made in other connections that the Departments have to administer the law as laid down by Parliament, and therefore cannot in some cases do what they might otherwise think reasonable, that a clear case, if it is a clear case, of the contrary principle being adopted might excite considerable comment'.[42] The chairman of the board remarked that this was 'embarrassing'.[43] The government would be in an impossible position if it had to admit in court, or indeed in Parliament, 'that the law was not being administered but that nothing was being done either to bring the practice in accordance with the law or the law in accordance with the practice'.[44] Knowing that the revenue practice would not stand up in a court of law[45] and that the government would be put in an indefensible position, even appreciating the 'administrative elasticity' that the revenue departments enjoyed,[46] the government determined this was not to be made public. The Chancellor of the Exchequer decided that a Select Committee should be appointed to examine the whole matter of the medicine stamp duty and to come to an agreement with Woolworth's that both suits would be dropped.[47] This agreement was not easily achieved, with Woolworth's being 'extremely troublesome',[48] but they ultimately concurred in the hope and expectation that that committee would address the very issue of the construction of the medicine stamp duty legislation.

---

[41] *Board of Customs and Excise and Predecessor: Private Office Papers, The Medicine Stamp Duties 1930–36*: TNA CUST 118/367 at p. 127.

[42] *Ibid.*, p. 128.

[43] *Ibid.*, p. 137.

[44] *Ibid.*, pp. 128–9.

[45] *Medicine Stamp Duty, 1936*: TNA T 172/1844.

[46] *Board of Customs and Excise and Predecessor: Private Office Papers, The Medicine Stamp Duties 1783–1936*: TNA CUST 118/366 at p. 121.

[47] Namely, the board's action against Woolworth's regarding the sale of *Milton Liquid* unstamped, and Woolworth's threatened action against the board with respect to the legality of the *known, admitted and approved* remedy exemption: *Board of Customs and Excise and Predecessor: Private Office Papers, The Medicine Stamp Duties 1930–36*: TNA CUST 118/367 at pp. 151–2.

[48] *Ibid.*, p. 180.

THE ROAD TO REPEAL

The Select Committee sat for some two months, heard evidence from a wide range of interested parties [49] and reported in February 1937.[50] The effect was relentlessly to expose to the professional, public and governmental gaze the fundamental defects of this long established tax. Views on the current state and the future of the medicine stamp duty were expressed by three distinct groups: the revenue board of the executive, unqualified vendors of proprietary medicines and qualified chemists and druggists. The key issues discussed were the state of the law of the medicine stamp duty, the possibility of reform, the privileges, if any, to be afforded to qualified chemists and druggists and the interface of the tax with public health concerns.

By the mid-1930s the archaic and confused state of the medicine stamp duty law, and the anomalies that it gave rise to, were recognised by everyone who came into contact with it – revenue officials, the medicine traders, the pharmaceutical profession and interested members of Parliament.[51] The revenue authorities agreed the law was difficult to administer, had been 'a source of trouble for many years'[52] and that in modern conditions it gave rise to serious anomalies. Indeed, it was 'bristling with anomalies'.[53] The abstruse and obsolete wording of the legislation had forced the board to 'admit certain concessions which are not strictly in accordance with the law'[54] and which had, accordingly, been the subject of 'adverse judicial criticism'.[55] These pragmatic imperatives had compounded the chaotic state of the law, and the revenue authorities acknowledged that the difficulties brought to a head by the threat of legal action had been brought about 'indirectly' by the 'antiquated

---

[49] *Medicine Stamp Duty, 1936*: TNA T 172/1844. The Treasury felt that 'no handle should be given for challenging the impartiality of the Committee' and accordingly the various interests were represented as witnesses rather than through membership of the Committee.

[50] Report and Minutes of Evidence from the Select Committee on Medicine Stamp Duties, *House of Commons Parliamentary Papers* (1937) (Cmd. 54) viii 129 at pp. 132–42.

[51] Thirty-sixth Report of the Commissioners of Customs and Excise, *House of Commons Parliamentary Papers* (1945–46) (Cmd. 6703) xi 1 at p. 20. The Select Committee on Patent Medicines in 1914 had said that the existing body of regulation, such as it was, and including the law of the medicine stamp duty, was 'chaotic and has proved inoperative' and that this was 'an intolerable state of things': Report and Minutes of Evidence from the Select Committee on Patent Medicines, *House of Commons Parliamentary Papers* (1914) (Cd. 414) ix 1 at p. xxvi.

[52] *Board of Customs and Excise and Predecessor: Private Office Papers, The Medicine Stamp Duties 1783–1936*: TNA CUST 118/366 at p. 122.

[53] Ibid.

[54] *Medicine Stamp Duty, 1936*: TNA T 172/1844.

[55] Thirty-sixth Report of the Commissioners of Customs and Excise, *House of Commons Parliamentary Papers* (1945–46) (Cmd. 6703) xi 1 at p. 20.

and obscure' provisions of the medicine stamp Acts and 'directly' by the grant of extra-statutory concessions, of which the most important was the 'glaring anomaly'[56] of the *known, admitted and approved* remedy exemption.[57] The medicine stamp legislation was 'archaic and confused and in need of revision'.[58] The board said that the 'defects of legal form', and 'obscurities and imperfections'[59] which had given rise to 'very elaborate and fine distinctions'[60] which in turn had resulted in a number of anomalies which complicated the administration of the duty and diminished its yield.[61] After its detailed investigation, the Select Committee was in complete agreement. It concluded that the medicine stamp Acts were 'out of date, largely obsolete and quite inappropriate to modern requirements'.[62] It was clearly absurd and anomalous that recommended articles such as single drugs sold under 'fancy' names, salines, asthma cigarettes, articles used as foods rather than medicines, and medicines referring to an organ of the body should all escape the charge, and that articles such as *Andrew's Liver Salts* should escape the charge after the *Lamplough* decision, but above all it condemned the implementation of the *known, admitted and approved* remedy exemption.[63]

The unqualified vendors of proprietary medicines – from the individual vendor to the large department stores such as Woolworth's – also condemned the medicine stamp duty Acts as 'confused and confusing in language [and] difficult and irritating in administration',[64] but also forcibly expressed the business view that they were 'a hindrance to legitimate trade, and ... wholly out of tune with modern ideas of commerce and taxation'.[65] Woolworth's aimed to distribute medicines in small quantities at low prices to the bulk of the population, which they said was good for trade and good for the public health and comfort. The company objected to the medicine stamp duty on the basis that the minimum tax being 3d, it effectively prevented the sale of medicines in

[56] *Board of Customs and Excise and Predecessor: Private Office Papers, The Medicine Stamp Duties: Last Phase: 1939–41*: TNA CUST 118/404 at p. 112.

[57] *Board of Customs and Excise and Predecessor: Private Office Papers, The Medicine Stamp Duties 1783–1936*: TNA CUST 118/366 at p. 130.

[58] Report and Minutes of Evidence from the Select Committee on Medicine Stamp Duties, *House of Commons Parliamentary Papers* (1937) (Cmd. 54) viii 129, Memorandum of C. J. Flynn of the Board of Customs and Excise at p. 166.

[59] *Ibid.*

[60] *Ibid.*, q. 175.

[61] *Ibid.*, p. 166.

[62] *Ibid.*, p. 140.

[63] *Ibid.*, pp. 136–7.

[64] *Ibid.*, Memorandum of F. W. Woolworth & Co Ltd at p. 311.

[65] *Ibid.*

small quantities.[66] Smaller retailers outside professional pharmacy believed that the rates of the tax were too high, constituted too great a burden on the poorer consumer and should be abolished, or at least reduced.[67]

Qualified chemists and druggists acknowledged the chaotic state of the legislation, and fully appreciated the need for reform. The administrative rulings developed to make the law workable could 'stand no further strain'.[68] However, after 150 years, the medicine stamp duty had become a matter of real importance to them. It had been the cause of developing certain rights that became embedded in their professional lives, was part of their culture, of pharmacy's legal and fiscal framework, and they expressed their views forcibly. They wanted to retain the tax and regarded its abolition as 'a serious thing'.[69] The commercial effect of advertisement by the appropriated stamp was still valued, with the presence of the stamp still providing a convincing aura of respectability which the public responded to.

Although the need for reform was universally accepted, how it could be achieved was more problematic. The official view in the mid-1930s was that reform of the tax to put it on a proper footing and therefore to retain it was difficult but possible. Such a view was strongly informed by the same official forces that had been at play since the late eighteenth century, throughout the nineteenth and into the new century. It was always understood that no government would easily abolish a tax that brought in a small but significant, and cheap, revenue stream. In 1884 the Chancellor of the Exchequer, Hugh Childers, had said he could 'hold out no hope of repealing this tax, which brings in £160,000 a year'.[70] Confirming the fiscal imperative that had been present since the inception of the tax, a predictable desire was expressed to retain it for its yield which, although now in decline, had for 150 years yielded a steady income, and one which as late as the 1920s was a material contribution to the public revenue. If reformed, it could continue to yield a useful sum.[71] As late as 1927 the notion of repeal was quietly but firmly resisted by the Treasury. Then yielding more than £1 million per year, this was an income

[66] *Ibid.*, p. 312.
[67] *Ibid.*, Memorandum of the Joint Parliamentary Committee of the Co-Operative Congress at p. 330.
[68] *Ibid.*, Memorandum of H. N. Linstead, Secretary of the Royal Pharmaceutical Society of Great Britain at p. 197.
[69] 'The Medicine Stamp Act', 28 *Chemist and Druggist* 11, 12 (15 January 1886).
[70] *Parl. Deb.*, vol. 292, ser. 3, col. 93, 7 August 1884 (HC).
[71] *Board of Customs and Excise and Predecessor: Private Office Papers, The Medicine Stamp Duties 1783–1936*: TNA CUST 118/366 at p. 130.

that 'cannot be altogether despised'.[72] Underlying this view of the executive was a strong culture favouring the status quo. If a tax yielded anything at all, it should be retained, on the basis that some revenue was better than none. No sources of income, however small, should be closed down once they were established, as the introduction of a new tax to replace it would always be fiercely resented by the taxpaying public and thus more difficult than retaining an existing one.

There was an official appreciation that the original definition of proprietary medicines for taxing purposes was the best that could be achieved and proposals for a reformed tax were not fundamentally different from the existing law.[73] The dominant sentiment was a desire to retain the status quo. So the internal inquiries of the revenue authorities in the 1920s had resulted in a recommendation that the law be left essentially unchanged, with the old words, phrases and concepts retained, but that the single drugs exemption for retailers be abolished, and that the medicine stamp duty be extended to all perfumes, cosmetics and toilet articles recommended for 'personal adornment or beautifying'.[74] The revenue department estimated that this would produce at least £4 million pa, suggesting that the policy underlying the proposal was entirely financial.[75] There was a difference of opinion, however, as to the retention or abolition of the *known, admitted and approved* remedy exemption.[76] The revenue authorities were clear that the abolition of any of the exemptions would be strenuously opposed by the trade and the pharmaceutical profession, indeed that it would provoke a 'storm of criticism' that would lead to a general condemnation of the entire duty that would be 'very difficult to meet'.[77] Accordingly, no 'real advantage would result from disturbing the existing position'.[78] This view was maintained and when in 1932 the board proposed four possible courses of action to the Chancellor of the Exchequer, namely abolition, reconstruction, partial reform or maintaining the present position,[79] the board recommended the last.

[72] *Parl. Deb.*, vol. 205, ser. 5, col. 750, 26 April 1927 (HC) *per* Ronald Mcneill, Financial Secretary to the Treasury.
[73] *Board of Customs and Excise and Predecessor, Private Office Papers, Entertainment Tax and Medicine Stamp Duties, 1927*: TNA CUST 118/230.
[74] *Board of Customs and Excise and Predecessor: Private Office Papers, The Medicine Stamp Duties 1783–1936*: TNA CUST 118/366 at p.100. See too *ibid.*, pp. 100–3; 172–7.
[75] *Ibid.*, pp. 100–1.
[76] See *ibid.*, p. 100 (abolition); *ibid.*, p.102 (retention).
[77] *Ibid.*, p. 102.
[78] *Board of Customs and Excise and Predecessor, Private Office Papers, Entertainment Tax and Medicine Stamp Duties, 1927*: TNA CUST 118/230.
[79] *Board of Customs and Excise and Predecessor: Private Office Papers, The Medicine Stamp Duties 1783–1936*: TNA CUST 118/366 at p. 117.

By 1936, however, it was clear that tinkering with the existing legislation would not suffice, and a total repeal of the old legislation and enactment of a fresh Act would be necessary.[80] There had to be 'a complete reconstruction of the duty'.[81] In this way, Sir Charles FitzRoy's suggestion for a 'remodelling on modern lines' of the tax would be possible, with the added advantage that the principle of the tax had already been accepted by Parliament.[82] The proposal was for a general charge to apply to all recommended, secret or proprietary remedies, and all exemptions abolished other than the dispensing concession, which would be made statutory.[83] In this way '[t]he tax would strike at prescribing without diagnosis, not at prescribing with diagnosis'.[84] There was a consensus within the revenue authorities that the definition of the object of charge – the medicine – that had existed since 1785 could not be materially improved upon. It could be cast more widely to cover common evasions, and refined to ensure that it reflected what had become the key characteristic of a proprietary medicine, namely its recommendation.[85] The duty could only be avoided by full disclosure of the ingredients of the medicine and an express disclaimer of any proprietary rights. The chairman of the board saw that 'doctors or chemists or both might be moved to strong protest'.[86] The Royal Pharmaceutical Society called for a statutory definition of dutiable medicines that was 'not capable of amendment by departmental rule'.[87] The society understood the difficulties – if not impossibilities – involved in effective definition, and suggested the formation of an expert advisory committee to address the question of boundaries and exemptions.[88] Their definition was too long and unwieldy and the idea of an advisory committee would probably simply cause a reversion to uncertain practice. Again, therefore, their proposals promised no real improvement on the law of 1785. The Select Committee, firmly of the view

[80] Letter from Sir A. J. Dyke to the chairman of the board of Customs and Excise, *Board of Customs and Excise and Predecessor: Private Office Papers, The Medicine Stamp Duties 1930–36*: TNA CUST 118/367 at p. 29.
[81] *Ibid.*, p. 48.
[82] *Board of Customs and Excise and Predecessor: Private Office Papers, The Medicine Stamp Duties 1783–1936*: TNA CUST 118/366 at p. 126.
[83] *Ibid.*, pp. 126–7.
[84] *Ibid.*, at p. 128.
[85] Letter from E. R. Forber, the chairman of the board of Customs and Excise, to Sir Arthur Robinson of the Ministry of Health, *Board of Customs and Excise and Predecessor: Private Office Papers, The Medicine Stamp Duties 1930–36*: TNA CUST 118/367 at pp. 32–3.
[86] *Ibid.*, p. 33.
[87] Report and Minutes of Evidence from the Select Committee on Medicine Stamp Duties, *House of Commons Parliamentary Papers* (1937) (Cmd. 54) viii 129, Memorandum of H. N. Linstead, Secretary of the Royal Pharmaceutical Society of Great Britain at p. 201.
[88] *Ibid.*, pp. 201–2.

that all existing legislation should be repealed, took the view that under a new statutory scheme all articles recommended for the prevention or relief of any human ailment, or to maintain bodily health, including medicines, cosmetics or toiletries should be chargeable; that the rates of duty should be reduced; that exempt preparations should include those supplied to registered medical practitioners and dentists or to pharmacists for use in dispensing prescribed medicines, all medicines exported for use abroad and all British spa waters consumed at place of origin.[89]

Although there was broad agreement in the mid-1930s that the medicine stamp duty should be retained but reformed, there was no such consensus in relation to the *known, admitted and approved* remedy exemption. A clear division of opinion emerged between the stakeholders. The revenue authorities, the Select Committee of 1937 and the unqualified vendors were all hostile to qualified chemists' and druggists' claim to the benefit of the exemption and pressed for its abolition. The official view was that on principle no one should be exempt from taxation on the basis of professional qualifications.[90] In relation to the *known, admitted and approved* remedy exemption, the board felt that the position of chemists and druggists was 'not a strong one'.[91] Their legitimate function was to dispense medical doctors' prescriptions and that should properly be exempt.[92] But if they traded in proprietary medicines, there was no reason why they should do so on different conditions to other traders because most dutiable medicines were prepared not by the chemist and druggist but by wholesale manufacturers and supplied to the vendors ready for sale. It was 'difficult to justify' placing the chemist in a more favourable position than the grocer because, as the solicitor to the revenue board observed uncompromisingly, '[i]t requires no professional qualifications to hand across the counter a packet of ready-made medicine, obtained from the makers or from wholesale dealers'.[93] The unqualified sector of the trade in proprietary medicines was unequivocally and unanimously of the same view. The Association of Wholesale Druggists and Manufacturers of Medicinal Preparations, whose members were mainly engaged in supplying the general poorer public with

---

[89] *Ibid.*, p. 141.
[90] *Board of Customs and Excise and Predecessor: Private Office Papers, The Medicine Stamp Duties 1783–1936:* TNA CUST 118/366 at pp. 129–30.
[91] *Ibid.*, p. 129.
[92] *Ibid.* But see the argument for retention by the Interdepartmental Committee of 1927: *Board of Customs and Excise and Predecessor, Private Office Papers, Entertainment Tax and Medicine Stamp Duties, 1927:* TNA CUST 118/230.
[93] *Board of Customs and Excise and Predecessor: Private Office Papers, The Medicine Stamp Duties 1783–1936:* TNA CUST 118/366 at p. 130.

cheaper proprietary medicines through unqualified small shopkeepers,[94] pressed for exemption from the tax and condemned the *known, admitted and approved* remedy exemption for chemists as unfair.[95] Similarly, the grocers argued that there should be no distinction in tax terms between any class of trader in dutiable medicines.[96] Not only did the exemption place the qualified and unqualified in unequal positions without proper justification, but also permitted the chemist to obtain 'an additional profit without rendering any additional service', because the medicines in question were almost invariably sold by the retailer, whether qualified chemist or unqualified grocer, in the same packet as obtained directly from the manufacturer, with the ingredients displayed and the wrapper intact.[97] And finally, the Select Committee concurred in condemning the exemption as obscure and out of date, seeing no reason why the chemists and druggists should be given this 'very valuable preference'.[98] The commercial inequalities between qualified and unqualified vendors selling the same product was untenable, the system of 'de-stamping' should be stopped and all dutiable preparations should be sold by chemists and unqualified individuals on equal terms.[99]

Predictably, the chemists and druggists argued to retain the tax and its accompanying *known, admitted and approved* remedy exemption, which they popularly named the 'Chemists' Privilege'. They had long since ceased to argue for the tax's repeal. Certainly by the 1890s and the early years of the following century, the consensus among their leaders was that a repeal of the medicine stamp duty would be severely damaging to their interests,[100] although it was generally presented as harmful in the public interest by removing the control on secret remedies. In 1903 a correspondent to the *Pharmaceutical Journal* said that the repeal of the medicine stamp duty legislation would be 'one of the greatest disasters that could happen to the drug trade', because it was the only existing restraint on a completely free trade in medicines.[101]

---

[94] Report and Minutes of Evidence from the Select Committee on Medicine Stamp Duties, *House of Commons Parliamentary Papers* (1937) (Cmd. 54) viii 129, Memorandum of the Association of Wholesale Druggists and Manufacturers of Medicinal Preparations at p. 304.

[95] *Ibid.*, p. 305. See too *ibid.*, Memorandum of the Proprietary Association of Great Britain, p. 222.

[96] *Ibid.*, Memorandum of the National Federation of Grocers' and Provision Dealers' Association, p. 290.

[97] *Ibid.*, Memorandum of the Joint Parliamentary Committee of the Co-Operative Congress, p. 331.

[98] *Ibid.*, Report, p. 137.

[99] *Ibid.*

[100] 'The Medicine Stamp Act', (1890) 20 *Pharmaceutical Journal* (series 3) 742.

[101] 'Liability to Medicine Stamp Duty', (1903) 71 *Pharmaceutical Journal* (series 4) 33. See too *ibid* p. 61.

Within their own circles they fully appreciated its commercial value in terms of promoting sales, and their special privileged position within it. Not only did the *known, admitted and approved* remedy exemption constitute a significant recognition of their qualified status and their value to the community, it conferred a commercial advantage of the utmost importance. Faced with unprecedented and intense competition from unqualified traders, the proprietary medicine trade was crucial to the commercial survival of qualified retail chemists, and, indeed, to their recruitment to the profession. In 1936 unqualified vendors outnumbered qualified vendors by nearly ten to one. The 135,000 unqualified vendors such as grocers – courted by the large manufacturing chemists – only had to pay a nominal five shillings annual licence fee to be able to sell dutiable medicines all over the country, particularly where no chemists' shops were established.[102] It was for this reason that the 15,000 qualified chemists felt so strongly about the *known, admitted and approved* remedy exemption. They felt their legitimate business, underpinned by historic privileges under the legislation, was at risk.[103] Were the tax to be abolished, or retained without the exemption, chemist, grocer and chain store would all be treated the same. No longer would they be able to undercut unqualified vendors by selling proprietary medicines more cheaply or, as was more common, selling the medicines at the same higher price but retaining the profit. Unable to enjoy any economies of scale, for small chemists and druggists the repeal of the tax would constitute the most important development in relation to their business that had ever occurred and the increased competition was feared to lead to commercial ruin.

The discussions as to the future of the *known, admitted and approved* remedy exemption revealed a fundamentally divergent view of the duty itself: the revenue authorities said that the principle of the duty was to charge proprietary medicines irrespective of the nature of the vendor, which was indeed the aim of the parent Act of 1785. The chemists and druggists, however, looked to the intention of the Act of 1783 to tax quackery as represented by unqualified

---

[102] This was less than the cost of a dog licence. The solicitor to the Board of Customs and Excise took the view that it was now regarded as no more than a registration fee, a means whereby vendors of dutiable medicines could be traced: Report and Minutes of Evidence from the Select Committee on Medicine Stamp Duties, *House of Commons Parliamentary Papers* (1937) (Cmd. 54) viii 129 at qq. 61–2 *per* Sir Charles FitzRoy. There was some evidence of wholesale chemists and druggists paying the licence duties for unqualified retailers to encourage them to sell their products: *ibid.*, qq. 253–4 *per* C. J. Flynn of the Board of Customs and Excise.

[103] *Ibid.*, qq. 694–702 *per* D. A. Bryan and G. A. Mallinson, Chairman and Secretary, respectively, of the National Pharmaceutical Association.

vendors recommending medicines.[104] They fought back strongly on this basis, stressing their special position, with legislative responsibilities for the sale of poisons and dangerous drugs, heavy financial and personal commitments in terms of state-required extensive training and regular registration of themselves and their premises.[105] They claimed to be 'the main bulwark between the public and quackery',[106] because where the formula was disclosed they could inform the customer about the likely effect of the medicine, whereas an ordinary licensed trader could not.[107] For these reasons, feeling that the tools of their trade, the very ingredients of the medicines on which their living depended, were being taxed, they felt strongly that they should be afforded 'special consideration in the matter of taxation'.[108] To them, the continuation of that right was 'an act of justice'.[109] In short, they felt they had a 'legal and moral right' to the privilege.[110] The clear consensus among qualified chemists and druggists, and of those involved in the manufacture of proprietary medicines, was that the tax should be retained and reformed, restricted to 'non-ethical' proprietary medicines for example,[111] but always and unanimously calling for qualified individuals to be given special treatment, namely exemption, within the fiscal regime.

It might have been expected that there would be a fourth stakeholder contributing to the debate on the future of the medicine stamp duty in the early decades of the twentieth century, namely those concerned with the dangers to the public health of self-medication. Since the inception of the medicine stamp duty there had always been two clear aspects to the issue of taxing

---

[104] Report and Minutes of Evidence from the Select Committee on Medicine Stamp Duties, *House of Commons Parliamentary Papers* (1937) (Cmd. 54) viii 129, Memorandum of H. N. Linstead, Secretary of the Royal Pharmaceutical Society of Great Britain at pp. 202–3.

[105] *Ibid.*, p. 195.

[106] *Ibid.*, q. 787.

[107] See the evidence of the directors of *Eno's Fruit Salts* and *Andrew's Liver Salts* where they are pressed as to whether their products are medicines or beverages: *ibid.*, qq. 858–91 *per* E. Stevens Spicer and F. A. S. Gwatkin.

[108] *Ibid.*, q. 370 *per* H. N. Linstead, Secretary of the Royal Pharmaceutical Society of Great Britain; *ibid.*, q. 738 *per* G. A. Mallinson, Secretary of the National Pharmaceutical Union. For the proposal of the Royal Pharmaceutical Society see *ibid.*, p. 200. For the similar view of the Company Chemists Association see *ibid.*, Precis of Evidence of the Company Chemists Association, p. 341. For the view of the National Pharmaceutical Union, see *ibid.*, p. 241. For the view of the Wholesale Drug Trade Association see *ibid.*, p. 265.

[109] *Board of Customs and Excise and Predecessor: Private Office Papers, The Medicine Stamp Duties 1936–39:* TNA CUST 118/391 at p. 221.

[110] 'Medicine Stamp Duty Acts', (1903) 71 *Pharmaceutical Journal* (series 4) 8.

[111] Report and Minutes of Evidence from the Select Committee on Medicine Stamp Duties, *House of Commons Parliamentary Papers* (1937) (Cmd. 54) viii 129 at qq. 424, 485–9 *per* H. N. Linstead, Secretary of the Royal Pharmaceutical Society of Great Britain.

proprietary medicines – public revenue and public health – and in its history the clear dichotomy in English law in relation to taxation and control was reflected. Considerations of public health had consistently and unambiguously been secondary to fiscal ones, and although there was a sense within the revenue boards that the original eighteenth-century object of the medicine stamp duty had been to restrain the sale of proprietary medicines as a dangerous and unwholesome commodity, by the end of its life the tax was regarded 'purely as a Revenue duty'[112] and proprietary medicines as a commodity like any other.[113] It was clear after 150 years that raising revenue and suppressing quackery could not successfully be combined, and that the eighteenth-century perception that tax could be a credible substitute for formal legal regulation had lost support. There were some arguments that retaining the tax would benefit public health, but these were rare and took their force from the fact that during the years of its existence there existed no other regulatory concepts. The consensus was that the medicine stamp duty had never achieved any material control over the quality of medicines in the interests of public health. Indeed, it was understood that the tax could even encourage the trade, and as early as 1856 its repeal was demanded for this reason alone.[114] Some physicians who did engage with the issue of the tax were eager for the tax to be replaced by a legislative prohibition on the sale of proprietary medicines, believing that the loss of revenue to the Exchequer was far outweighed by the benefits to the 'health and morality' of the public.[115]

As scientific and medical advances were made in the late nineteenth and early twentieth centuries, so public health concerns became more prominent and the interface between them and the fiscal regime increasingly questioned. The danger to public health of a legally unregulated trade in proprietary medicines was recognised, and, beyond a hope expressed by the Royal Pharmaceutical Society that raising revenue and suppressing quackery could be combined in some way,[116] it was generally understood that the issue was not a fiscal one. From the early twentieth century the dominant view was

---

[112] *Ibid.*, q. 57 *per* Sir Charles FitzRoy, solicitor to the Board of Customs and Excise. Sir Charles FitzRoy's performance before the Select Committee was surprisingly lacklustre and ill informed.

[113] *Ibid.*, q. 58.

[114] Report and Minutes of Evidence, Select Committee to inquire into Adulteration of Food, Drinks and Drugs, *House of Commons Parliamentary Papers* (1856) (379) viii 1 at p. ix.

[115] Report and Minutes of Evidence from the Select Committee on the Pharmacy Bill, *House of Commons Parliamentary Papers* (1852) (387) xiii 275 at q. 2207 *per* G. Webster, physician.

[116] Report and Minutes of Evidence from the Select Committee on Medicine Stamp Duties, *House of Commons Parliamentary Papers* (1937) (Cmd. 54) viii 129 at qq. 485–9 *per* H. N. Linstead, Secretary of the Royal Pharmaceutical Society of Great Britain.

that the advertisement and sale of proprietary medicines had to be controlled, and that that was a task for the Ministry of Health in the interests of public health. Successive governments were accordingly principally concerned, largely unsuccessfully, with addressing the problem of uncontrolled advertising of proprietary medicines.[117] The Select Committee on Patent Medicines in 1914 was directed to consider the content, sale and advertisement of proprietary medicines, terms of reference that extended far beyond the medicine stamp duty, and to suggest any reform in the law.[118] The revenue authorities provided a memorandum of evidence to the inquiry in 1914, but as the board itself observed, the taxation aspect was 'merely incidental or subsidiary'.[119] The Select Committee concluded that secret remedies constituted 'a grave and widespread public evil',[120] which the law as it stood was powerless to prevent, and recommended the establishment of a system of registration of makers and their medicines under one single central government authority and that the content of advertisements for proprietary medicines be more closely controlled.[121] In relation to the medicine stamp duty, the Select Committee stopped short of suggesting its abolition, and instead recommended a programme of legislative consolidation and amendment to ensure the removal of the 'numerous existing anomalies and unreasonable exceptions'.[122] It also recommended the abolition of the appropriated stamp, and said that any reference to the government stamp in an advertisement for a proprietary medicine should be prohibited.[123] The committee made no further recommendations about the taxation aspect, and did not touch on the *known, admitted and approved* remedy exemption, which had caused the revenue authorities so much difficulty, even though – or possibly because – William Glyn-Jones was a member. After the committee made its recommendations, and once the pressure of war legislation had ceased, the public health aspects were addressed in a number of bills, notably the Proprietary Medicines Bill 1920 which, following the Canadian and Australian models, aimed to ensure that proprietary medicines were registered with the Ministry of Health with details

---

[117] *Ibid.*, Memorandum of H. N. Linstead, Secretary of the Royal Pharmaceutical Society of Great Britain at p. 195.

[118] Report and Minutes of Evidence from the Select Committee on Patent Medicines, *House of Commons Parliamentary Papers* (1914) (Cd. 414) ix 1.

[119] *Board of Customs and Excise and Predecessor: Private Office Papers, The Medicine Stamp Duties 1783–1936*: TNA CUST 118/366 at p. 97.

[120] Report and Minutes of Evidence from the Select Committee on Patent Medicines, *House of Commons Parliamentary Papers* (1914) (Cd. 414) ix 1 at p. xxvi.

[121] *Ibid.*, pp. xxvii-xxviii.

[122] *Ibid.*, p. xxvii.

[123] *Ibid.*

as to their composition, and scrutinised by the ministry as a requirement for sale to the public.[124] The bill was, however, dropped after the committee stage. Tax played no part in such initiatives.

More significant with regard to the public health debate in the fiscal context was the establishment of an interdepartmental committee in 1926, representing the Treasury and the Ministry of Health, solely to discuss the reform of the medicine stamp duty.[125] It suggested that were the tax to be abolished in its entirety, it would 'give a new and unnecessary fillip to the quack medicine trade'[126] – an observation revealing that a nexus between the imposition of a duty and a perceived measure of repressive control still existed in relation to the taxation of proprietary medicines, however obliquely and indefinitely it was expressed and however slight its effect in practice.[127] In considering its future, the revenue authorities referred to the 'at least questionable advantages to the general interest, qua public health' of the tax's repeal.[128]

Despite such initiatives, neither party in the fisco-medical debate was profoundly concerned with the other. The British Medical Association was more concerned with the effect on the public health of unrestricted advertising of proprietary medicines than with the revenue aspect of the trade, believing such publicity led to self-diagnosis and self-medication, both harmful in tending to delay proper skilled medical treatment.[129] It was not particularly interested in the medicine stamp duty, beyond being certain that it had done nothing to control the trade in proprietary medicines. In explaining to the Select Committee in 1936 why its representatives had not examined the tax, the association said '[i]t is not the sort of thing a Medical Association would care to examine'.[130] A similar attitude was exhibited by a representative of the Board of Customs and Excise when he observed in 1936 that '[w]e, as a Department, are not

[124] *Board of Customs and Excise and Predecessor, Private Office Papers, Entertainment Tax and Medicine Stamp Duties*, 1927: TNA CUST 118/230; *Memorandum by the Minister of Health on the Proposed Patent Medicines Bill*, 17th February 1920: TNA CAB/24/98. For the history and background to the Proprietary Medicines Bill 1920 see Report and Minutes of Evidence from the Select Committee on Medicine Stamp Duties, *House of Commons Parliamentary Papers* (1937) (Cmd. 54) viii 129 at qq. 674–8 *per* J. Kenningham, Secretary of the Proprietary Association of Great Britain.

[125] *Board of Customs and Excise and Predecessor, Private Office Papers, Entertainment Tax and Medicine Stamp Duties*, 1927: TNA CUST 118/230.

[126] *Board of Customs and Excise and Predecessor: Private Office Papers, The Medicine Stamp Duties 1783–1936*: TNA CUST 118/366 at p. 125.

[127] *Ibid.*, p. 125.

[128] *Ibid.*

[129] Report and Minutes of Evidence from the Select Committee on Medicine Stamp Duties, *House of Commons Parliamentary Papers* (1937) (Cmd. 54) viii 129 at pp. 277–8.

[130] *Ibid.*, q. 1048 *per* Dr J. W. Bone, British Medical Association.

responsible from the public health point of view. We are merely responsible for the collection of those duties'.[131] This had always been so. When at the end of the nineteenth century it was realised that the reduction of the licence duty had caused the trade in proprietary medicines to expand, it was observed that that was not the business of the revenue authorities, whose duty it was 'simply to collect the revenue, in accordance with statutory provisions, and to see that those provisions are not evaded'.[132] And again, when considering the scope of the statutory definitions, Sir A. J. Dyke said:

> The first thing to do is to say what we mean by "medicine." We need not worry too much about what the pundits will think of the definition. We want a definition for Revenue purposes and so long as this is made clear it doesn't matter whether the definition is approved by the Faculty.[133]

Indeed, it was complained in 1926 during a debate on the tax that no representative of the Ministry of Health was present in the House.[134] As a result of such attitudes, in general the two issues of tax and public health were kept firmly distinct.

Although the terms of reference of the Select Committee on Medicine Stamp Duties in 1937 restricted the investigation to the fiscal aspect of the tax, in the course of the evidence a number of witnesses maintained that some form of control of the trade in proprietary medicines was desirable. Even the Royal Pharmaceutical Society called for a full inquiry into the public health aspect of proprietary medicines.[135] The evidence showed that the poor and ill-educated, motivated by fear engendered by advertisement, tended to spend excessively on such medicines.[136] It was accepted that for the most part proprietary medicines were no longer the dangerous or useless preparations with impossible claims that had characterised them in the eighteenth and nineteenth centuries, but were generally recommended, often by medical practitioners, for the relief of minor ailments, in a specified dose and known

---

[131] *Ibid.*, q. 129 *per* C. J. Flynn of the Board of Customs and Excise.

[132] 'Medicine Stamp Duty', (1893) 23 *Pharmaceutical Journal* (series 3) 597.

[133] Letter from Sir A. J. Dyke to the chairman of the board of Customs and Excise, *Board of Customs and Excise and Predecessor: Private Office Papers, The Medicine Stamp Duties 1930–36*: TNA CUST 118/367 at p. 29.

[134] *Parl. Deb.*, vol. 205, ser. 5, cols. 756–8, 26 April 1927 (HC) *per* Messrs Thurtle and Mosely.

[135] Report and Minutes of Evidence from the Select Committee on Medicine Stamp Duties, *House of Commons Parliamentary Papers* (1937) (Cmd. 54) viii 129 at p. 202 *per* H. N. Linstead.

[136] Two-thirds of the entire medicine stamp duty revenue was derived from stamps on the two lowest denominations, namely medicines costing 3d and 6d: *Board of Customs and Excise and Predecessor: Private Office Papers, The Medicine Stamp Duties 1783–1936*: TNA CUST 118/366 at p. 123.

ingredients. As such they provided a useful service to the public, who could purchase, inexpensively and safely, such remedies as analgesics and laxatives. The problem was that they encouraged consumers to delay seeking qualified medical treatment for their ailments.[137] The committee concluded in its report in 1937 that if it were deemed desirable to control the trade in medicines, that should be by a system of examination and registration of all advertised articles.[138]

THE DEMISE OF THE TAX

The recommendation of the Select Committee on the Medicine Stamp Duty in 1937 to the effect that the tax should be retained in principle but repealed and recast in fresh legislation to apply to all articles used as medicines and recommended as such, with fewer exemptions[139] and no preferential treatment for chemists and druggists with respect to proprietary medicines, was strongly objected to by all parties. The Royal Pharmaceutical Society said the proposals constituted a 'tax ... on the practice of pharmacy', and, because they were 'hasty and ill-considered' and the 'implications not thought out',[140] would result in 'a fresh period of uncertainty, compromise and litigation,'[141] replacing the settled conventions of revenue practice with chaos.[142] The Voluntary Hospitals Committee objected because some of their medicines would become liable, the Federation of British Industries and the Food Manufacturers' Federation objected because it would bring many articles that were not medicines into charge, the National Association of Cider makers because it would bring some ciders into charge and cripple the industry and advertising bodies because recommendation was the sole criterion for liability. The revenue authorities saw that the alternatives recommended by the Select Committee included no adequate definitions, and that administration would be impossible.

Most significant, however, was the public health perspective, and this was ultimately to prove decisive. The Ministry of Health objected because the Select Committee's proposed scheme was too wide and would attach to a range of simple, effective remedies that the public were accustomed to purchasing

---

[137] Report and Minutes of Evidence from the Select Committee on Medicine Stamp Duties, *House of Commons Parliamentary Papers* (1937) (Cmd. 54) viii 129 at p. 139.

[138] *Ibid.*, p. 142.

[139] *Ibid.*, pp. 140–1.

[140] *Board of Customs and Excise and Predecessor: Private Office Papers, The Medicine Stamp Duties 1936–39*: TNA CUST 118/391 at p. 39.

[141] *Ibid.*, p. 34.

[142] *Ibid.*

unstamped, and should continue to be able to do so. Despite the commit-tee's conclusion that medicines were a proper object of taxation, a contrary view could be discerned among many of the witnesses examined, along with a clear understanding that if a tax on medicines were to be introduced as a new tax now, it would be rejected out of hand. Certainly the Ministry of Health was quite clear in its view that medicines were not a suitable subject for tax-ation, and was happy to see the medicine stamp duty abolished. It believed all good medicines should be untaxed, and all bad medicines prohibited.[143] 'In the interests of public health', the minister had said in 1920, 'it is essen-tial that this traffic should be brought under strict control without delay'.[144] It seems, however, that the ministry was not prepared to assist in drawing the line between good and bad medicines and proposing a scheme for control.[145] It was clear that the revenue board could not hope to succeed where the Ministry of Health had failed. Any tax would catch both good and bad medicines, and would lay itself open to the criticism that it was a tax on health.[146]

At this point it was becoming clear that abolition was the only practical solution. The untenable legal position of the tax caused by bureaucratic law-making could not be solved by reforming the tax, because none of the pro-posed schemes – including that of the Select Committee itself – could be expressed in legislation in such a way as to be fair and secure and have any chance of getting through a critical and astute House of Commons. But it was clear now that the public health imperative made any recasting of medicine stamp duty, even if that were possible, politically indefensible. The revenue authorities themselves believed that '[c]ontrol and not taxation is the proper method of dealing with the abuses of extravagant advertisement or recom-mendation'.[147] Left with no option, in August 1937, a mere six months after the Select Committee report was printed, and following internal discussions, the revenue authorities decided the tax should be abolished.[148] In March 1938 they recommended to the Chancellor of the Exchequer that he should 'aban-don the duty altogether'[149] and Sir John Simon accordingly proposed it in his budget of April 1939. Advised that the medicine stamp duty had become

[143] *Ibid.*, pp. 63–4.
[144] *Memorandum by the Minister of Health on the Proposed Patent Medicines Bill*, 17th February 1920: TNA CAB/24/98.
[145] *Board of Customs and Excise and Predecessor: Private Office Papers, The Medicine Stamp Duties 1936–39*: TNA CUST 118/391 at p. 68.
[146] *Ibid.*, p. 90.
[147] *Ibid.*, p. 103.
[148] *Ibid.*
[149] *Ibid.*, p. 135.

administratively unworkable, that the alternative scheme suggested by the Select Committee in 1937 was unworkable and that repeal would not affect the public health,[150] he proposed complete abolition.[151]

The budget announcement was met with widespread, almost unanimous, resistance. Opposition centred on the two issues of loss of revenue and damage to the public health, but both stemmed from the determination of the chemists and druggists to retain the commercial advantages they enjoyed under the current fiscal regime.[152] The professional pharmaceutical bodies had grown considerably in political power and public influence, and they launched an intensive campaign of resistance to the proposed repeal.[153] They engineered opposition in the House of Commons, persuading members of Parliament to oppose the repeal.[154] The first, obvious, reason for opposition was the voluntary abandonment of any source of revenue at such a politically sensitive time, and for no better reason than difficulties in its administration.[155] The second reason was that the repeal of the tax would damage the public health. Despite the Chancellor's assurance that neither the Ministry of Health nor the medical profession as represented in the Select Committee of 1937 felt abolition would constitute any such danger, successive speakers urged that other than the poisons legislation, the medicine stamp duty constituted the only control over the sale of proprietary medicines. Without it, proprietary medicines would be freely sold by anyone, 'without let or hindrance as to place, quantity, or description'.[156] 'Control without taxation', argued Sir Arnold Wilson, 'is impossible'.[157] The medical profession objected to the repeal on this basis, arguing that it would lead to even greater self-medication.[158] In this same context of damage to the public health, the chemists urged one valid and persuasive point: the medicine stamp duty, through the operation of the *known, admitted and approved* remedy exemption, had encouraged disclosure of the formulae of proprietary medicines and if the tax and its exemption were

---

[150] *Parl. Deb.*, vol. 346, ser. 5, col. 990, 25 April 1939 (HC); *ibid.*, vol. 347, ser. 5, col. 2587, 25 May 1939 *per* Sir John Simon.

[151] *Ibid.*, vol. 348, ser. 5, cols. 2597–2603, 22 June 1939 (HC).

[152] One of the few members of Parliament to make this point clearly was Mr Alexander: *ibid.*, cols. 2595–7.

[153] *Board of Customs and Excise and Predecessor: Private Office Papers, The Medicine Stamp Duties 1936–39*: TNA CUST 118/391 at pp. 190–3.

[154] 'On the Floor of the House', (1939) 234 *The Lancet* 43.

[155] *Parl. Deb.*, vol. 348, ser. 5, cols. 2575–6, 22 June 1939 (HC) *per* Graham White; *ibid.*, col. 2589 *per* Sir Henry Morris-Jones.

[156] *Ibid.*, col. 2576 *per* Graham White.

[157] *Ibid.*, col. 2582 *per* Sir Arnold Wilson.

[158] 'Repeal of the Medicine Stamp Duties', (1941) 237 *The Lancet* 513.

repealed, there would be no incentive to disclose and a return to secret remedies.[159] The danger was that '[t]he fog of complete pharmaceutical obscurity will again fall on the market for proprietary preparations and there will be no check on what is being sold'.[160] This was recognised by the House, and for the medical profession it was a key issue.[161] *The Lancet* commented that '[w]hatever its fiscal convenience, the repeal of the medicine stamp duty] ... is socially and medically a retrograde step'.[162] The strength of this parliamentary opposition proved too strong. Without a scheme of control to replace it, the Chancellor of the Exchequer was forced to postpone the abolition of the tax to allow for a further inquiry.[163]

In August the Chancellor of the Exchequer and the Minister of Health met a deputation of members of Parliament and agreed that they would set up a small departmental committee to discuss the two distinct issues of control and taxation. The proposal got no further, being postponed due to the outbreak of war in the autumn of 1939. But the revenue authorities were nervous: Woolworth's – understandably, because they had withdrawn their action on the promise that the matter would be addressed by the government – were not happy with the postponement of the abolition. They acted provocatively in selling a dutiable toothpaste unstamped, and also threatened renewed legal action. The revenue authorities could 'never know when the volcano may erupt'.[164]

Having reached an impasse, it was not until the introduction of the purchase tax, a direct ad valorem tax, in 1940 that there came an incontrovertible reason to abolish the medicine stamp duty entirely rather than merely reform it.[165] Its arrival in the fiscal code marked the final phase of the medicine stamp duty. The new tax applied to transactions between wholesalers and retailers, including sales of all medicines except 'certain essential and costly drugs and medicines',[166] with other drugs and medicines being charged at a reduced

---

[159] *Board of Customs and Excise and Predecessor: Private Office Papers, The Medicine Stamp Duties 1936–39*: TNA CUST 118/391 at pp. 191–2; *Parl. Deb.*, vol. 348, ser. 5, col. 2584, 22 June 1939 (HC) *per* Sir Arnold Wilson.

[160] 'Parliamentary Intelligence', (1939) 233 *The Lancet* 1238.

[161] See for example *Parl. Deb.*, vol. 348, ser. 5, cols. 2590–92, 22 June 1939 (HC) *per* Dr Edith Summerskill.

[162] 'The Budget', (1939) 233 *The Lancet* 999.

[163] *Parl. Deb.*, vol. 348, ser. 5, col. 2604, 22 June 1939 (HC) *per* Sir John Simon.

[164] *Board of Customs and Excise and Predecessor: Private Office Papers, The Medicine Stamp Duties: Last Phase: 1939–41*: TNA CUST 118/404 at p. 26.

[165] Finance (No. 2) Act 1940 (3 & 4 Geo. VI c.48) ss. 18–41.

[166] Such as cocaine and insulin: 'Purchase Tax: Proposed List of Essential Drugs', (1940) *British Medical Journal* 427; 'Drugs Exempt from Purchase Tax', (1941) *British Medical Journal* 663.

rate.[167] There was no suggestion or expectation that the purchase tax would be anything other than a revenue-raising instrument, and care was taken that standard drugs were not subject to it. It strikingly illustrated not only a tenacious belief that medicines were suitable objects of taxation,[168] but also a persistent reluctance entirely to disassociate tax from the question of control.[169] Nevertheless, because the purchase tax would be charged on the price of the medicine including the medicine stamp duty where sold to an unqualified trader, it constituted a tax upon a tax. It would also thereby increase the economic benefit enjoyed by qualified chemists through the application of the *known, admitted and approved* remedy exemption under the medicine stamp duty. Purchase tax thus provided the ideal political opportunity to call for the complete repeal of the medicine stamp duty. Double taxation was evidently unjustifiable, and the Proprietary Association of Great Britain made an 'emphatic protest' against it, arguing that it would place an unacceptably heavy burden on the very large section of the public who bought these simple remedies for minor ailments. It was 'unjustifiable', would 'penalise severely the sick,' jeopardise businesses and adversely affect the export trade.[170]

While privately the Chancellor of the Exchequer, Sir Kingsley Wood, admitted that it was an 'appallingly difficult problem',[171] he saw this was an opportunity not to be missed, and he determined to bring together the various pharmaceutical unions and bodies representing retail, manufacturing and wholesale chemists, as well as representatives of the grocery trade, to arrive at a compromise that would 'maintain a fair balance between the interests of the pharmacists and those of other vendors'.[172] The chemists would accept the repeal of the medicine stamp duty in return for a new statutory equivalent privilege to compensate them for the loss of the *known, admitted*

[167] The basic rate of purchase tax was 33⅓ per cent of the wholesale value of chargeable goods. Certain 'essential and costly' drugs and medicines were free of tax, and other drugs and medicines were chargeable at the reduced rate of 16⅔ per cent. See Thirty-seventh Report of the Commissioners of Customs and Excise, *House of Commons Parliamentary Papers* (1945–46) (Cmd. 6951) xi 171 at pp. 314–5. See 'Medicines and the Purchase Tax', (1940) 236 *The Lancet* 458.

[168] Second reading of the Pharmacy and Medicines Bill, *Parl. Deb.*, vol. 373, ser. 5, col. 65, 8 July 1941 (HC) *per* Ernest Brown.

[169] See the correspondence between the revenue authorities and the Chancellor of the Exchequer in *Board of Customs and Excise and Predecessor: Private Office Papers, The Medicine Stamp Duties 1936–39*: TNA CUST 118/391 at pp. 251–8.

[170] *Board of Customs and Excise and Predecessor: Private Office Papers, The Medicine Stamp Duties: Last Phase: 1939–41*: TNA CUST 118/404 at pp. 26–7.

[171] *Ibid.*, p. 47.

[172] *Parl. Deb.*, vol. 370 ser. 5, col. 1313, 7 April 1941 (HC) *per* Sir Kingsley Wood. See too *ibid.*, vol. 364, ser. 5, cols. 740–1, 13 August 1940, (HC) Sir Kingsley Wood.

and approved remedy advantage. The agreement – arrived at by the various vendors and with their widespread support – was that only qualified chemists or medical practitioners could sell by retail any medicine recommended for the prevention, cure or relief of a human ailment – essentially, *known, admitted and approved* remedies. Single drugs, mineral waters and proprietary medicines not described in the *British Pharmacopoeia* or the *British Pharmaceutical Codex*, could be sold freely by unqualified individuals, even if recommended.[173] Essentially, the agreement left the sale of recommended medicines with known composition to the qualified chemist, and the sale of recommended medicines of unknown composition to the unqualified vendor – an anomaly not lost on the editor of *The Lancet*.[174]

The scheme ostensibly addressed the medicine stamp duty problem, removing double taxation, and doing so with the support of the chemists and other vendors,[175] and retaining existing trade practices and usages. What the scheme patently did not do was to control proprietary medicines. The Ministry of Health described it as 'an ingenious and tolerably successful attempt to preserve the balance between the two Trade interests', but it had 'no other merits whatever'.[176] Nevertheless the consensus in government in early 1941 was that the medicine stamp duty, that 'museum piece of administrative complexity',[177] should be repealed for fiscal reasons alone, because until the end of hostilities there was no realistic prospect of formulating a scheme to control proprietary medicines in the interests of public health. The Chancellor of the Exchequer announced in his budget of 1941 that the medicine stamp duty would be repealed and the trade agreement given legal force.[178] Again, the loss of some £800,000 a year in revenue caused some concern in Parliament, as did the removal of the only measure of control over the consumption of proprietary medicines. It was feared that the repeal would cause an increase in drug taking and self-medication, that such medicines would be available so easily and widely that 'it will be inviting the people to go in for an orgy of self-medication'.[179] Following tortuous political wrangling, the view emerged that the tax could not be repealed until some controlling legislation

---

[173] *Board of Customs and Excise and Predecessor: Private Office Papers, The Medicine Stamp Duties: Last Phase: 1939–41*: TNA CUST 118/404 at pp. 80–1, 85.

[174] 'Impending Drug Legislation', (1941) 237 *The Lancet* 762.

[175] *Board of Customs and Excise and Predecessor: Private Office Papers, The Medicine Stamp Duties: Last Phase: 1939–41*: TNA CUST 118/404 at p. 96.

[176] *Ibid.*, p. 98.

[177] *Parl. Deb.*, vol. 370, ser. 5, cols. 1314–15, 7 April 1941 (HC) *per* Sir Kingsley Wood, Chancellor of the Exchequer.

[178] *Ibid.*

[179] *Ibid.*, vol. 370, ser. 5, cols. 1651–4, 9 April 1941 (HC) *per* Captain Elliston.

was introduced.[180] At that point, any provision for the control of proprietary medicines passed out of the hands of the revenue authorities and squarely into those of the Ministry of Health. Because the trade arrangement had no fiscal content, it could not be part of a finance bill, and it was clear that repeal of the medicine stamp duty should be included in any controlling legislation rather than a finance bill, only because opposition was feared if the two matters of the repeal and the trade agreement were not dealt with together.

The Pharmacy and Medicines Act 1941 embodied the control measures that had become generally accepted as necessary.[181] It brought together a number of regulatory provisions relating to the preparation, retail and advertisement of medicines, providing that dispensing and compounding drugs on the premises was prohibited where the sale of drugs was not a substantial part of the business, and that advertising cures for certain diseases such as tuberculosis, glaucoma, diabetes and cancer outside the regular medical profession was forbidden.[182] The only fiscal provision in the Act was that which abolished the medicine stamp duty.[183] It simply provided that all duties charged under the medicine stamp Acts would be repealed as from 2 September 1941, the interval being included to allow for the disposal of stamped stock. It followed from the repeal that the Act embodied the trade agreement that aimed to compensate the chemists for the fiscal advantage they had enjoyed under the medicine stamp duty by introducing a trading privilege. The Act restricted the retail sale of recommended medicines to certain classes of qualified individuals, including medical practitioners, dentists and chemists, but it also provided that the composition and active ingredients of any article recommended as a medicine had to be disclosed by listing on the packet or by reference to the *British Pharmacopoeia* or the *British Pharmaceutical Codex*.[184] This was the 'monopolistic privilege in lieu' of the *known, admitted and approved* remedy exemption.[185] 'It is in the public interest', it was said in Commons Committee on the bill,

> that the future of the chemists' profession should be safeguarded and that the repeal of the medicine duties should not lead to such a reduction in the

[180] *Board of Customs and Excise and Predecessor: Private Office Papers, The Medicine Stamp Duties: Last Phase: 1939–41*: TNA CUST 118/404 at pp. 115–24.
[181] 4 & 5 Geo. VI c. 42.
[182] Reputable newspapers had been abiding by a voluntary code to this effect for many years.
[183] 4 & 5 Geo. VI c. 42 s. 14.
[184] *Ibid.*, s. 11.
[185] See the secret memorandum by the Home Secretary and others dated June 1941 in *Board of Customs and Excise and Predecessor: Private Office Papers, The Medicine Stamp Duties: Last Phase: 1939–41*: TNA CUST 118/404 at p. 127.

numbers of those at present engaged in a vitally necessary profession, or in the numbers of those willing to come forward as recruits to it, that an essential link in the Nation's health services would be broken. This might well be the effect of depriving chemists of the fiscal advantages which they at present possess from their right to sell known, admitted and approved remedies free of stamp duty without conferring on them some compensating privilege of a reasonable nature.[186]

The government's view was that the clause gave the chemists proper protection, and yet permitted the repeal of an antiquated and unsatisfactory tax. Furthermore, in so doing, it interfered hardly at all with established trade practices: the normal channels and methods of retailing medicines remained largely unchanged. There was, therefore, 'no justification for representing the clause as a frontal attack on legitimate trading or as an attempt to set up in favour of qualified persons a monopoly which would be detrimental to public welfare'.[187] Nevertheless, the Act was soon perceived by the chemists and druggists as a hollow victory. They were 'very unhappy' about the legislation[188] and 'filled with rage',[189] because they finally realised what the government had known all along: that they had 'sacrificed the substance for the shadow'.[190]

A FISCAL NONENTITY OR REVEALING PARADIGM?

A tax as specialised, as relatively insignificant in monetary terms and as highly circumscribed in its field of operation as the medicine stamp duty could appear, on those criteria, to be a fiscal nonentity. In terms of yield and scope, most other taxes in the British fiscal system of the nineteenth century had a far greater and more obvious presence among the taxpaying public, the officers of the revenue boards, the legislature and, increasingly, the judiciary. This study has shown that despite such a modest position within the formal structures of tax and law, and social perceptions, the medicine stamp duty was a tax of exceptional importance as a revealing paradigm. Through an almost unique combination of legal, fiscal and social features it exposed with remarkable clarity three broad themes that transcended its own operation and was relevant to all taxes within the British tax system as they developed in the nineteenth and early twentieth centuries. It is in permitting this exceptional degree of

[186] *Ibid.*, in Notes to Amendments, pp. 155ff. (clause 7).
[187] *Ibid.*
[188] *Ibid.*, p. 130.
[189] *Board of Customs and Excise and Predecessor: Private Office Papers, The Medicine Stamp Duties: Last Phase: 1939–41*: TNA CUST 118/404 at p. 143.
[190] *Ibid.*, p. 130.

insight that the story of the medicine stamp duty is significant in the history of British tax law.

First, it has been seen that the medicine stamp duty was driven by political imperatives to raise urgently needed public revenue. Despite the object of charge being both dangerous and morally undesirable, it eschewed any pretensions to a material regulatory effect and recognised the subsidiary market control only for its political effect. In this, the tax displayed the often hidden forces at play in the introduction of an impost into the tax system. It demonstrates the potency of orthodox views on the purpose of taxation as purely revenue-raising, and the negative – or indifferent – official attitudes to regulatory objectives or effects.

Second, the deeply flawed legislation, deteriorating as the years passed without reform, required the revenue boards to implement it as best they could, resulting in a code of law so encrusted with bureaucratic practice that it became fiscally, legally and politically untenable. It shows bureaucratic lawmaking at its zenith and starkly reveals its extremes. There were some positive aspects, notably a desire on the part of the revenue authorities to ensure fairness in tax administration and a mitigation of the law's severity, official courtesy and assistance to taxpayers, and a strongly supportive and knowledgeable professional press to assist those liable to the tax. Nevertheless the tax constituted the most powerful example of the profound dangers, not only to individual legal regimes but to the entire legal order, of both fiscal and legal complacency, the impossibility of tax officials' position in the face of legislative inertia and the power of pragmatic necessity. It reveals where the limits of bureaucratic lawmaking lay, and these were not within the executive, which was driven by necessity, nor indeed the Treasury, which was largely ineffectual with respect to the Crown-appointed revenue commissioners,[191] nor Parliament, which allowed the law to stagnate, nor within the judiciary, which was necessarily reactive. Instead, the medicine stamp duty shows that the limit to bureaucratic lawmaking was a practical one: administering a tax through reliance on extensive administrative practice was not sustainable and ultimately failed in its objective of rendering the tax viable. Left to the executive department, and without the controls of considered and up-to-date legislation and the scrutiny of the courts, the law became even more uncertain, more inconsistent and more inaccessible. It was said to bristle with anomalies.[192] In short, it became

---

[191] Twentieth Report of the Commissioners of Inquiry (Excise Establishment), *House of Commons Parliamentary Papers* (1836) (22) xxvi 181 at pp. 303–6.

[192] *Board of Customs and Excise and Predecessor: Private Office Papers, The Medicine Stamp Duties 1783–1936*: TNA CUST 118/366 at p. 122.

chaotic with no possibility of coherent development. Confidence, compliance and enforcement were utterly undermined.

Third, in unifying chemists and druggists and recognising them as belonging to a skilled occupation, the medicine stamp duty showed how a tax could have unintended social effects and constitute a largely unrecognised factor, both positive and negative, in a range of social phenomena. Professionalisation, with the modern pharmacy profession being, to some extent at least, a social product of tax law and its bureaucratic practice, was one such phenomenon, but another was the longer-term integrity and authenticity of therapeutic drugs. Here the medicine stamp duty promoted major advances in the scientific analysis of medicines and was responsible for introducing widespread disclosure of the active ingredients of medicines sold to the public without prescription.

Finally, these themes of fiscal imperatives, bureaucratic lawmaking and social effects combine to demonstrate the intensely isolationist nature of tax law and its administration within the British legal system. The medicine stamp duty acutely shows its nature and extent. In distancing itself from any non-fiscal objective, its attitudes to public health epitomised its isolation. From its inception the medicine stamp duty was officially regarded and popularly perceived as a tax and not as an instrument of medical regulation. Like all tax legislation, the medicine stamp duty Acts were designed with the needs of the state and not of the taxpayer in mind. The fact that the medicine stamp duty was allowed to operate as a tax like any other meant that fiscal concerns dominated, and any wider considerations as to its impact on the field of activity in which it operated were ignored. So its efficacy or inefficiency as a control on dangerous medicines was disregarded, and any regulatory effect it might have had was not allowed to operate outside the constraints of the essential nature of taxation. The fiscal character dominated, and the medicine stamp duty brought with it all the consequences of its character as a tax. This exclusivity as a financial instrument, its expression in tax law and the fisco-medical construct in which it operated was an inherent and probably unavoidable limitation of the tax regime.

It was the acceptance of its flagrant and extensive undermining of the orthodox conception of the authority of law that demonstrated above all the isolation of tax law. Although ultimately this caused its demise, the manifest undermining of the authority of law exhibited by the medicine stamp duty was seen as exceptional and not regarded as a threat to the integrity of the authority of law in general. The reason for this passivity was, essentially, the isolation of tax law from the rest of English law. There was no reason or principle in English law that suggested that tax law was in any way different from any other branch of law. Indeed, such was the importance of the control of tax-raising powers in the struggle for democratic rights; it was all the more crucial to ensure that the authority of Parliament and of the judiciary was maintained as paramount and inviolable. Tax law was, indubitably, formal law, but it possessed certain characteristics that set it apart and made it stand outside the norms of the legal system. It had a rare and prominent constitutional underpinning, its own special parliamentary process, remarkably little judge-made law, and its administration was so highly specialised that it inevitably became dominated by expert civil servants responsible for its implementation and given extensive powers to do so. These special characteristics led the legislature, the executive, the taxpayer and to some extent the judiciary to perceive tax law as distinct from the rest of the law – indeed, often not as real law at all. Tax law and its administration was a closed and inward-looking institution, a self-referential system, looking to itself, concerned with its own operation, setting its own and almost invariably exclusively financial criteria for success within an operational culture that excluded both the taxpayer as an individual carrying on an activity that gave rise to that state and the orthodox conception of the authority of the law. As a result of this perception of tax law, the threat to the authority of law so sharply exemplified by the medicine stamp duty was regarded by the legal establishment as entirely confined to the sphere of taxation, an exceptional occurrence in English law resulting from the unique nature of tax law. As such it was not considered to reflect a wider undermining of the law by the executive, nor any kind of generalised reluctance of the law to engage with it.

Appendix

MEDICINE STAMP DUTY ACT 1785

25 Geo. III c. 79

An Act for repealing an Act, made in the twenty-third Year of the Reign of his present Majesty, intituled, *An Act for granting to his Majesty a Stamp-duty on Licences to be taken out by certain Persons uttering or vending Medicines; and certain Stamp-duties on all Medicines sold under such Licences, or under the Authority of his Majesty's Letters Patent*; and for granting other Duties in lieu thereof.

WHEREAS by an Act, made in the twenty-third Year of the Reign of his present Majesty King George the Third, intituled, *An Act for granting to his Majesty a Stamp-duty on Licences to be taken out by certain Persons uttering or vending Medicines; and certain Stamp-duties on all Medicines sold under such Licences, or under the Authority of his Majesty's Letters Patent*; it was enacted, That, from and after the first Day of *September* one thousand seven hundred and eighty-three, there should be charged, levied, and paid, unto and for the Use of his Majesty, his Heirs and Successors, the several Rates and Duties following; (that is to say,) All Persons (except such as had served a regular Apprenticeship to any Surgeon, Apothecary, Druggist, or Chymist, or such as had kept a Shop for the Space of three Years before the passing of that Act, for the vending of Drugs or Medicines only (not being Drugs or Medicines sold by virtue of his Majesty's Letters Patent), uttering or vending Medicines in *Great Britain*, should annually take out a Licence for that Purpose, in Manner therein prescribed; and where the Persons so uttering or vending Drugs or Medicines, should reside within the Cities of *London* and *Westminster*, or within the Distance of the Penny Post, on every such Licence there should be charged a Stamp-duty of twenty Shillings; and where the Persons, so uttering or vending such Drugs or Medicines, should reside in any other Part of *Great Britain*, there should be charged on every such Licence a Stamp-duty of five Shillings: Upon every Box, Packet, Bottle, or Phial, or other Inclosure of any Medicine under the Price or Value of two Shillings and six Pence, which should be uttered, vended, or sold, by any Person or Persons taking out such Licences, or by any Person or Persons under the Authority of his Majesty's Letters Patent, there should be charged a Stamp-duty of three Pence: Upon every Box, Packet, Bottle, or Phial, or other Inclosure of any Medicine of the Price or Value of two Shillings and six Pence, and under the Price or Value of five Shillings, which should be uttered, vended, or sold, by any Person or Persons taking out such Licences, or by any Person or Persons under the Authority of his Majesty's Letters Patent, there should be charged a Stamp-duty of six Pence: Upon every Box, Packet, Bottle, or Phial, or other Inclosure of any Medicine of the Price or Value of five Shillings and upwards, which should be uttered, vended, or sold, by any Persons taking out such Licences, or by any Persons under the Authority of his Majesty's Letters Patent, there should be charged a Stamp-duty of one Shilling: Now, we, your Majesty's most dutiful and loyal Subjects, the Commons of *Great Britain*, in Parliament assembled, finding that it will be convenient and for the Publick Service to repeal the said Stamp-duties, so made payable by the said recited Act, and to grant unto your Majesty the several new Stamp-duties herein after mentioned, for securing a certain Fund for the Payment of such Annuities as by the said recited Act were charged upon the said Stamp-duties; therefore do most humbly beseech your Majesty that it may be enacted; and be it enacted by the King's most Excellent Majesty, by and with the Advice and Consent of the Lords Spiritual and Temporal, and Commons, in this present Parliament assembled, and by the Authority of the same, That, from and after the first Day of *September* one thousand seven hundred and eighty-five, the Rates and Duties granted by an Act, made and passed in the twenty-third Year of his present Majesty, intituled, *An Act for granting to his Majesty a Stamp-duty on Licences to be taken out by certain Persons uttering or vending Medicines; and certain Stamp-duties on all Medicines sold under such Licences, or under the Authority of his Majesty's Letters Patent*; shall cease, determine, and be no longer paid or payable.

II. And be it further enacted by the Authority aforesaid, That, from and after the said first Day of *September* one thousand seven hundred and eighty-five, there shall be raised, levied, collected, and paid, throughout the Kingdom of *Great Britain*, unto and for the Use of his Majesty, his Heirs and Successors, the several Rates and Duties following; (that is to say),

That for and upon every Packet, Box, Bottle, Phial, or other Inclosure containing any Drugs, Oils, Waters, Essences, Tinctures, Powders, or other Preparation or Composition whatsoever, used or applied, or to be used or applied, externally or internally, as Medicines or Medicaments for the Prevention, Cure, or Relief of any Disorder or Complaint incident to, or in any wise affecting the Human Body, which shall be uttered or vended in *Great Britain*, there shall be charged a Stamp-duty according to the Rates following; (that is to say,) Where the Contents of any such Packet, Box, Bottle, Phial, or other Inclosure aforesaid, shall not exceed the Price or Value of one Shilling, there shall be charged a Stamp-duty of one Penny Halfpenny:

And where the Contents of any such Packet, Box, Bottle, Phial, or other Inclosure aforesaid, shall exceed the Price or Value of one Shilling, and not exceed the Price or Value of two Shillings and six Pence, there shall be charged a Stamp-duty of three Pence:

And where the Contents of any such Packet, Box, Bottle, Phial, or other Inclosure aforesaid, shall be above the Price or Value of two Shillings and six Pence, and under the Price or Value of five Shillings, there shall be charged a Stamp-duty of six Pence:

And where the Contents of any such Packet, Box, Bottle, Phial, or other Inclosure, shall be of the Price or Value of five Shillings or upwards, there shall be charged a Stamp-duty of one Shilling.

III. Provided always, That nothing herein before contained shall extend, or be construed to extend, to charge with the Rates or Duties hereby imposed, any Drug or Drugs named or contained in either of the Books of Rates; (that is to say,) The Book of Rates, subscribed with the Name of Sir *Harbottle Grimstone* Baronet, and mentioned and referred to by the Act of Tonnage and Poundage, made in the twelfth Year of the Reign of King CHARLES the Second; or in the other Book of Rates, intituled, *An additional Book of Rates of Goods and Merchandizes usually imported, and not particularly rated in the Book of Rates referred to in the Act of Tonnage and Poundage, made in the twelfth Year of the Reign of King* CHARLES *the Second, with Rules, Orders, and Regulations, signed by the Right Honourable* Spencer Compton, *Speaker of the Honourable House of Commons*, and mentioned and referred to by an Act made and passed in the eleventh Year of the Reign of his Majesty King GEORGE the First; nor to any Medicinal Drug or Drugs whatsoever, which shall be uttered or vended entire, without any Mixture or Composition with any other Drug or Ingredient whatsoever, by any Surgeon, Apothecary, Chemist, or Druggist, who hath served a regular Apprenticeship, or by any Person who hath served as a Surgeon in the Navy or Army, under any Commission or Appointment which shall have been duly entered at the War Office or Navy Office, or by any other Person whatsoever licensed in pursuance of this Act; but that all such Drugs shall and may be uttered and vended by all such Surgeons, Apothecaries, Chymists, and Druggists, or other Persons licensed as aforesaid, freed and discharged from the Rates and Duties by this Act imposed on Drugs, in such Manner as they respectively, before the passing of this Act, and the said herein recited Act, might have done.

IV. Provided also, That nothing herein before contained shall extend, or be construed to extend, to charge with the like Rates or Duties any Mixture, Composition, or Preparation whatsoever, mixed or compounded with, or prepared from Medicinal Drugs, medicated or chymical Preparations or Compositions, or other Ingredients bearing different Denominations, or having different Properties, Qualities, Virtues, or Efficacies, which shall be uttered or vended by any such Surgeon, Apothecary, Chymist, or Druggist, as aforesaid, or by any such Person who hath served as a Surgeon in the Navy or Army, under any such Commission or Appointment as aforesaid, the different Denominations, Properties, Qualities, Virtues, and Efficacies of which Mixtures, Compositions, and Preparations, are known, admitted, and approved of, in the Prevention, Cure, or Relief of any Disorder, Malady, Ailment, or Complaint incident to, or in anywise affecting the human Body; and wherein the Person mixing, compounding, preparing, or uttering or vending the same, hath not, nor claims to have, any occult, secret, or unknown Art for the mixing, compounding, or preparing the same, nor hath, nor claims to have, any exclusive Right or Title to the mixing, compounding, or preparing, or to the vending of the same, and which Mixtures, Compositions, or Preparations, have not been, are not, nor hereafter shall be prepared, uttered, vended, or exposed to Sale, under the Authority of any Letters Patent under the Great Seal, nor at any Time heretofore have been, now are, or hereafter shall be, by any publick Notice, Advertisement, or by written or printed Papers or Hand Bills, held out or recommended to the Publick by the Makers, Proprietors, or Venders thereof, as Nostrums or Proprietary Medicines, or as Specifics, or otherwise, for the Prevention, Cure, or Relief of any such Distemper, Malady, Ailment, or Complaint as aforesaid.

V. And be it further enacted by the Authority aforesaid, That every Person in *Great Britain,* uttering or vending any Drugs, Oils, Waters, Essences, Tinctures, Powders, or other Preparations or Compositions whatsoever, used or applied, or to be used or applied, externally or internally, as Medicines or Medicaments for the Prevention, Cure, or Relief of any Disorder or Complaint incident to, or in anywise affecting the human Body, subject to the Duties herein before imposed, shall, annually, take out a Licence for that Purpose and that, for and upon every Licence so taken out by any such Person who shall reside within the Cities of *London* or *Westminster*, the Borough of *Southwark*, or within the Limits of the Penny Post, or within the City of *Edinburgh*, there shall be charged a Stamp-duty of twenty Shillings; and for and upon every Licence, so taken out by any other such Person, there shall be charged a Stamp-duty of five Shillings.

VI. And be it further enacted by the Authority aforesaid, That, for the better and more effectual levying and collecting all the said Duties herein before granted, the same shall be under the Government, Care, and Management of the Commissioners for the Time being appointed to manage the Duties charged on stamped Vellum, Parchment, and Paper; who, or the major Part of them, are hereby required and impowered to appoint and employ such Officers under them for that Purpose, and to allow such Salaries and incidental Charges as may be necessary, and to provide and use such Stamps to denote the said several Duties as shall be requisite in that Behalf, and to do all other Things necessary to be done for putting this Act in Execution with relation to the said Rates and Duties herein before granted, in the like, and in as full and ample Manner, as they, or the major Part of them, are or is authorised to put in Execution any former Law concerning stamped Vellum, Parchment, and Paper.

VII. And be it further enacted by the Authority aforesaid, That, from and after the passing of this Act, any two or more of his Majesty's Commissioners appointed for managing the Duties arising by Stamps on Vellum, Parchment, and Paper, or some Person duly authorised by them, shall grant Licences to such Persons who shall apply for the same, to utter or vend, in any City, Town, or other Place within *Great Britain*, any Drugs, Oils, Waters, Essences, Tinctures, Powders, or other Preparation or Composition whatsoever, used or applied, or to be used or applied, externally or internally, as Medicines or Medicaments for the Prevention, Cure, or Relief of any Disorder or Complaint incident to, or in anywise affecting the human Body, and subject to the Duties by this Act imposed; and the said Licences shall continue in force for the Space of one Year, commencing from the first Day of *September* one thousand seven hundred and eighty-five, upon all Licences to be granted on or before that Day; and upon Licences to be first granted to any Person or Persons after the said first Day of *September* one thousand seven hundred and eighty-five, to commence from the Day of the Date of every such Licence; and all and every Person and Persons, who shall take out such Licence for uttering or vending any such Drugs, Medicines, Medicaments, or other Preparations or Compositions aforesaid, shall take out a fresh Licence for another Year, ten Days at the least before the Expiration of that Year for which he or she shall be so licensed, if he or she shall continue to utter or sell such Drugs, Medicines, Medicaments, or other Preparations or Compositions aforesaid; and shall, in like Manner, renew such Licence, from Year to Year, paying down the respective Sums due for the Stamps on such Licences, as long as he or she shall continue to utter or vend such Drugs, Medicines, Medicaments, or other Preparations or Compositions as aforesaid.

VIII. And be it further enacted by the Authority aforesaid, That, from and after the said first Day of *September* one thousand seven hundred and eighty-five, no Person whatsoever shall utter, vend, or expose to Sale, any Drugs, Medicines, Medicaments, or other Preparations or Compositions aforesaid, which shall be subject to the Duty herein before imposed, unless he or she shall have first obtained a Licence in such Manner as is herein before directed, upon Pain to forfeit, for every such Offence, the Sum of five Pounds, to be recovered and applied as herein after is directed.

IX. And, in order to secure the Duty hereby imposed, be it further enacted by the Authority aforesaid, That every Person making, preparing, or vending any such Drugs, Medicines, or Medicaments, or other Preparations or Compositions aforesaid, which are subject to the Duty herein before imposed, shall, from Time to Time, send, or cause to be sent, to the said Commissioners of Stamps, or to their Officers appointed by them for that Purpose, Paper Covers, Wrappers, or Labels, made for inclosing such Packets, Boxes, Bottles, Phials, or other Inclosures, containing or intended to contain any such Drugs, Medicines, Medicaments, or other Preparations or Compositions aforesaid, with his, her, or their Name or Names, and any other particular Word or Thing printed thereon, to denote the Value at which the same are respectively intended to be sold, in such Manner and Form as the said Commissioners shall from Time to Time direct, in order that the same may be stamped with the several and respective Duties hereby directed to be imposed, and marked, impressed, and distinguished with such other Mark or Device as the said Commissioners shall direct, and delivered again from Time to Time to such Maker or Vender, as Occasion shall require; and all and every the Packets, Boxes, Bottles, or Phials, or other Inclosures, containing any Drugs, Medicines, Medicaments, or other Preparations or Compositions aforesaid, uttered, vended, or exposed to Sale, by any Person or Persons whatsoever, shall have pasted, stuck, fastened, or affixed thereto, such Covers, Wrappers, or Labels, stamped, marked, impressed, and distinguished as aforesaid, in such Manner as the said Commissioners shall from Time to Time direct.

X. And be it further enacted by the Authority aforesaid, That no Person or Persons shall utter, vend, or expose to Sale, any Packet, Box, Bottle, or Phial, or any other Inclosure, containing any Drug, Medicine, Medicament, or other Preparation or Composition aforesaid, subject to the Stamp-duties hereby imposed, unless the Cover, Wrapper, or Label, hereby directed to be pasted, stuck, fastened, or affixed to the same, shall be pasted, stuck, fastened, or affixed thereto, and marked and stamped as by this Act is directed; or that shall have any Cover, Wrapper, or Label pasted, stuck, fastened, or affixed thereto, marked or stamped with a Mark or Stamp of less Denomination or Value than by this Act is directed, under Pain that all and every such Person and Persons so offending shall forfeit and pay, for every Packet, Box, Bottle, or Phial, or other Inclosure, containing any such Drug, Medicine, Medicament, or other Preparation or Composition aforesaid, so uttered, vended, or exposed to Sale, the Sum of five Pounds, to be recovered and applied as herein after is directed.

XI. And, to prevent the Cover, Wrapper, or Label, and the Mark or Stamp thereon, hereby directed to be pasted, stuck, fastened, or affixed to every Packet, Box, Bottle, Phial, or other Inclosure, containing any Drug, Medicine, Medicament, or other Preparation or Composition aforesaid, from being made use of again after they have been sold and disposed of, to be affixed to other Packets, Boxes, Bottles, Phials, or other Inclosures, containing any Drugs, Medicines, Medicaments, or other Preparations or Compositions aforesaid, by which Practices his Majesty's Revenue might be lessened and diminished; be it further enacted by the Authority aforesaid, That if any Person or Persons shall, from and after the first Day of *September* one thousand seven hundred and eighty-five, fraudulently cut, tear, or take off any Mark or Stamp, in respect whereof or whereby any Duties are hereby payable, or denoted to be paid or payable to his Majesty, on any Packet, Box, Bottle, or Phial, or other Inclosure, containing any Drug, Medicine, Medicament, or other Preparation or Composition aforesaid, subject to the Duties hereby imposed, after the same shall have been sold or disposed of as aforesaid; or shall fraudulently paste, stick, fasten, or affix to any such Packet, Box, Bottle, or Phial, any Cover, Wrapper, or Label, so marked and stamped as aforesaid, the same having once been made use of for the Purpose aforesaid; or shall utter, vend, or expose to Sale, any Packet, Box, Bottle, Phial, or other Inclosure, containing any Drug, Medicine, Medicament, or other Preparation or Composition aforesaid, with such Cover, Wrapper, or Label, so fraudulently cut, torn, or taken off as afore-said, and pasted, stuck, fastened, or affixed thereto; all and every Person and Persons so offending, in any of the Particulars before mentioned, shall, for every such Offence, forfeit and pay the Sum of ten Pounds, to be recovered and applied as herein after is directed.

XII. And, to prevent Persons from fraudulently selling or buying any Covers, Wrappers, or Labels, which have been before made use of for denoting any of the Duties by this Act imposed, or any Packets, Boxes, Bottles, Phials, or other Inclosures, wherein any Drugs, Medicines, Medicaments, or other Preparations or Compositions aforesaid, have been contained, and sold and disposed of with such Covers, Wrappers, or Labels, pasted, stuck, fastened, or affixed thereto; be it further enacted by the Authority aforesaid, That if any Person or Persons shall, from and after the first Day of *September* one thousand seven hundred and eighty-five, sell or buy any such Cover, Wrapper, or Label, which hath before been made use for the inclosing any Packet, Box, Bottle, or Phial, or other Inclosure of any Drug, Medicine, Medicament, or other Preparation or Composition, liable to the Duty hereby imposed, in order to be again made use of for the like Purpose; or shall sell or buy any Packet, Box, Bottle, Phial, or other Inclosure, with such Cover, Wrapper, or Label, which hath before been made use of as aforesaid, pasted, stuck, fastened, or affixed thereto; every such Person so offending shall, for every such Offence, forfeit and pay the Sum of ten Pounds, to be recovered and applied as herein after is directed.

XIII. Provided always, and be it further enacted by the Authority aforesaid, That if either the Buyer or Seller of any such Cover, Wrapper, or Label, or any such Packet, Box, Bottle, Phial, or other Inclosure, shall inform against the other Party concerned in buying or selling such Cover, Wrapper, or Label, or such Packet, Box, Bottle, Phial, or other Inclosure, the Party so informing shall be admitted to give Evidence against the Party informed against, and shall be indemnified from the Penalties by him or her incurred, and shall receive the same Benefit and Advantage as any other Informer shall be intitled to by virtue of this Act for such Information.

XIV. And be it further enacted by the Authority aforesaid, That the said Commissioners for the Time being appointed to manage the Duties upon stamped Vellum, Parchment, and Paper, shall allow and pay to every Person that shall be supplied with, or shall bring any Paper Covers, or Wrappers, or Labels as aforesaid, to the Head Office of Stamps, to be stamped in pursuance of this Act, the Duty whereof, hereby imposed, shall amount to the Sum of ten Pounds or upwards, after the Rate of two Pounds in the hundred Pounds *per Annum*; and if such Duty shall amount to the Sum of fifty Pounds or upwards, after the Rate of five Pounds in the hundred Pounds *per Annum*, upon present

Payment of the said Duty upon the said Paper Covers, Wrappers or Labels, so to them supplied or by them brought.

XV. And be it further enacted by the Authority aforesaid, That, from and after the said first Day of *September* one thousand seven hundred and eighty-five, every Person and Persons who shall make, prepare, utter, vend, or expose to Sale, any such Medicines, Medicaments, or other Preparations or Compositions aforesaid, liable to the Duties imposed by this Act, before they respectively shall make, prepare, utter, vend, or expose to Sale, any such Medicines, Medicaments, or other Preparations or Compositions aforesaid, shall give or send Notice in Writing of the usual House or Place, Houses or Places, where they respectively shall make, prepare, utter, vend, or expose to Sale, the same; and also of all Drugs, Oils, Waters, Essences, Tinctures, Powders, and other Preparations and Compositions subject to the Duties by this Act imposed, that shall be made, prepared, uttered, vended, or exposed to Sale by them respectively, or intended so to be; which Notice shall be given or sent to the Commissioners for the Time being for managing the Duties on stamped Vellum, Parchment, and Paper, or to their Officers next adjacent to the Place where such Medicines, Medicaments, or other Preparations or Compositions, shall be made, prepared, uttered, vended, or sold; and the like Notice shall be given or sent by every such Person or Persons as often as they respectively shall change their Places for that Purpose, or shall change or vary the Articles, or any of them, in which they shall so deal: and which Notice shall contain the true and just Name and Names of all such Drugs, Oils, Waters, Essences, Tinctures, Powders, or other Preparations or Compositions aforesaid, by which the same respectively have been, or now are, or at any Time hereafter, shall be called, known, or distinguished, and the Kinds and Qualities thereof, and the Price or Prices at which the same shall be intended to be vended or exposed to Sale, upon Pain that every Person, making Default in giving such Notice as aforesaid, for every such Offence, shall forfeit and pay the Sum of ten Pounds, to be recovered and applied as herein after is directed.

XVI. And, in order to obviate any Doubts which may arise in the Construction of this Act for want of a particular Specification, Denomination, and Enumeration of the different Drugs, Oils, Waters, Essences, Tinctures, Powders, or Preparations or Compositions which are charged with, or subject to the Rates or Duties by this Act imposed, or to which the same shall extend; be it declared and further enacted, That the Rates and Duties hereby imposed on Drugs, Oils, Waters, Essences, Tinctures, Powders, and other Preparations or Compositions used or applied, or to be used or applied, as Medicines or Medicaments for the Prevention, Cure, or Relief of any Distemper, Malady,

Ailment, or Disorder, incident to or in any wise affecting the human Body, and upon Persons uttering or vending the same; and all the Powers, Provisions, Articles, Clauses, Distributions of Penalties and Forfeitures, and all other Matters and Things prescribed or appointed by this Act for the raising, levying, collecting, and securing the said Rates and Duties, shall extend, and be deemed and adjudged to extend, to charge with the said Rates and Duties all and every the Article and Articles mentioned, named, enumerated, or specified in the Schedule hereunto annexed, by the respective Names therein mentioned, or by whatsoever other Name or Names the same have heretofore been, now are, or hereafter shall be called, known, or distinguished; and also all Pills, Powders, Lozenges, Tinctures, Potions, Cordials, Electuaries, Plaisters, Unguents, Salves, Ointments, Drops, Lotions, Oils, Spirits, medicated Herbs, and Waters, Chemical and Officinal Preparations whatsoever, of the same or the like Properties, Qualities, Virtues, or Efficacies, with those Articles so mentioned, named, enumerated, or specified therein, or any of them, made, prepared, uttered, vended, or exposed to Sale by any Person or Persons whatsoever, wherein the Person making, preparing, uttering, vending, or exposing to Sale the same, hath, or claims to have, any occult, secret, or unknown Art for the making or preparing the same, or hath or claims to have any exclusive Right or Title to the making or preparing the same, or which at any Time heretofore have been, now are, or hereafter shall be prepared, uttered, vended, or exposed to Sale, under the Authority of any Letters Patent under the Great Seal, or which at any Time heretofore have been, now are, or hereafter shall be, by any publick Notice or Advertisement, or by written or printed Papers or Hand Bills, held out or recommended to the Publick, by the Makers, Venders, or Proprietors thereof, as Nostrums or Proprietary Medicines, or as Specifics, or otherwise, for the Prevention, Cure, or Relief of any such Distemper, Malady, Ailment, or Complaint as aforesaid; and shall also extend, and be deemed and adjudged to extend, to charge with the Rates or Duties imposed on Licences, all and every Person and Persons respectively who shall utter, vend, or expose to Sale, any such Preparations or Compositions as aforesaid.

XVII. And be it further enacted, That if any Person or Persons shall counterfeit or forge, or procure to be counterfeited or forged, any Seal, Stamp, or Mark, directed or allowed to be used, or provided, made or used, in pursuance of this Act, for the Purpose of denoting the Duties by this Act granted, or shall counterfeit or resemble the Impression of the same upon any Vellum, Parchment, or Paper, with an Intent to defraud his Majesty, his Heirs or Successors, of any of the said Duties; or shall utter, vend, or sell any Vellum, Parchment, or

Paper, directed to be marked or stamped with any Mark or Stamp provided
and used in pursuance of this or any other Act or Acts of Parliament, for denoting the Duties thereby granted with a counterfeit Mark or Stamp thereupon,
knowing such Mark or Stamp to be counterfeit; or if any Person shall privately
and fraudulently use any Seal, Stamp, or Mark, directed or allowed to be used
by this Act, with Intent to defraud his Majesty, his Heirs or Successors, of any
of the said Duties; then every such Person so offending, and being thereof
convicted, shall be adjudged a Felon, and shall suffer Death as in Cases of
Felony, without Benefit of Clergy.

XVIII. And be it further enacted by the Authority aforesaid, That all Powers,
Provisions, Articles, Clauses, and all other Matters and Things, prescribed
or appointed by any former Act or Acts of Parliament, relating to the Stamp-
duties on Vellum, Parchment, and Paper, shall be of full Force and Effect with
relation to the Rates and Duties hereby imposed, and shall be applied and
put in Execution, for raising, levying, collecting, and securing the said new
Rates and Duties hereby imposed, according to the true Intent and Meaning
of this Act, as fully, to all Intents and Purposes, as if the same had severally
and respectively been hereby enacted, with relation to the said new Rates and
Duties hereby imposed.

XIX. And be it further enacted by the Authority aforesaid, That all pecuniary
Penalties, hereby imposed, shall be divided and distributed (if sued for within
the Space of six Calendar Months from the Time of any such Penalty being
incurred) in Manner following; One Moiety thereof, to his Majesty, his Heirs
and Successors, and the other Moiety thereof, with full Costs of Suit, to the
Person or Persons who shall inform and sue for the same.

XX. And be it further enacted by the Authority aforesaid, That all pecuniary
Penalties, imposed on any Person or Persons for Offences committed against
this Act, shall and may be sued for and recovered in any of his Majesty's Courts
at *Westminster*, for Offences committed in that Part of *Great Britain* called
England, the Dominion of *Wales*, or the Town of *Berwick upon Tweed*; and in
his Majesty's Court of Sessions, Court of Justiciary, or Court of Exchequer in
Scotland, for Offences committed in that Part of *Great Britain* called *Scotland*,
by Action of Debt, Bill, Plaint, or Information, wherein no Essoin, Protection,
Privilege, Wager of Law, or more than one Imparlance, shall be allowed.

XXI. Provided always, and be it further enacted by the Authority aforesaid,
That such Division or Distribution of the Penalties as aforesaid, shall be,
and is hereby confined and restricted to the prosecuting for the same within
the Time herein before for that Purpose limited; and that in Default of such

Prosecution within the Time aforesaid, no Informer or Informers shall have or be intitled to any Part or Share of such Penalties, but that the Whole thereof shall belong to his Majesty, his Heirs and Successors, and shall be recoverable in Manner aforesaid; any Thing herein contained to the contrary notwithstanding.

XXII. Provided always, and it is hereby enacted by the Authority aforesaid, That it shall and maybe lawful to and for any Justice of the Peace, residing near the Place where the Offence shall be committed, to hear and determine any Offence against this Act, which subjects the Offender to any pecuniary Penalty, at any Time within six Months after the Offence committed, or to be committed, against this Act; which said Justice of the Peace is hereby authorised and required, upon any such Information exhibited, or Complaint made in that Behalf, to summon the Party accused, and also the Witnesses on either Side, and shall examine into the Matter of Fact; and upon due Proof made thereof, either by the voluntary Confession of the Party, or by the Oath of one or more credible Witness or Witnesses, to give Judgement or Sentence for the Penalty or Forfeiture according as in and by this Act is directed, and to award and issue out his Warrant under his Hand and Seal, for the levying any pecuniary Penalties or Forfeitures so adjudged on the Goods of the Offender, and to cause Sale to be made thereof, in case they shall not be redeemed within six Days, rendering to the Party the Overplus, if any; and where the Goods of the Offender cannot be found sufficient to answer the Penalty, to commit such Offender to Prison, there to remain for the Space of three Months, unless such pecuniary Penalty shall be sooner paid and satisfied; and if any Person or Persons shall find himself or themselves aggrieved by the Judgement of any such Justice, then he or they shall and may, upon giving Security to the Amount of the Value of such Penalty and Forfeiture, together with such Costs as shall be awarded in case such Judgement shall be affirmed, appeal to the Justices of the Peace at the next General Quarter Sessions for the County, Riding, Shire, Stewartry, or Place, who are hereby impowered to summon and examine Witnesses upon Oath, and finally to hear and determine the same; and in case the Judgement shall be affirmed, it shall be lawful for such Justices to award the Person or Persons to pay such Costs occasioned by such Appeal as to them shall seem meet.

XXIII. And be it further enacted by the Authority aforesaid, That if any Person or Persons shall be summoned as a Witness or Witnesses to give Evidence before such Justice or Justices of the Peace, touching any of the Matters relative to this Act, either on the Part of the Prosecutor, or of the Person or Persons accused, and shall neglect or refuse to appear at the Time and Place to be for that Purpose appointed, without a reasonable Excuse for such his, her, or their Neglect or Refusal, to be allowed of by such Justice or Justices of the Peace before whom the Prosecution shall be depending, that then every such Person shall forfeit, for every such Offence, the Sum of forty Shillings, to be levied and paid in such Manner, and by such Means, as herein before directed as to other Penalties.

XXIV. And be it further enacted by the Authority aforesaid, That the Justice or Justices of the Peace before whom any Offender shall be convicted as afore-said, shall cause the said Conviction to be made out in the Manner and Form following, or in any other Form of Words to the same Effect, *mutatis mutandis*; (that is to say:)

'BE it remembered, That on the   Day of   in the Year of our Lord in the County of   A. B. of   was convicted before me C. D. one of his Majesty's Justices of the Peace for the said County, resid-ing near the Place where the Offence was committed, for that the said A. B. on the   Day of now last past, did, contrary to the Form of the Statute in that Case made and provided [*here state the Offence against the Act*]; and I do declare and adjudge that he the said A. B. hath forfeited the Sum of   of lawful Money of *Great Britain*, for the Offence aforesaid, to be distributed as the Law directs.

Given under my Hand and Seal, the   Day of

XXV. Provided nevertheless, That it shall and may be lawful to and for the said Justice, where he shall see Cause, to mitigate and lessen any such Penalties as he shall think fit, reasonable Costs and Charges of the Officers and Informers, as well in making the Discovery as in prosecuting the same, being always allowed, over and above such Mitigation, and so as such Mitigation do not reduce the Penalties to less than one Moiety of the Penalties incurred, over and above the said Costs and Charges; any Thing contained in this Act, or any other Act of Parliament to the contrary notwithstanding; and no such Conviction shall be removed by *Certiorari* into any Court whatsoever.

XXVI. And be it further enacted by the Authority aforesaid, That the several Duties herein before granted shall be paid, from Time to Time, into the Hands of the Receiver General for the Time being of the Duties on stamped Vellum, Parchment, and Paper, who shall keep a separate and distinct Account of the several Rates and Duties, and pay the same (the necessary Charges of raising, paying, and accounting for the same, being deducted) into the Receipt of the

Exchequer, at such Time, and in such Manner, as the Duties now charged on stamped Vellum, Parchment, and Paper, are directed to be paid; and that in the Office of the Auditor of the said Receipt shall be provided and kept a Book or Books, in which all the Monies arising from the said several Rates and Duties, and paid into the said Receipt as aforesaid, shall be entered separate and apart from all other Monies paid or payable to his Majesty, his Heirs or Successors, upon any Account whatsoever; and the said Money so paid into the said Receipt of Exchequer as aforesaid shall be a Fund for the Payment of the several Annuities, and all other Charges and Expences as are directed to be paid and payable pursuant to an Act of Parliament, passed in the twenty-third Year of the Reign of his present Majesty, intituled, *An Act for raising a certain Sum of Money by way of Annuities, and for establishing a Lottery.*

XXVII. And be it further enacted by the Authority aforesaid, That if any Person or Persons shall at any Time or Times be sued, molested, or prosecuted, for any Thing by him or them done or executed in pursuance of this Act, or of any Clause, Matter, or Thing, herein contained, such Person or Persons shall or may plead the General Issue, and give the Special Matter in Evidence, for his or their Defence; and if upon the Trial a Verdict shall pass for the Defendant or Defendants, or the Plaintiff or Plaintiffs become nonsuited, then such Defendant or Defendants shall have Treble Costs awarded to him or them against such Plaintiff or Plaintiffs.

SCHEDULE

To which this ACT refers:

Containing the Names by which many medicinal Preparations now in Use, subject to the Duties by this Act imposed, are known and distinguished.

D R U G S, O I L S, W A T E R S, *etcetera, used as Medicines; commonly called*

ANALEPTIC Pills, Doctor James's.
Ague and Fever Drops.
Anderson's Scotch Pills.
Andalusia Water.
Anodyne Necklace.
Antipertussis.
Antirheumatic Drops.
Balsamic Electuary for the

Jesuit Drops.
Johnson's Yellow Ointment.
Keyser's Pills.
Leake's Pills.
Lozenges of Blois.
Ditto _____ of Tolu.
Ditto _____ Stomachic.
Ditto _____ Specific.
Ditto _____ for the Heartburn.

Bateman's Drops.

Betton's original British Oil.

Beaume de Vie.

Birt's Martial Balsam.

Bostock's Grand Elixir.

Cox's Tincture.

Daffy's Elixir.

Dalby's Carminative.

Dawson's Lozenges.

Doctor Dickinson's Cephalic Drops.

Edwards's Ague Tincture.

Essence of Water Dock.

Falck's Universal Pills.

Freeman's Bathing Spirits.

Fryar's Balsam.

Fendon's Drops.

Godfrey's Cordial.

Grant's Drops.

Griffin's Tinctura Asthmatica.

Hickman's Pills.

Hill's Pectoral Balsam of Honey.

Ditto Tincture of Sage.

Ditto Tincture of Valerian.

Ditto Essence of Waterdock.

Ditto Elixir of Bardana.

Ditto Tincture of Centaury.

Ditto Canada Balsam.

Hamilton's Cinnamon Drops.

Ditto _____ Asthmatic Effluvia.

Hooper's Female Pills.

Holdsworth's Lozenges.

Hunter's Elixir.

Ditto_____ Restorative.

James's Fever Powder.

Lockyer's Pills.

Le Cour's Imperial Oil.

Norris's Drops.

Peters's Tincture.

Ditto_____Pills.

Peke's Ointment.

Ratcliff's Elixir.

Spilsbury's Antiscorbutic Drops

Speedman's Stomach Pills.

Spirits of Scurvy Grass.

Stomachic Lozenges.

Stoughton's Elixir.

Sterne's Balsamic Aether.

Squire's Elixir.

Steer's Opodeldoc.

Ditto_____Oil.

Ditto_____Purging Elixir.

Tuberosa Vitae, or Chilblain Water.

Turlington's Balsam.

Vandour's Nervous Pills.

Velno's Vegetable Syrup.

Wace's Asthmatic Drops.

Ward's White Drops.

Ditto_____ Essence for the Head Ach.

Ditto_____Liquid Sweat.

Ditto_____Red Pills.

Ditto_____Sack Drops.

Ditto_____Sweating Powders.

Ditto_____Paste.

Worm Cakes, Storey's.

Worm Sugar Plumbs.

Wray's Ague Pills.

Index

Printed in the United States
By Bookmasters